Praise For How To Be A Great Astrologer

"This is James Braha's first non-Hindu book and it is very fine... It is the best book out that is dedicated solely to interpreting traditional Western natal aspects. Not to go unmentioned is an excellent chapter dedicated to the lunar nodes, which Braha correctly observes are "the single most important feature of a Western astrological birthchart." ...To the point and elegantly executed, it's a good buy."

Planetary Focus Magazine

"*How To Be A Great Astrologer* is James Braha's best book to date. The aspect interpretations that make up the bulk of this book are alone worth the cover price. No less valuable are Braha's introductory words, in which he provides a thoughtful explanation of how astrology works, and a chapter on planetary aspect theory, which addresses issues like research-oriented astrology and the house system controversy. This is an intelligent, well-reasoned approach to the cosmic craft, one that will help all students of the subject get a clearer grasp of the issues involved. Congratulations James Braha, on a well-done piece of work!"

Dell Horoscope

"This is more than just another well-written aspects book. It is a work of art... The aspect delineations are well written and astrologically accurate. The book is lavishly illustrated with angelic celestial pictures and includes quotes and aphorisms from the great figures of this age... The section on the nodes is one of the clearest explanations I have ever seen in print. *How To Be A Great Astrologer* is going to become one of the important reference texts for practicing astrologers!"

Diamond Fire Magazine

"This is not just another beginning astrology book. James Braha's background is steeped in Indian lore and his latest book is again based on Eastern concepts. *How To Be A Great Astrologer* offers new insights that Western astrologers may not be aware of."

Aspects Magazine

OTHER BOOKS BY JAMES BRAHA:

How To Predict Your Future:
    Secrets of Eastern and Western Astrology
Ancient Hindu Astrology
    For the Modern Western Astrologer
Astro-Logos, Revelations of a Hindu Astrologer
The Art and Practice of Ancient Hindu Astrology:
    Nine Intimate Sessions Between Teacher and Student

HOW TO BE
A GREAT
ASTROLOGER

THE PLANETARY ASPECTS EXPLAINED

BY JAMES BRAHA

Hermetician Press / Hollywood, Florida

James Braha
Hermetician Press
P.O. Box 552
Longboat Key, Florida 34228

How To Be A Great Astrologer - The planetary aspects explained

© 1992 Copyright James Braha

Cover design by Paul Pettys
Copyright free illustrations by Gustav Doré

I.S.B.N. # 0-935895-02-7

Library of Congress Catalogue Card Number: 91-65831

Printed in Hong Kong by Liang Yu Printing Factory, Ltd.
6 7 8 9 10 15 20

To those who dare to be great.

ACKNOWLEDGEMENTS

I would like to express my gratitude to the following individuals. To my editor, Patrick Bosold for his expertise and valuable suggestions. To Vashti Alezannah, Howard and Shane Dugan, Rebecca Buckley, Jane Tobal, Laura Walz, Lauren Braha, Emmett Walz, Sheppard Root, Sam Benjamin, Kevin Quartarone, Rudy Gillmann, Walter Gillmann, Bob and Terry Fitzpatrick, Mike Donnelly, Moira Collins, Joy Billings, Lisa Hawley, Marcus and Imal Wagner, and Thor Thorgeirsson. And to Kerry Breitbart, for his friendship and profound generosity.

There is no such thing as a definitive, absolute interpretation of an astrological aspect. By the tender grace of God, humankind is granted the experience of free will united with justice — the opportunity to reap the consequences of, and thereby learn from, all our actions. If, in past lives, a person has greatly misused aggressiveness (the Mars energy), he or she may be born this time around with a Mars-Saturn opposition, indicating significant restrictiveness and a built-in check on the desire nature. The Mars-Saturn opposition can clearly, even systematically, be defined through personal observation as well as proper analysis of the core meanings of the two planets; nonetheless, the miracle of human life is that we possess, at every instant, the freedom to act as we choose regardless of planetary influences. How then can any aspect be interpreted in exact, all-conclusive terms?

The gentle reader may well ask, "If this is so why does this text treat each aspect so authoritatively?" Quite simply, I made this choice because nearly all conventionally-written, modern-day Western astrology books on planetary aspects leave readers desperate for a VISCERAL EXPERIENCE of astrological knowledge. The style of this text parallels the writings of the ancient sages of the Hindu, or Vedic, predictive astrology of the East. I purposely chose this style because it delivers the most potent presentation of PURE, ESSENTIAL, ARCHETYPAL information.

I consider this work to be extremely traditional and conventional. In order for practicing astrologers to utilize the interpretations properly, however, it is absolutely crucial to bear in mind the reason that I wrote this book. Otherwise, the delineations found herein may be taken as some form of gospel truth, which is not my intent.

For example, one typical description in this book reads as follows: "If the Moon is square or opposite Mars the person is selfish. He thinks of himself before anyone else..." Does this mean that all individuals possessing this astrological configuration act so crudely? Of course not. However this description does reveal (hopefully) the essential symbology of the ASPECT. Whether the person possessing the aspect behaves as indicated is a matter of several different considerations.

2   One of the most important factors astrologers have in their analytical favor is the "orb of influence." Put simply, an exact conjunction will act far more powerfully and genuinely than, say, one which occurs within five or six degrees. In hopes of expressing the purity and essence of each aspect, the configurations have been described as if they occur at a point of extreme intensity, i.e. exact or within one or two degrees. The purpose of this writing, I say again, is to give the astrologer a visceral experience of astrological information. This should give astrologers who are dealing with a certain feature, a workable understanding FROM WHICH TO BEGIN.

Traditional Western astrology is not, basically, a predictive, event-oriented system. Unlike the interpretations of the ancient Hindus, our deciphering of the star language deals more with the genetic, inborn, behavioral patterns which give rise to the actions and circumstances of one's existence. In a culture where a peanut farmer can grow up to be president it is fitting and proper that our astrological system should support the glory and magnificence of free will. This text is not an attempt to deny or distort such a natural, indigenous cultural heritage; however, it could appear so because of the factual writing style I have used.

Most importantly, knowledge means power. Therefore, if this book succeeds in expressing highly potent astrological descriptions, the work can be used to profound advantage or destructiveness. The text is direct, candid, and quite forthright. It has been composed, as the title indicates, for astrologers — those whom I see as the healers and counselors of the new age. Some professionals may wish to read portions of this work directly to their clients. However, great care should be taken, especially in the case of the hard aspects (the squares and oppositions).

Non-astrologers hearing blunt, authoritative descriptions of their own hard aspects could be psychologically harmed or damaged. Therefore, I repeat, care should be taken. If these pages are ever to be read aloud verbatim, I recommend giving the client an explanation of free will, or asking the client to read this introduction, before hearing his or her particular aspect descriptions.

Another important point regarding proper use of this book concerns the variable effects of aspects. Having practiced the star language for some time now, I am only too aware that trines do not always produce good effects, and squares and oppositions do not absolutely generate negative effects. I strongly recommend that the reader consider the conjunction as the "main aspect" of each series. For example, when attempting to comprehend a Moon-Venus square or Moon-Venus trine, please read the description of Moon Conjunct Venus first. This will help enormously by providing a sense of the natures, compatibilities, etc. of the two planets involved. And, because conjunctions are neutral in nature, they will generally render the most accurate and reliable descriptions. (Experience reveals that the "hard" and "soft" aspects are more subject to the free will factor, i.e., how the person decides to use his or her energy and talents once aware of them). Furthermore, always remember that each delineation in this book represents the SYMBOLOGY OF AN ASPECT, not necessarily a PERSON.

As for the way I have treated each planetary aspect as an end unto itself, as an almost major "life directive," an explanation is in order. Clearly, there can be no real precision and accuracy in an astrological interpretation until the entire birthchart, with all its multitudinous factors, is considered. However, there is also a marvelous phenomenon, which nearly every seasoned astrologer has experienced, that occurs when one particular feature is understood in totality. It is as if by tuning in to one distinctly personal aspect of a person, the whole of the being can be known. This miracle of a sort occurs by way of "synergy" (similar to the "hundredth monkey" concept) and it is profoundly useful to practicing counselors, psychologists, and astrologers. The planetary aspects in this book have been written with such a concept in mind.

I am pleased with this text. However, I do wish to apologize to female astrologers for the use of the masculine gender throughout the work. Putting myself in the place of a woman reading the aspects, I feel a subtle sense of pain, a sense of being somewhat ignored or neglected. At one point, I tried to write using both genders, but to no avail. The problem is that to use the term "he or she" approximately 5,000 times would not merely be extremely tedious, it would dilute the simplicity, directness, power, and potency of the knowledge. That would defeat the entire purpose of the book. I found that using "he" and "him" at certain times and "she" and "her" at others not only weakened the text, but seemed to create some new-fashioned, avant garde brand of astrology.

To my mind, the only solution which would not undermine the objective of the work would be to produce two separate volumes, one for women and one for men. This, unfortunately, is financially infeasible at present. I therefore beg the readers' forbearance and pray I have not committed a major indiscretion. Positively no chauvinism or disrespect is intended. For the time being, I ask readers to insert "she" and "her" for female clients where the text reads "he" and "him."

Finally, I wish to say that the delineations enclosed are but a minimum explanation of the planetary aspects. Astrologers wishing to contribute insights should send findings to me, via Hermetician Press.

4   Knowledge of the star language is a profound blessing. It is a sublime and wonderful way to serve and assist humanity, and make a real difference in the world. We are truly privileged. In the words of Isabel Hickey, one of the Western world's best astrological authors, Godspeed and God Bless.

October 1991

Love and serve all humanity. Assist everyone.

Be cheerful, be courteous.

Be a dynamo of irrepressible happiness.

See God and good in every face.

There is no saint without a past.

There is no sinner without a future.

Praise every soul.

If you cannot praise someone, let them pass out of your life.

Be original, be inventive.

Dare, dare, and then dare more.

Do not imitate. Stand on your own ground.

Do not lean on the borrowed staff of others.

Think your own thoughts. Be yourself.

All perfection and all virtues of the Deity are hidden inside you - reveal them.

The savior also is already within you - reveal Him.

Let his grace emancipate you. Let your life be that of a rose.

Through silence it speaks in the language of fragrance.

There is no saint without a past.

There is no sinner without a future.

"The heavens declare the glory of God; and the firmament showeth His handiwork. Day unto day uttereth speech, and night unto night showeth knowledge. There is no speech nor language where their voice is not heard."

THE 19TH PSALM

The following is an explanation of how and why astrology, the star language, works. It is not a proof, it is merely food for thought. Within existence there is, necessarily, language. Within language there is, always, existence. The two actually cannot be separated. This precept is now being consistently expounded in philosophical circles. Bear in mind that what is meant by language is not merely words and symbols, but also the underlying function — the ability to distinguish. This point is crucial.

That the existence of a thing depends upon language, or the ability to distinguish, may be easily grasped by considering different cultures. For example, there are cases of less-civilized tribes who have been shown photographs but have seen nothing other than a piece of paper, because they were not yet educated to the concept of photograph. The same natives cannot see themselves in a mirror because there is no word (distinction) for "mirror" in their language. Quite simply, without language, or the ability to distinguish, there is no existence. One of the best illustrations is the case of Helen Keller. She writes, "Suddenly, I knew not how or where or when, I awoke to language, to knowledge of love, to the usual concepts of nature, of good and evil." Of her life before languaging ability she says, "For nearly six years I had no concepts whatever of nature or mind or death or God. There was not one spark of rational thought...I was like an unconscious clod of earth." Helen Keller's entire experience of existence was based on language, her ability to distinguish.

Another example of the significance of language can be seen by considering "picture puzzles." One of the most famous of these involves two silhouettes, which upon closer examination reveal a vase hidden within the picture. Most typically, a person sees either the vase or the silhouettes. The person does not perceive both until told to examine the picture more closely. For the person experiencing only the silhouettes, the vase does not exist until it is created through language, until it is distinguished.

For those familiar with Sanskrit, the language of the Vedas, the intertwining of language and existence is no surprise. Sanskrit is known as a "name and form" language where there is literally no difference between the symbol (word or vibration) and the object it describes. Some believe that the perfected yogi's supernatural power to materialize objects at will is connected to the yogi's ability to PURELY speak a Sanskrit word and thus invoke its actual form. Also, according to Vedic philosophy, there is the special mantra OM, the primordial sound continually reverberating through the universe, considered to be the vibratory power behind all energies.

If existence for humans is based largely, perhaps entirely, upon language, and if a human is a microcosm of the universe, then what logically must the universe also require for its existence? Language, of course. Now we see a reason for astrology, an actual purpose for the cosmos to speak, to distinguish. For that is what the star language does — it distinguishes who and what we are. In the same way humans get to enjoy existence because of language, so does the universe have its own similar way of functioning. Understand, however, that since the cosmos does not have awareness of itself in the same way that humans do, the universe can only experience its existence by distinguishing or "languaging" beings capable of returning the communication. How do we humans respond back to the cosmos? By either accepting the dictates and prophecies the cosmos has made about our lives (via the stars), or by using our free will, our own "languaging" ability to live as we choose. Thus, what ultimately occurs is a kind of continual dance between nature, or the cosmos, and individuals.

Most fascinating is the fact that the communications from the universe come to us in the form of fate or predestiny, while we recipients must necessarily possess free will, or the universe would lose its enjoyment of existence. This is how free will and predestiny exist side by side without infringement upon each other. Indeed, one could not even exist without the other.

The question then becomes, "If our free will is every bit as vital as the fateful communications of the heavens, why are the stars so accurate in their distinguishing of our lives? How is it that astrological predictions and personality descriptions often come true with such startling accuracy?" Do the planets and stars cause these effects? Not in the sense of heavenly bodies being physically connected to our lives. Quite simply, the universe "languages," or distinguishes, certain features of our existence with such precision, such extreme definitiveness and clarity, that in these realms we are essentially unable to create ourselves differently. What occurs is a kind of conversation between the individual and the cosmos, in which the universe sometimes speaks louder, clearer, and with greater certainty. The best way to grasp this concept is to consider how human behavior changes in the presence of different people. Brilliant children may become dullards when around relatives who see them as such. Extremely capable people become inept around critical, fault-finding individuals. This is simply the interplay of two beings who are simultaneously creating a reality. So it is with the human being and the cosmos. Nature distinguishes who we are, and what will happen to us, and we are free to choose and create our own reality. Our lives depend upon whose distinguishing power (or "languaging" ability) predominates at any given point in time.

There is no darkness without the possibility of light. One is not a mother without a child. Likewise, there is no free will without predestiny. The two are dependent upon each other. The universe, by distinguishing communicative beings, gets to exist. If not for human choice, the language of the heavens would be pointless. If not for astrology, the element of fate, our experience of free will would cease to exist. The universe exists by virtue of the star language!

"In the beginning was the Word, and the Word was with God. And the Word was God."

The Bible

The Moon's nodes are the single most important feature of a Western astrological birthchart. The South Node reveals a person's past (previous incarnations) and the North Node indicates a person's future (where he or she is headed). Most significantly, the North Node represents the purposes, intentions, and objectives of an entire lifetime. Individuals who follow the path symbolized by their North Node are the most fulfilled, content, and self-actualized of all people. The beauty and profundity of the nodes are that they serve as a primary explanation, a genuine solution and answer, to every person's essential question in life: "What, specifically, am I here for?" Whereas all other birthchart aspects reveal behavior, tendencies, or events likely to occur, the nodes function as a marvelous guidance system. Not only do the nodes advise what realms of activity to pursue, but the South Node reveals the reason for such interests. The nodes are always exactly opposite each other. If the South Node is in the third house, the person has already learned and mastered teaching, debating, detailed analysis, skepticism, etc. With the North Node in the ninth house (the house opposite from the third), the person must now develop faith, intuition, religion, and philosophical knowledge. Those who, through laziness or fear, pursue the easy, comfortable ways of their South Node (past-life) inclinations remain frustrated, discouraged, and disappointed with life. South Node activities carry no vital challenge, growth, or meaning. If the person engages in South Node endeavors in any significant way (especially negative attributes of the South Node house and sign symbolism), there will be disturbance and suffering.

Despite all this, some astrologers consider the nodes meaningless, and disregard them in their birthchart interpretations. How can such a dichotomy exist in such an experiential discipline as astrology? The answer is simple. The nodes function as a pair, and only one of them (the South Node) reveals actual behavior. The South Node, through its sign and house position, indicates the tendencies, characteristics, and affinities that the person is born with. These are readily discernible traits. The North Node, however, does not confer anything. It merely POINTS THE WAY to fulfilling, evolutionary activity which the person may undertake if he or she desires. The North Node does not indicate likely or probable behavior. Unlike planetary aspects and planets in signs and houses, there is no inherent pressure or compulsion to enter North Node realms. Each person has, of course, a natural, intuitive sense about the areas of life that will bring the most fulfillment, those activities that are "the right things to do." However, North Node territory, being new and untested, is often scary or intimidating. Thus, many individuals never succeed in reaching their North Node directives. Astrologers looking for proof that the North Node "causes" anything will not find it. Ten different people with the North Node in Pisces will not necessarily appear similar in any "Piscean" behavioral way. However, validation of the North Node in a sign (or house) is easily ascertained: simply describe the particular meaning of the North Node position to each individual, and note how well the explanations match the person's innate sense of purpose and intention. Astrologers who ignore the nodes or overlook their vast importance and magnificence make a grave error.

There are always two segments of information revealed by each node: 1) its sign placement, and 2) its house position. Therefore, these obviously must be blended. For example, if the North Node is in the tenth house (career focus) and in the sign of Pisces (selfless, sacrificial, healing activities, etc.), then the person may wish to be devoted to a powerful medical career. Or the path to follow may be an intense spiritual mission. But, if the North Node is in the tenth house in a different sign, say Aquarius (fads, original creations, activities which are ahead of the times, etc.), then the person may wish to focus on creating inventions for the good of society. The sign and house placements of the nodes must both be taken into account.

The most arduous of all node positions occurs when the house and sign of the North Node are diametrically opposed. For instance, if the North Node is in the sign of Aries, but it is also in the seventh house (as in the case of Richard Nixon), a difficult situation exists. The North Node in Aries means that the person must let go of relationship dependency, and develop his or her own personality. The individual must not be too influenced by the partner's desires. However, the North Node in the seventh house means the exact opposite. It indicates that the person has been selfish or very self-contained in past lives, and must now pursue a deep, meaningful love relationship where extreme compromise and pleasing the spouse is the order of the day. In delicate node cases such as this, the object is to strike a balance. What makes the task extraordinarily difficult is that the person must, alternately, pursue both paths. If one course is followed to the exclusion of the other, there will be quick retribution and suffering. Both ways must be cultivated, as the person is on Earth to learn equilibrium between the two spheres symbolized.

The Western astrological method of analyzing the nodes is entirely different from the method employed in Hindu predictive astrology. I must issue a crucial warning to all Hindu astrologers, especially to those who are now using my text, "Ancient Hindu Astrology For The Modern Western Astrologer." The node descriptions given in this book must NOT be used to describe the node positions in Hindu (sidereal-based) astrology. They will not work, and will not provide accurate information for sidereal planetary positions. The following descriptions of the nodes are for traditional Western astrological charts using the tropical planetary locations only. This point cannot be overemphasized.

At the end of each node description, I have included a brief explanation of the Hindu method of node analysis. I have done this to whet the reader's appetite for learning more about Hindu (sometimes called Vedic) astrology. It is my experience that Hindu predictive astrology complements our Western, psychologically-based system in a magnificent way. Hindu astrology excels in revealing the actual karma and fate of a person. The Western system is profound in delineating an individual's personality, psychology, behavioral patterns, and the areas for growth and evolution. Astrologers using both methods for each birthchart interpretation have a great advantage over those who do not. In Hindu astrology, the North Node is called "Rahu" and the South Node is known as "Ketu." Regarding the brief Hindu delineations which are given, Western astrologers should USE THE INFORMATION SOLELY FOR THEIR OWN REFLECTION AND INTEREST. The material should NOT be presented to clients. The reason for this is that in many cases, perhaps thirty percent, house positions will vary between the two systems. In other words, a person's North Node may be in the fourth house of the Western chart, but in the fifth house of the Hindu chart. The Rahu and Ketu descriptions given in this book are included only to pique the reader's interest in Hindu predictive astrology (or "jyotish," the science of light, as it is known in India).

If the North Node is in Aries or the first house, the person's greatest growth, evolution, and fulfillment come through developing his own personality and personal power. He has been too dependent on marriage partners in past lives, and has relinquished his individuality and authority to his mates. The person must follow his instincts and impulses, and learn to care for his own destiny. He must not allow himself to be dominated, manipulated, or overshadowed by the feelings and wishes of others. There is a great likelihood that the person will become enmeshed in an early marriage and soon feel smothered and controlled. He may (with great effort, pain, and struggle) eventually free himself in order to develop and nurture his own personality, ambitions, and self-expression. Then the possibility of growth, satisfaction, and a sense of accomplishment becomes a reality.

The person should beware of compromising too quickly and easily. He must work on confidence and self-reliance, and use his own judgement. He will be happier and healthier when he learns to value his own opinions and stand up for himself. The person gains a great deal from decisiveness and dynamic action, and should therefore take the initiative as much as possible. Men or women with this North Node placement are well-advised to cultivate and nurture their masculine side. The person should be more assertive, and express his emotions when provoked. He must not, in the event of anger or irritability, give in to his habitual patterns of suppression and self-denial. In this lifetime his individuality, self-esteem, and ego needs are of the essence.

The person must let go of his compulsion to create peace and harmony in the environment. Toward this end, he will be forever thrust into circumstances where he feels compelled to declare his convictions and take appropriate action. The person should focus on his physical body, be more daring, and allow the fiery element of his personality to come through more often. In ancient Hindu astrology, the North Node (Rahu) in the first house and the South Node (Ketu) in the seventh indicates a beautiful and powerful appearance, serious ups and downs in married life, and a strange, eccentric, or highly spiritual spouse. John Lennon is a good example. Sign positions of the nodes are of much less significance.

NORTH NODE IN TAURUS OR THE SECOND HOUSE
SOUTH NODE IN SCORPIO OR THE EIGHTH HOUSE

If the North Node is in Taurus or the second house, the person's greatest growth, evolution, and fulfillment come through appreciation and enjoyment of earthly pleasures. In past lives, the person has been preoccupied with the profundity of life, mysticism, spiritual development, and helping others find their values and self-worth. It is now time to expand the practical side of being, and cherish God's creation to the fullest. The person should focus on wealth, comforts, the arts etc. Collections of any kind are very much to be favored. The person must let go of patterns of detachment and indifference, and engage fully and passionately in life. Enjoyment of the physical universe is his path to happiness, spiritual integration, and higher realms of awareness.

The person should concern himself with personal security. He needs to take jobs that are steady and stable, and that allow him to cultivate a conservative, systematic manner. Endeavors involving agriculture, gardening, or archeology will bring satisfaction and delight. The person should surround himself with beauty, and take his appearance very seriously. He must honor the qualities of patience, consistency, firmness, and determination. Above all, he must learn to acknowledge and value his own personal needs and desires. He should seek out the real and tangible, and remain somewhat skeptical of that which he cannot see, smell, hear, touch, or taste. Self-identity is extremely important during this lifetime, and the person is developing loyalty, balance, and equanimity.

Sex may be enjoyed for the sensuality and sheer pleasure of the experience, but not as a means of gaining power, indulging in passion, or losing his identity to another. Unless other aspects of the birthchart indicate otherwise, the person may have little desire for the occult or mystical side of life. He is not much concerned with psychological transformation and spiritual methods of evolutionary growth. In Hindu astrology, the North Node (Rahu) in the second house and the South Node (Ketu) in the eighth house (or vice versa) are the most troublesome node placements. The reason is that the second house, in the ancient predictive system, is considered family life; either node there causes serious harm and suffering. Happiness in general is much disturbed, and there may be marital strife and discord. Ketu in the eighth house is good for intuition and psychic ability. Sign positions are of little significance.

If the North Node is in Gemini or the third house, the person's greatest growth, evolution, and fulfillment come through mental expression and rational analysis of objective truth. In past lifetimes, the person may have been idealistic and emotional in his thinking. Now he must use discrimination, and focus on facts and figures in the here and now. He should follow his instincts of avoiding dogmas, creeds, religions, and higher philosophies. The person gains little from meditation, astrology, metaphysics, and any disciplines which are not verifiable through traditional science. The person suffers when he goes by faith and intuition. He does not fare well whenever he follows blindly. He must abide by his newfound skepticism, and make his way to the truth by way of logic and reasoning.

Happiness will be found in mental professions such as teaching, lecturing, debating, and writing. The person is a good salesman. He thrives on city life and should be as active as possible. Public relations or coordinating-type careers are favored. During previous incarnations, the person was sentimental, philosophical, and too taken with theories, principles, doctrines, and conjectures. Now he must plant his feet firmly on the ground and embrace the notion that "what you see is what you get." The person should cultivate good relations with siblings and relatives. He must work on versatility and adaptability, and try to experience as much variety and "spice of life" as possible. The person may often find himself thrust into situations that require great precision and attention to details.

The daily environment is important, long-distance travel is not. The person is well-advised to meet as many people as possible and continually expand his social life. He should avoid gambling or trying to predict the future, except through serious investigation and statistical research. The more he gains of useful information and practical knowledge, the happier he will be and the greater his growth and evolution. He must not allow his feelings and emotions to interfere when trying to understand an issue. The person should not concern himself with broad viewpoints, abstract ideas, fanciful inspirations, and spiritual realities. He must learn through personal experience, not gurus and mentors.

Many Western astrologers consider the North Node in Gemini to be exalted. This is interesting because, at first glance, the person appears cursed in the realms of religion, philosophy, and higher knowledge. How, then, is he to make his way to enlightenment and final liberation? It may be that the person is exceedingly blessed because he is making great evolutionary strides simply by living with physical reality. Perhaps he has had such unshakeable faith in previous lives that his only present necessity is to deal squarely with life as it is. The person feels no need whatsoever to inject meaning and significance into his existence through conceptual and philosophical beliefs. Certainly, the person with the North Node in Gemini or the third house has an easier time with practicalities than anyone else. He pays attention and quickly learns how things work here on planet Earth. In ancient Hindu astrology, the North Node (Rahu) in the third house indicates an enormously strong will and an interesting personality. The person is courageous and adventurous. He works well with his hands, has intense cravings, and fulfills his desires easily. The South Node (Ketu) in the ninth house may indicate troubles with religious or spiritual teachers. Or the person may have a guru or mentor who is strange, weird, occultish, extremely introverted, or invisible in a way. The sign positions in Hindu astrology are much less significant.

If the North Node is in Cancer or the fourth house, the person's greatest growth, evolution, and fulfillment come through taking care of his home and family life. In previous incarnations there may have been an overabundance of professional activities and social responsibility. Now the person must concentrate on his own soul growth and fulfillment of emotional needs. All activities involving land, property, and homes are favored. The person should develop his feminine and maternal energy, and seek to nurture all those in his presence. He should dedicate his life to family, children, relatives, and loved ones. He may do well in healing professions, nursing, cooking, catering, innkeeping, or any domestically-oriented jobs. Although career focus is neither psychologically significant nor a main objective of this life, the person is extremely concerned with the well-being of all members of his immediate community. He must do his best to see that everyone has a sense of belonging.

The person should not look for a life of profound philosophical meaning. His actions are not based upon compelling drives towards particularly ambitious goals. Rather, he is here to experience and appreciate the full value of his emotions, senses, passions, sensitivities, and vulnerabilities. His job is to keep his family and the human species alive and well. Tradition, rituals, and cultural values are of very great importance. The person is on a lifelong journey back to his roots. Spiritually, this means he is very well-advised to engage in meditation, contemplation, and all inner-directed self-development techniques. Also, he gains tremendous benefits from periods of self-imposed seclusion and isolation. On a more mundane level, the person wants to learn everything possible about the lives, history, and circumstances of his ancestors and predecessors. At the very beginning of life the person is organically connected to his father. However, as his consciousness grows, he quickly realizes there is no progress to made in this realm. He then shifts his attention to his mother and all other tenderhearted expressions of creation.

The person is devoted to practicalities, not ideals. He is wonderfully sympathetic and functions as a magnificent support system to those in need. He is like a rock of stability, always emotionally available for others. In this lifetime the person is learning extreme devotion and loyalty to his loved ones. He may derive tremendous pleasure from gardening, landscaping, or farming. Collectibles and material possessions are very important. The person must have absolute control over his daily environment. He should surround himself with beauty and whatever else appeals to his personal tastes. Living near water is preferred, and the person may wish to develop his psychic, sensitive nature to the fullest. He is here for a highly subjective, even sentimental, experience of life and is now relinquishing his obsession with objective realities and ultimate truths. The person may do well in mining, archeology, or any ecological vocation.

In ancient Hindu astrology, the North Node (Rahu) in the fourth house indicates problems with a forceful or domineering mother and troubles in gaining educational degrees. There are strong cravings in the heart and a possibility of attaining large homes or mansions. The South Node (Ketu) in the tenth house reveals a good reputation and successful professional life. Careers may involve any spiritual activity which raises the consciousness of the common person. There is distinct talent in metaphysical or natural healing techniques. The sign positions of the nodes are of much less significance.

If the North Node is in Leo or the fifth house, the person's greatest growth, evolution, and fulfillment come through performing creative acts, attaining recognition, and developing the ego. Self-expression and personal power are essential. In past lives, the person may have been detached, unemotional, and indifferent to approval and acknowledgment. Now he must seek out status, accolades, leadership, and honor. Above all, he must create a life which is regarded as significant and meaningful. Theatre and film are favored, as are all other artistic endeavors. The person should strive for prominence and fame. He should promote himself and his work. He must abandon his old tendencies of modesty, altruism, and obscurity.

In previous incarnations, the person may have lived a life of group activity, always being with friends and companions. Now he must delve deeply into passionate love affairs and all matters of the heart. He should enjoy the pleasures of romance, sensuality, and eroticism. Children are extremely important and fulfilling. The person finds great value in working with youth. He may decide to teach, so that his influence will live on through his pupils. He must act with integrity, honesty, and warmth. He should strive for individuality, and resist the temptation to follow the dictates and opinions of others. He is here for his own needs, concerns, and pleasures, not for those of society. He should honor his desires and instincts more than his rational mind.

Pride, dignity, and self-respect should be cultivated. The person has to realize the unique and special nature of his personality. He should work on developing confidence and a regal demeanor. The more he becomes the center of attention, the greater his evolution will be and the faster he will attain perfection. He should guard against shyness, timidity, and an unassuming manner. He gains great benefit from fun and pleasure, and should immerse himself completely in earthly matters. The person may enjoy sports, stocks, and all other forms of speculation. Careers involving entertainment and personal creativity are favored. Faith and loyalty in this life are important.

22   In Hindu astrology, the North Node (Rahu) in the fifth house indicates powerful or worldly children, cravings for material benefits, and unsettled peace of mind. The person is considered to have died in his last life while contemplating his money and possessions. Now he is easily able to fulfill his materialistic desires. Unfortunately, however, his cravings may be never-ending. The South Node (Ketu) in the eleventh house means spiritual or psychic friends, difficulties with groups, and strong ability to realize major goals and ambitions in life.

"If you do not change your direction, you are likely to end up where you are headed."

ANCIENT CHINESE PROVERB

If the North Node is in Virgo or the sixth house, the person's greatest growth, evolution, and fulfillment come through routine service, daily work, and attention to details. In past lives, the person has been dreamy, idealistic, religious, and spiritual. Now he must focus on practical matters and learn to deal with boundaries, essentials, and necessities. Careers involving nursing, cooking, haircutting, etc. are all favored. Or the person may fulfill his destiny in any pursuit dealing with knowledge and information. He may be a good writer, editor, accountant, or bookkeeper. The person must investigate, analyze, and evaluate on a daily basis.

The person may have been born wanting to help everyone else, with little concern for his own personal needs. Now he is here to focus on self-improvement, progress, and full development of his talents. He should take care of the quality of his appearance and the food he eats. Health matters are important, and the person should exercise and learn about preventative medicine and healing techniques. He has to relinquish his easygoing ways, and make a lifestyle of discriminating, judging, and attaining perfection in earthly matters. He should work on precision, manual dexterity, technical skills, and any crafts of his choice. Duty and discipline are crucial in this lifetime.

The person should be picky. He should be cautious, careful, and intensely examine all issues. He should seek to understand the details and mechanics of things. The more knowledge he gains, the happier he will be. His task is to categorize and compartmentalize, and create order wherever chaos exists. He should leave wisdom, idealism, and broad perspectives to philosophers. His efforts should be directed toward solving problems and overcoming obstacles. Old tendencies of profound, compassionate sacrifice should be avoided. The person is here for minor service and he will suffer if he acts the part of "savior," or allows others to take advantage of his generous nature. Enjoyment of small pets is favored. Purity and innocence are essential, and the person must never function out of improper motives.

24   In Hindu astrology, the North Node (Rahu) in the sixth house indicates extreme good health and a powerful appetite. The person defeats his enemies and competitors with ease, and therefore may reach the top of his chosen field with little interference or resistance. The South Node (Ketu) in the twelfth is good for spiritual growth and enlightenment. The nodes in the signs are of much less significance.

"For a long time, it had seemed to me that life was about to begin - real life. But there was always some obstacle in the way, something to be gotten through first, some unfinished business, time still to be served, a debt to be paid. Then life would begin. At last it dawned on me that these obstacles were my life."

ALFRED D'SOUZA

If the North Node is in Libra or the seventh house, the person's greatest growth, evolution, and fulfillment come through intimate contact in love unions. In past lifetimes the person was too selfish or self-directed and now must learn how to compromise and cooperate with the individual of his heart's desire. Love relationships and marriage are essential and must not be resisted or opposed, except under extenuating circumstances for brief intervals. The person must discover how to surrender his personal motives and viewpoints, and open up to the needs and concerns of his companion. He is born with confidence, assertiveness, and self-reliance. He has an over-developed personality and sense of independence.

Because the person has had his way for so many lifetimes, he now, unconsciously, finds the experience empty. Consequently, he immerses himself only in relationships which entail great surrender and compromise. To counter this tendency, he should be extremely careful before marrying. He must not in any way assume that a marriage partner will change or alter their desires, behavior, or lifestyle sometime in the future. The sacrifices and concessions necessary in the beginning of the relationship, though they may actually be quite intense and unfair, are certain to continue during the duration of the union. A tremendous amount of devotion is to be learned. It is crucial to note that evolution occurs through affinity with the love partner, not with friends, teachers, or gurus.

The person should develop his social life. Happiness comes from lending a sympathetic ear and cultivating sensitivity to the cares and needs of others. Any activities involving beauty, arts, sweets, jewelry, or other Venusian expressions are to be favored. The person should work on being more idealistic, generous, and affectionate. He should nurture his intellectual, contemplative side and forego his habitual impulsive tendencies. He should try to create balance, harmony, and serenity wherever he goes. The more the person lets go of his personal ego desires, and the more he cultivates tolerance, love, and appreciation, the happier and more fulfilled he will be.

In Hindu predictive astrology, the North Node (Rahu) in the seventh house indicates intense cravings for love relationships, as well as significant ups and downs in married life. Minor issues which need to be addressed are constantly arising (to be dealt with). The spouse is worldly, materialistic, powerful, and manipulative or domineering. The South Node (Ketu) in the first house indicates a spiritual, ascetic, and psychic personality. However, confidence is weakened and the person may be shy, impish, or rather invisible. The nodes in the signs are of much less significance.

"We are all faced with great possibilities brilliantly disguised as impossible situations."

AUTHOR UNKNOWN
QUOTED BY SARAH DOHERTY
FIRST ONE-LEGGED PERSON TO CLIMB MT. MCKINLEY

If the North Node is in Scorpio or the eighth house, the person's greatest growth, evolution, and fulfillment come through relinquishing his desires for possessions, and helping others to determine their values. In past lifetimes, the person has been attached to his acquisitions and engrossed in his cravings for personal security. Now he is learning how to surrender and merge with energies separate from his own. Success and happiness will be found in pursuits involving the occult, metaphysics, mysticism, and psychic work. The person may also do well in politics or other fields which promote causes or campaigns for the good of others. The person should not concern himself too much with his own self-identity and intimate pleasures. He is here for greater purpose and profundity.

Good results occur when the person concentrates on spiritual evolution, soul growth, and psychological transformation. He should focus on ideals, paradigms, and ultimate realities rather than what can be gained from the mundane, physical universe. Sexual experiences are deep, significant, and valuable. The person transcends individuality and merges profoundly through the orgasmic experience. Appearances and physical beauty are not so important. The person must seek that which is deep, real, spiritual, and lasting. He should open himself to all kinds of experiences, without trying to pick and choose the good versus the bad. Passion, power, and self-control are to be cultivated. The person should welcome his newly-vulnerable nature and embrace whatever ego death-and-rebirth experiences come his way.

In Hindu astrology, the North Node (Rahu) in the eighth house and the South Node (Ketu) in the second (or vice versa) are considered the most painful and troublesome node positions. Family life is harmed and there are disturbances in married life. Happiness is not favored. However, there may be good spiritual and mystical experiences. Also, money can be earned from metaphysical or natural healing techniques. The sign positions of the nodes are much less significant.

NORTH NODE IN SAGITTARIUS OR THE NINTH HOUSE
SOUTH NODE IN GEMINI OR THE THIRD HOUSE

If the North Node is in Sagittarius or the ninth house, the person's greatest growth, evolution, and fulfillment come through pursuing religion, philosophy, and higher knowledge. In past lives the person was intellectual, analytical, meticulous, precise, and skeptical. Now he is to cultivate faith, and concentrate on ideals, paradigms, and the ultimate truth of existence. The person should use wisdom and seek broad viewpoints. He must give credence to his intuition, feelings, and inspirations. He must take his visions and prophecies seriously, and give little importance to the petty and inconsequential in daily life. The person gains his greatest happiness by devoting his energies to spiritual ideals, mystical movements, and enlightened gurus. He is exceedingly gifted in promoting religion or any other knowledge which raise the consciousness of the masses. Publishing, as a career, is greatly favored.

The person must continually discriminate between right and wrong, and even make a discipline of the process. He should seek freedom and liberation, and develop his social conscience. Beliefs, principles, and morals are everything, and the person must maintain a positive outlook under all circumstances. The person is eternally concerned with profundities. He knows the meaning of life is to find perfection and God. Money, possessions, and material comforts are of little consideration. The person should seek to increase his generosity and charitable nature. Travel is a source of evolution, and the person may wish to engage in foreign affairs. He should take fun and recreation seriously, and enjoy speculations when he feels the impulse.

The person may pay little attention to relationships with siblings and relatives. He must relinquish his previously constricted or microscopic way of thinking and allow his perception and insights to take him to the highest interpretation of life that is possible. In Hindu astrology, the North Node (Rahu) in the ninth house indicates cravings for religion and higher knowledge, and great power after the age of forty-one. However, there may also be difficulties with the father and religious or spiritual teachers. The South Node (Ketu) in the third house means that the person is strong-willed, exciting and adventurous, and good at fulfilling his desires. It also signifies a spiritual, introspective, or introverted younger sibling. The nodes in the signs are of much less significance.

If the North Node is in Capricorn or the tenth house, the person's greatest growth, evolution, and fulfillment come through concentrated career activity. In previous lives, the person may have led existences that were extremely personal and emotionally acute. Now he must come out to the public and direct his energies toward society. The person is born with deep, organic ties to his mother. He is extraordinarily sensitive to his early family life and all the surrounding conditions and circumstances. However, he soon learns that his niche in the world derives from activities that capture the attention and notice of humankind at large. He becomes increasingly intimate with his father and other authoritarians with each passing year. More than any other astrological placement, the person with this North Node placement may feel a sense of purpose and destiny. He is very ambitious and likely to succeed in his professional life. He may find his calling early on and move toward the work like an arrow to its target. There is leadership ability and the possibility of fame. Although the North Node signifies new realms for the soul to master (realms that may seem scary or intimidating), the person is exceptionally courageous about pursuing his ultimate dreams and visions. Homes, land, and property are not much favored unless the person has decided that real estate is the domain in which to make his mark. Though he never forgets his connection to family, ancestors, and the past, the person is actively forging a new path toward a much broader base of influence. The person should beware of workaholic tendencies or his personal life will suffer. He is likely to marry a partner who is particularly devoted to home and domesticity, a spouse who will not disturb his involvement in his mission. He must direct his attentions to large-scale organizing rather than close friends and loved ones.

The person should concern himself with fame, prestige, and status. He should seek to become an authority figure in his field. His sense of security comes from his work and reputation, not possessions or home life. He is moving away from a highly subjective, feeling-oriented existence to one of hard work and fulfillment of ideals. He is conservative, worldly, serious, and rational. He sets high goals and allows nothing to stand in his way. The person is of extremely developed spirit and soul powers. The task of this life is to make the greatest use of his conscious-

30 ness. He should not engage in contemplation, meditation, introspection, and seclusion for more than brief, intermittent periods of time. His duties are social and his greatest happiness comes from being with people on a regular basis. His work must produce results that withstand the test of time. He should never lose himself in theories and abstractions.

In dealing with the masses, the person must be careful not to get trapped into giving too much time and energy to specific individuals. He must always remember his larger purpose. Professions involving one-on-one contact are not desirable; they will not be fulfilling for any length of time. In Hindu astrology, the North Node (Rahu) in the tenth house indicates a potent and thriving career. The person is especially capable of affecting and influencing "mllechas," peasants or non-Hindus. Career success grows stronger after the age of forty-one when Rahu is considered to "mature." The South Node (Ketu) in the fourth house means difficulties with homes, cars, and mother. It also indicates an innately spiritual nature and religious pilgrimages throughout the lifetime. The nodes in the signs are much less significant.

If the North Node is in Aquarius or the eleventh house, the person's greatest growth, evolution, and fulfillment come through performing altruistic acts for society, getting involved with groups and friends, and developing a sense of detachment. In past lives the person may have been extremely proud, renowned, and ego-oriented. Now he is here to care for the citizenry of the world. He must let go of emotional attachments, and seek to improve existing conditions of the common person. He should try to locate and abolish outdated forms and structures, and implement new, innovative, efficient methods wherever he can. The person should not place great attention on children, intense love affairs, and deeply personal pursuits.

The person should favor his mind, not his impulse. He must cultivate the intellect and allow his rational mind to take precedence. Science and research endeavors are favored. Rules, regulations, dogma, and rhetoric are not to be greatly regarded. The person is learning a much more impersonal style of functioning. He is concerned with knowledge, information, and truth, and is relinquishing old habits of sentimental convictions and individual preferences. Commitment to ideals, especially the betterment of humankind, is crucial. The person must perceive life from the viewpoint of society. He should take life easy, not intensely. He should meet with friends and groups regularly, and effortlessly discover causes and campaigns worth furthering. Freedom, liberty, and equality for all must always be supported.

Fame and recognition are psychologically unimportant. The person may be a pioneer or revolutionary, but he is never to allow his reputation to go to his head. He should always favor activities which have never been done before. He does well with utopian movements, current fads, and prevailing crazes. He should generally avoid speculations, gambling, intense passions, and profound romance. His purpose is humanitarian. In Hindu astrology, the North Node (Rahu) in the eleventh house indicates great ability to fulfill major goals and desires. The person earns plenty of wealth from "side ventures," and has powerful, influential, and worldly friends. The South Node (Ketu) in the fifth house means the person's "poorvapunya" or past life credit is connected to spirituality and psychic experience. In other words, in previous lifetimes the person worked hard on attaining enlightenment and evolutionary growth, and in this life he gains the benefits. Ketu in the fifth does not produce many children. But those that are born will be introspective, psychic, contemplative, and decidedly spiritual.

"The important thing is this: to be able at any moment to sacrifice what we are for what we could become."

CHARLES DUBOIS

If the North Node is in Pisces or the twelfth house, the person's greatest growth, evolution, and fulfillment come through serving others in a profound way. In past lives, the person concentrated on daily work, mundane tasks, and his own perfection and self-improvement. Now he is to devote his energy to idealistic callings, benevolent endeavors, and the betterment of humankind. He may be drawn to medicine, psychology, metaphysics, mysticism, religion, or any activity which heals or uplifts others. Or he may relieve the pain and suffering of the masses through heartfelt artistic expression. Singing is especially favored. The person is learning to let go of his old patterns of criticizing, evaluating, and picking things apart. Now he must be as generous as he can be. He should give, give, and then give more. He should live from the heart, not the mind. Happiness comes from working to further the highest vision of human life, with no thought of personal gain. The more noble and virtuous the person's motives, the faster and greater his evolution will be.

The person should cultivate faith and develop his spiritual nature. His main task is to transcend self-interest. He should adopt a lifestyle of love, compassion, and understanding. Above all, he must never condemn or judge others, even the worst of the human race. When he does, he brings sorrow, grief, and shame onto himself. The higher part of his being simply will not tolerate small and narrow behavior. The person should champion the cause of peace, harmony, and brotherhood. He must look for the best in others and refrain from gossip, negativity, and pessimism. Of all possible life paths, his is the highest and most majestic. He should consider the spirit behind peoples' actions, and bear in mind the complexity and rigor of human life.

The person is not here to be cautious, careful, and sensible. He is seeking enlightenment and ultimate freedom. He wants to live a life of purity, devotion, and union with the Infinite. He must pursue his ideals, visions, and inspirations. Material comforts are of little importance. The person may wish to perform major service. He may work in hospitals, clinics, nursing homes, or other institutions which aid society. He must follow his intuition and feelings. He will be happy living near the sea.

34 Artistic endeavors are favored. In Hindu astrology, the North Node (Rahu) in the twelfth house indicates cravings for spiritual growth and "moksha" — final liberation. There may also be intense sexual enjoyment. The South Node (Ketu) in the sixth house reveals very strong health, excellent ability to defeat enemies and competitors, and daily work involving metaphysical healing techniques. The nodes in the signs are of much less significance.

"For unto whomsoever much is given, of him shall much be required: and to whom men have committed much, of him they will ask the more."

LUKE 12:48

Planetary aspects are the most powerful and consistently accurate feature of Western birthchart analysis. Aspects are the heart and soul of the system.

Aspects are planetary relationships based upon divisions of the 360° zodiac. 360° divided by two = 180°. If two planets are 180° apart, they are said to be in an "opposition" aspect. 360° divided by three = 120° (the trine aspect). 360° divided by four = 90° (the square). 360° divided by six = 60° (the sextile). 360° divided by one = 360° (the conjunction — planets very close together). The conjunction, square, sextile, trine, and opposition are the "major" aspects in the birthchart, and are the ones described in this book. (The quincunx, or 150° aspect is regarded as a major aspect by some, but it is not discussed here.)

Aspects symbolize psychological and behavior patterns, as well as karmic events and circumstances that are likely to occur. Aspects reveal fundamental characteristics and attributes of a person. Despite the variables and multitudinous factors which must be taken into account when analyzing planetary relationships (signs, elements, orbs, applying motion versus separating motion, etc.), aspects always work. Because of free will, environmental factors, spiritual evolution, and the nature of life itself, no astrological feature is to be categorized or pigeonholed with absolute definitiveness. Yet, every significant (strong by degree) planetary aspect operates in some definite, *perceptible* way.

Planets in houses and planetary rulerships, on the other hand, are a source of much debate. Most practicing astrologers, after three or four years of experience, begin to question the accuracy of information symbolized by the planets in houses. What usually occurs at this point is a good deal of experimentation with various "house systems" (Koch, Placidus, Campanus, Regiomontanus, etc.). Eventually each astrologer finds a house system that he or she is comfortable with, one that seems to give reliable results *for the particular charts researched*. My belief, however, is that there may be fundamental problems with the Western method of distinguishing birthchart houses. Or at best, it may be that planets-in-houses in the Western system are useful only in symbolizing the character and psychological profile of a person. Thus, they are not reliable to an astrologer interested in any kind of predictive work.

Because I am not a technical (investigative or research-oriented) astrologer, I cannot speak conclusively about the matter. I do not feel that planets-in-houses should be ignored. In the cases of the North and South Nodes, they work extremely well in providing information about the motives and psychology of a person. But, having studied and practiced Hindu astrology, where house rulerships and planets-in-houses function very much like clockwork, it is clear that Western house systems do not work with a respectable degree of consistency. I would not consider Western house systems to be fundamentally inaccurate just because they work only sixty or seventy percent of the time. (After all, astrology never reaches complete accuracy anyway.) But my experience indicates that Western houses and house rulerships produce accurate results only when they exactly match the Hindu positions for the same chart! Time and time again, when I have noted a planet in a certain house in the Western chart that resides in a different house of the Hindu chart, the symbolism of the planet in the Hindu chart yields the objectively verifiable results in the person's life.

        Furthermore, the curious results of the Gauquelin studies, which showed planets in cadent (third, sixth, ninth, and twelfth) houses to be strong, may be better understood in light of Hindu astrology. Gauquelin's findings were in blatant opposition to the traditional teachings that consider the angular (first, fourth, seventh, and tenth) houses the most powerful, and the cadent houses the weakest. I have practiced Hindu and Western astrology, side by side, over the past ten years or so. I have continually noticed planets in <u>cadent</u> houses in Western charts falling in <u>angular</u> houses in the same person's Hindu chart. Thus, I consider it more likely that the cadent planets that Gauquelin proved to be so powerful were really angular. Gauquelin might have discovered this himself, had he used a consistently accurate house system such as the ancient traditional Hindu method. (There are actually two different Hindu house systems in use. Most astrologers use both concurrently, but give more weight to the older method.).

        Suffice it to say, Western astrology's house rulerships and planets-in-houses do not produce results as accurate and precise as Western astrology's planetary aspects or zodiac sign placements. Aspects and zodiac sign symbolism, quite simply, are the core of Western astrology; house rulerships and planets in houses are the basis and beauty of the Hindu system. Those who are practicing Western astrology should, of course, continue analyzing and interpreting planets-in-houses, but place greater significance, and trust, in planetary aspects. As for using house rulerships in Western astrology, I advise caution even to the extent of skepticism. However, one should not fret unduly about the matter. The star language is, most definitely, a cosmic science. Practitioners often succeed in spite of faulty techniques due to their intuition, inspiration, psychic ability, etc.

Finally, in order not to be accused of favoring one system over the other (I believe astrologers should use both systems, side by side), I wish to say that there is nothing in astrology so magnificent as Western planetary aspects. I would be lost in my practice without them.

"People do not care how much you know until they know how much you care."

POWELL

CONJUNCTIONS

Conjunctions are often considered the most powerful of all aspects and are neutral in nature. Conjunction indicates a blending of the energies involved, and yields either positive or negative effects depending upon the natures and compatibilities of the planets in aspect. Two benefic planets close together produce harmony, while a conjunction involving even one malefic planet generally causes some grief and discord. Planets conjunct the Sun are said to be "combust" or burned up by the rays of the hot Sun. The closer the conjunction with the Sun, the more afflicted the planet will be. Modern astrologers tend to ignore, or downplay, the effects of combustion. However, this is a serious mistake. Combustion is a significant astrological condition which symbolizes noticeable results in a person's life. This book takes such effects into account. Finally, it is worth noting that planets conjunct the Sun have the effect of coloring, or shading, the Sun sign. For example, if the Sun is in the sign of Virgo, but conjunct Saturn, the person will behave somewhat like a Capricorn because Saturn rules that sign. If the Sun is conjunct Venus, the person will be somewhat Libran and/or Taurean, no matter what their Sun sign.

SQUARES

The square (the 90° aspect) is often regarded as the most difficult planetary relationship. Part of the intense strain is caused by the fact that the two planets involved occupy incompatible elements. (Earth-sign energy is compatible with water-sign energy. Air-sign energy is compatible with fire-sign energy). Two planets involved in a square aspect not only fail to function harmoniously, they operate at definite cross-purposes. Each planet symbolizes a particular feature of the personality trying to get its own way, while ignoring the needs of the other feature. Unfortunately, fulfilling the needs of both is important to the person's happiness. Furthermore, squares are characterized by a lack of awareness. In other words, people with a strong square aspect are largely unaware that they have an actual problem; they are also unaware that the problem is caused by their own inharmonious and unintegrated psyche and behavior. These people simply think they are periodically harassed or victimized, for no good reason.

Most importantly, the dilemma of hard aspects (squares and oppositions) has its roots in two "ignorant" ways of functioning: The first is a deep attachment to some personal desire or agenda that the person feels they cannot relinquish or surrender to the ways of nature. The second is the arrogance of believing that one's obstacles are caused by external circumstances, other people, or anything outside the self. This makes dealing with square aspects especially difficult. Handling hard aspects cannot even begin until the person adopts a significant degree of humility, and openness to the advice and support of others. The remedy lies in the willingness to see one's responsibility in causing all personal experience. Also, the person must make use of the intellect, and consider that feelings are not necessarily useful, accurate, or even particularly real (ultimately). Surrender is definitely required.

OPPOSITIONS

When two planets are 180° apart, or exactly opposite each other, the energies involved manifest themselves with a marked lack of balance, perspective, and proportion. Behavioral extremes are quite likely. The person feels a perpetual "either/or" influence, as if receiving either the benefits of one planet's energies or the benefits of other planet's energies — but never both. More than anything, compromise is needed. Having planets in opposition to each other is similar to having a planet in the first house and a planet in the seventh house. Therefore, experiences generated by opposition aspects nearly always involve other people. In this sense, the opposition is perhaps more specific in its karmic nature. For example, if Venus is square Pluto, a person may be vulnerable in love matters and experience painful emotional incidents with many different lovers throughout life. Such love affairs, however, could involve any individuals, in order for the person to learn his or her required lessons. But, if Venus is opposite Pluto, the person is more likely to undergo one or two distinctly "fated" relationships, wherein the karmic retribution is extremely unique and specific. The person may feel that the difficulties experienced with the other person are EXACTLY deserved, even though there is no logical reason to feel this way, and even though the circumstances may be incredibly unfair.

Like square aspects, oppositions always indicate a good deal of struggle, friction, and resistance. Indeed, oppositions cause as much, and often more, pain than squares. However, oppositions are somewhat easier to deal with than squares, because the problems created through oppositions manifest on a more external or circumstantial level, rather than internally, deep within the psyche. Thus, the person becomes aware of his or her opposition problems fairly quickly. Furthermore, after continually encountering difficult predicaments of the same nature, one

42 eventually comes to realize that they are creating the situations from their own unconscious. Unlike the effects of a square aspect, the person soon notices a pattern of "projection" (creating problems in the outer world in order to become aware of inner complexes). Once the awareness dawns, the person can then begin to assume personal responsibility. From that point on, the problem can be consciously addressed. Handling opposition aspects requires adjustment, moderation, and a sense of appropriateness. The person absolutely must consider the opinions and feelings of the others with whom he or she is involved. Clearly, the task is to gain as much objectivity as possible.

The <u>benefit</u> of squares and oppositions is that they often produce tremendous growth and evolution, depending upon the integrity, commitment, and intention of the individual. Persons with hard aspects are constantly being tested. Moreover, humans need a certain degree of struggle and inner strife to arouse ambition, aspiration, and accomplishment. It is extremely rare to see a great and powerful person who does not have at least a few very intense squares or oppositions in his or her birthchart. Hard aspects are dynamic in nature and they promote constant challenge and confrontation. It is the hard aspects, not the trines and sextiles, which create strength, fortitude, and character.

TRINES

The 120° aspect is an influence of good luck, grace, charm, and benefit. A trine aspect indicates talent that a person is simply born with. Trines do not require struggle or effort in order to manifest and give value. However, trines should definitely be activated and appreciated. Individuals with trines should consciously try to make the most of their ability and good fortune. Unfortunately, because the aspect confers abilities which come so easily, there is a great tendency to take the particular aptitude or genius indicated for granted. In fact, it is undesirable to have many trines in a birthchart without also having some significant squares and oppositions present. In such cases, the person is likely to be lazy, superficial, and wasteful. Astrologers witness this quite regularly. On the other hand, a chart with no trines at all may indicate a lifetime of too much struggle, strain, and scarcity.

Although trines appear to manifest as gifts from God, there is certainly a corresponding behavioral pattern which may be understood as causing the easy and graceful experiences. The person has a tremendous sense of optimism. Regarding the particular energies indicated by the planets in trine aspect, the person absolutely expects good results to occur. He or she has no doubts whatsoever, nor any negative thoughts, about fulfillment of desires. Since thought is the creative power of the universe, the person naturally succeeds. Trines also mean that the person behaves with openness, flexibility, and a marked lack of attachment or arrogance in the realms symbolized by the particular aspect.

SEXTILES

The sextile (60° aspect) is, like the trine, quite harmonious. However, rather than producing sheer luck and fortune, it indicates the OPPOR-TUNITY to create good results concerning the two planets in aspect. To make the most of a sextile, the person must be willing to seriously and patiently work on the energies indicated. Many people tend to ignore the talent and beneficial results a sextile can bring, unless the rest of the birthchart is quite afflicted or difficult. In such cases, the person feels he or she has little choice but to develop and nurture what few opportunities exist. However, there will almost certainly be good effects in the end if one concentrates on the energies of the existing sextiles. There is to no way to know whether or not a person is making use of their sextiles without asking them. However, sextiles can only be considered a potential benefit to a birthchart.

ORB OF INFLUENCE

The orb of influence has to do with how exact a planetary relationship must be in order to still produce recognizable results. For example, the square aspect occurs when planets are exactly ninety degrees away from each other. But a square still exists if the planets are, say, ninety-three or ninety-four degrees apart. Those three or four degrees are considered the orb of influence.

Astrologers differ in their opinions of workable orbs. Many textbooks advocate allowing eight or ten degree orbs for aspects, depending on the planets involved and other particulars. However, in practice I believe such an orb is generally too wide. Robert Hand, in his superb book "Horoscope Symbols," suggests an orb of five degrees for the conjunction, square, trine, and opposition, and three degrees for the sextile. In my own practice, I take note of aspects which occur within eight degrees, but speak to clients only about aspects within five degrees (or six at most). The main reason for considering seven- or eight-degree orb aspects is that if a person has very few planetary relationships, or only very weak ones, "wide" aspects may indeed play a part in the person's life. Also, if a particular planet is "aspected" by five or six other planets, even though those aspects all have wide orbs, there will be a significant result. For instance, if Mercury forms trines with three planets, and sextiles with two or three others, even if the aspects are of very wide orbs, the person is likely to be extremely communicative or gifted in writing. Finally, it is a rule of thumb that the personal planets (Sun, Moon, and Mercury) may be allowed wider orbs of influence because of their sensitive natures and the great importance of their energies in a person's life.

"APPLYING" ASPECTS VERSUS "SEPARATING" ASPECTS

When analyzing two planets in a relationship, it is important to note whether the faster-moving planet is moving <u>toward</u> the exact aspect or <u>away</u> from it. Let us use, for example, a Moon-Pluto conjunction. If the Moon is in five degrees Libra, and Pluto occupies nine degrees Libra, then the Moon (the faster of the two heavenly bodies) is moving <u>toward</u> the exact conjunction (which would occur in nine degrees Libra). This would be an "applying" conjunction, and its influence is more intense than it would be if the planets were moving away from an exact aspect. If the Moon is in twelve degrees Libra, moving further away from Pluto (in nine degrees Libra), the aspect would be "separating" and its effects would be slightly lessened.

Although "applying" and "separating" motion is certainly significant, one should not take the matter too rigidly. If an aspect is separating but extremely close by degree (i.e. a ninety-two degree separating square), the influence in the person's life is still very intense. Furthermore, some studies have indicated that the strongest effect of an aspect occurs very shortly after the exact aspect! Perhaps the most effective use of "applying" versus "separating" motion is to consider "applying" aspects within three degrees of exactness as very profound, and "separating" aspects which are three or four degrees away from exact as decidedly less potent. It is all, of course, relative. Aspects will always have varying grades of impact. It is also worth mentioning that a retrograde planet involved in a planetary aspect is either backing away from a perfect aspect or backing toward one. A planet retrograding toward the exact aspect obviously indicates a more intense effect.

VERY FEW ASPECTS IN A BIRTHCHART

Having very few aspects in a birthchart can mean several things. Most typically, a person with few aspects feels more free will than most people. The person is not much pulled or driven to any particular behavior or activity. Such individuals experience little sense of destiny, and have difficulty finding their niche in life. Great depth and worldly accomplishment is rather unlikely. The person feels a definite frustration, but never feels it intensely enough to be moved to action. On the positive side, if a person with few aspects makes a serious commitment to something, other obligations will not distract from the task. Lack of determination or perseverance is certainly possible, but other karmic obligations are unlikely to intrude.

I am reminded of my early days in astrology, before owning a computer. I wanted to examine the chart of a very renowned Indian guru, Swami

Brahmananda Saraswati (also known as Guru Dev, the spiritual master of Maharishi Mahesh Yogi). Guru Dev left home at the tender age of nine and spent four years seeking an enlightened guru. Having found his teacher, he spent the next fifty or sixty years meditating in a cave! Eventually, the people of India implored the great saint to come out of silence and assume the seat of "Shankaracharya" (a priestly position that involves ministering to the masses of Northern India — the seat had been vacant over one hundred years). The reason I wanted to see Guru Dev's birthchart was to examine the astrological symbolism indicating his spiritual and worldly greatness. The problem was that Guru Dev was born on December 20th, 1868 and my ephemeris only went back as far as 1900.

When I finally obtained a computer that could produce the desired birthchart, I was shocked to find that the chart had a dearth of planetary aspects. There were four trines (one strong by degree, the others fairly weak) and one or two POSSIBLE hard aspects to the Moon (depending upon the exact time of birth). Aside from some distinct spiritual talent and grace, the chart did not appear special by any stretch of the imagination. I eventually concluded that having few aspects could be quite beneficial if the soul is highly evolved and if, somehow, the person does decide firmly about his or her commitment in life. In such cases, the person is wonderfully free to act without the hindrance of all sorts of obligations, duties, and past karmas continually coming due.

ASPECTS TO BIRTHCHART ANGLES AND NODES

Aspects to the Ascendant, Midheaven, and lunar nodes are significant and important. Unfortunately, they are beyond the scope of this work and may be covered in a future text. Regarding nodal conjunctions, planets conjunct the South Node function poorly because the South Node represents a kind of "dead end," evolution wise. In Hindu astrology, Ketu (the South Node) is a psychic, astral, otherworldly influence. As such, any planet coming close to Ketu becomes a seriously uncontrollable influence, as if lost in a kind of black hole. For example, Venus conjunct the South Node indicates strange luck in love matters (i.e. attractions to alcoholics, unavailable partners, or weird individuals etc.). Mercury conjunct Ketu indicates an indecisive, confused, or wavering mind that functions partially in the present and partially in the astral plane. Some Western astrologers believe that planets conjunct the South Node indicate karmic retribution for failing to pursue North Node activities lifetime after lifetime. Planets conjunct the North Node function well because the North Node represents a point of positive focus. If Venus is conjunct the North Node, the person is talented in artistic and aesthetic endeavors. If the Moon is conjunct the North Node, the person does well with agriculture or the public, etc. Hindu astrology considers even conjunctions to the North Node to be somewhat malefic, but that should not concern Western astrologers for now.

If the Sun is conjunct the Moon, the person is of a feeling or moody nature. He may be domestic and family-oriented. The person has great common sense. He is ambitious and successful. He is good at caring for others and may be a wonderful cook. His ties to his mother and father are extreme. This may create resentment in his wife and children, who feel they do not come first. There is much pain or suffering on account of the mother, due to the Moon (ruler of mother) being "combust" or burned by the hot Sun. However, the relationship is a most important one. The person strongly desires his mother's affection and wants to be close to her. He will give more than he receives in the relationship. The closer the aspect (by degree), the more intense (and/or difficult) the results will be.

The person is well-integrated in that his willpower and emotions function as one. He knows his wants and needs. However, because he is so affected by moods and feelings, he is constantly beginning new projects which he does not finish. Since the Moon rules females, a man with this placement gets a "Sun-type" woman. The wife may be powerful, dignified, or authoritative. As the Sun rules men, a woman with this conjunction gets a "Moon-type" or nurturing, emotional, caring husband. Most importantly, the person lives a life of great singularity. He is concerned with a few affairs and is absolutely one-pointed in them. The nature of his interests will be shown by the sign and house placements of the Sun and Moon. The element (or sign) involved is also crucial. In an air sign, this conjunction indicates a great intellectual or mental nature; a fire sign element will produce an ambitious, impulsive, and creative type; and so on.

Because the Sun and Moon represent the two most important and personal planetary energies in the birthchart, their conjunction is complex. The person is more intricate than he seems. In this conjunction, the Sun (being the indicator of the spirit, soul, and individuality) is affected by all the significations of the Moon. Therefore, the person is emotional, sensitive, receptive, nurturing, etc. However, the Moon (indicator of the personality, emotional response, and habit patterns) is being affected by the energy of the Sun. Thus, the person is strong-willed, powerful, dignified, confident, and authoritative. In effect, the person is a perfect combination of "yin" and "yang" (masculine and feminine) energy. Both ways of being are essential and at the person's disposal. Marlon Brando has the Sun-Moon conjunction within one degree. Harrison Ford, Enrico Caruso, and Jackie Robinson all have (or had) very close Sun-Moon conjunctions.

The most difficult feature of this aspect is that even though the person is exceedingly logical, he may lack a certain objectivity. The person experiences life in a much more personal and self-oriented way than others. This is because both aspects of his being, the personality and the spirit, are responding to every stimulus in nearly the exact same manner. The person is likely to be selfish, self-centered, or self-obsessed — but not purposefully, malevolently, or even consciously so. In other words, the person is self-absorbed or self-interested, but not in a "Mars-type," aggressive way. Depending on the extremity of his actions, the person's behavior may be somewhat appropriate because it corresponds to the "double" personal experience he lives with.

The person must be made aware of his "difference" if he is to get along well in close relationships. It is likely that others will have difficulty in genuinely knowing the person. There is also a possibility that he is repressed, isolated, or psychologically affected by latent or subconscious factors. The Sun rules the father, and in this case the Sun gains by its association with the benefic Moon. Therefore, the person's father may be powerful, special, or successful. The person loves his father and benefits from him. The person is "Cancerian" in nature. He is security-oriented, good with the public, and absorbs experience like a sponge. However, he may also be quiet or often "in his own world." He also may be slow, lazy, lethargic, or indulgent. He is popular and excited about life. There may be strong possessiveness and tenacity in relationships. The person is psychically sensitive. He is tremendously adaptable but may, at times, be too impressionable or changing.

In Hindu astrology, the brighter the Moon at the time of birth, the more comfortable and fortunate the life of the person and his mother. A dim Moon is considered weak and afflicted. The Sun-Moon conjunction occurs at the time of the new, or dim, Moon. Therefore a person with the aspect may lack confidence and the ability to gain recognition. Life is generally more strenuous and there may be problems with the breast, brain, and (for women) the menstrual cycle.

If the Sun is square or opposite the Moon, the person feels like a split being. He is torn in different directions and feels a major dichotomy between his emotions and spirit. His feelings take him one way, his willpower another. Because the Sun and Moon rule father and mother, the hard aspects indicate that the person's parents were discordant at the time of the child's conception. Thus, the person feels a significant lack of inner harmony. He is pulled between his masculine, aggressive tendencies and his soft, feminine side. There is a lifelong ambition, and uphill struggle, to achieve fulfillment and happiness. The person experiences difficulty in making decisions because of his inner turmoil, but is quite successful in his undertakings. His drive to achieve wholeness and self-completion is so strong that he is determined to reach his goals. And he does (especially the person with the Sun opposite Moon). He eventually concludes, of course, that achievements in the outer world do not produce inner peace. But his search is an essential part of his path.

The person suffers, unwittingly, due to imbalanced perspective. Because his emotions are at odds with his spirit he is disadvantaged in comprehending the whole of things. He perceives matters in terms of good and bad, right and wrong, either/or. He is almost entirely incapable of dealing with paradox and is definitely prone to passing judgement. There is plenty of intelligence and shrewdness, and great ability to get his way. But there is little wisdom or depth of understanding. The life is simply too subjective. The person is possessive and strongly attached to material benefits. There may be emotional insecurity and a somewhat poor sense of self which is revealed most dramatically in the person's difficulty with the opposite sex. He is likely to choose a love mate who is extremely different in nature from himself. Thus, the partner is ultimately unable to accept him for who he truly is. Though he blames his mate, it is obvious that he has chosen that person in order to deal with the issues of self-love and self-acceptance, major themes of his life.

The person may be stubborn and defensive. He will definitely have many subconscious habit patterns that are difficult to break. There will be much self-analysis and psychological growth, and the most difficult part of the process is that the person is always looking for objective realities. He does not deal with abstracts, complexities, or intangibles.

Regarding his own evolution, he seeks the simple way out. He looks for physical, concrete symptoms he can alter and be done with, once and for all. He is restless and craves new experiences to fill the void he feels. He wants to find perfection and knows it is "out there." The person is popular and competitive. Relationships are important, indeed crucial, because the person believes his only chance to create wholeness is through outside stimulus, possessions, and resources. Some individuals with Sun-Moon squares or oppositions are inconsistent, because their emotional stability wavers too much. They are also apt to give up on certain features of their lives they feel unable to control.

In Hindu astrology, a lunar-based system, it is extremely desirable to be born under a bright Moon. Therefore the Sun opposite Moon, indicating a full Moon birth, is one of the most auspicious astrological possibilities. One born on a full Moon will be successful, powerful, wealthy, famous, and enjoy many comforts. However, he still has difficulty finding contentment. Vivien Leigh, who suffered from depression, had the Sun-Moon square within three and one half degrees. Richard Dreyfuss has the Sun-Moon opposition within two degrees. Though he is one of the world's most successful actors, he was plagued with drug abuse problems for several years.

If the Sun is trine or sextile the Moon, the person is emotionally well-balanced. His parents were harmonious at the time of his conception and he is happy, healthy, and well-integrated. His energy flows smoothly, and he feels peaceful and at ease with himself. There is a strong constitution and the person recovers quickly from debilitating experiences. There is dignity, charm, and magnetism. The person is stable and adaptable. He is optimistic and has good instinct. The willpower is strong and the person feels directed and purposeful. His goals and aspirations are in tune with his heart.

The person is sincere, natural, and sees no reason to lie. He takes things as they come and does not resist life. He is consistent and dependable. The only drawback to harmonious Sun-Moon aspects is a potential laziness or lack of ambition and urgency. Unless other aspects in the birthchart indicate significant friction and struggle, the person may be too complacent for his own good. Relationships with the opposite sex are favored and the person follows in the footsteps of his compatibly-married parents. Family life is a source of joy. The person is social and popular and there is success in dealings with the public. Respect is easily earned. Most of all, the person moves through life gracefully, with little regret, bitterness, or remorse. He is self-responsible, mature, and does not make an issue of his abilities.

The trine aspect is significantly more powerful than the sextile. The sextile indicates the opportunity to make the above characteristics a reality.

If the Sun is conjunct Mercury, the person is mentally active. He is intellectual, self-expressive, and talkative. He is curious and wants to know about everything. The person is ambitious, creative, and has especially good business sense. He may excel in writing, lecturing, debating, or any intellectual field. He has great mental energy and excellent learning capacity. He is optimistic. Because Mercury rules the nervous system and in this case is "combust" or burned by the hot Sun, the person is nervous, restless, and often lacking in patience. The person may be high-strung. His mind, in working too fast, may sometimes lack depth. Health-wise, the person is susceptible to lung problems and difficulties with the intestines and nervous system. It is crucial to note the closeness, by degree, of the conjunction of the Sun and Mercury. The stronger the "combustion," the more intense the effects will be all the way around.

The person is a fine teacher. He possesses the qualities of a Virgo and a Gemini. He is perceptive, analytical, and critical. He can sell anything. However, Mercury's combustion with the Sun limits the person's objectivity and impartiality. The person lacks perspective regarding himself and his actions. He is unaware of his chronic "blind spots." The person may be somewhat egocentric and occasionally dogmatic, stubborn, or narrow in thought. This is because the Sun and Mercury (representing the spirit and mind) are in the same sign. This creates a "double experience" of everything.

The person has good willpower. He is witty, humorous, and has a dramatic mind. He will benefit from his father, who may be intelligent, intellectual, and expressive. The person may be extremely talkative and he may need to develop better listening skills. Because Mercury and the Sun are never more than ninety degrees apart, their conjunction is a very common aspect. It is also the only aspect that is possible between the two.

If the Sun is conjunct Venus, the person is kind, gentle, and warmhearted. He is adept at making others feel good. He is highly refined and excels in music, dance, drama or any artistic profession. There will be an abundance of charm and personal magnetism. The person is protected throughout life by a sort of divine grace or "guardian angel" which manifests as intuition against danger and plain old luck. There is almost no possibility of ever being harmed, in a major way, by violence or accident. The person is loved by all, especially the opposite sex. A woman with this placement is the most desired of all females. She may also be a beauty queen or fashion model. The Sun-Venus conjunction is an aspect of extreme good karma and therefore the person gains benefits and fulfills desires with little effort. The person is optimistic, happy, and innately content. However, because he is devoid of struggle, he may be too easygoing or lazy, or have a tendency to procrastinate. Compared to the rest of society, the person is spoiled. This aspect, by itself, is more detrimental than beneficial to hard work and accomplishment. In the long run, there may be suffering on such account.

The person has great feminine energy and therefore the aspect is more useful to females. The person is occasionally taken advantage of, in a big way, because of an overdeveloped desire to compromise. He is appreciative, aesthetically-oriented, and likes to be surrounded by beauty and comforts. Although the person is capable of charming anyone and obtaining nearly any love partner he desires, there will be difficulties in the love life. This is due to Venus being "combust" or burned by the rays of the hot Sun. The closer the aspect, the more harm there will be in relationships or married life. The person is sensual, passionate, and good-looking. He is a romantic and desires total peace and harmony. He will love life, parties, and all social activities. Since the Sun rules the father, and is conjunct benefic Venus, there are good results in that realm. The person is much loved by his father, who may be beautiful, refined, artistic and special. There may be problems with the throat or reproductive system. A woman with the aspect may get a powerful or domineering husband.

Business magnate Ted Turner has the Sun conjunct Venus within one and one half degrees. Renaissance artist Rafael and the great English poet Percy Shelley also had very close Sun-Venus conjunctions.

If the Sun is conjunct Mars, the person is strong, energetic, and assertive. He is adventurous and lives an exciting life. The person has great courage and never backs down from a challenge. Indeed, he is highly competitive and driven by his ego. He likes to stir things up and may occasionally argue or provoke a fight for no reason. The person is stubborn in fulfilling his desires. He may intimidate or overpower others to get his way. Life may be a personal and selfish endeavor to this person. He is overly subjective. The person is talented in mechanics or any technical field. He may be attracted to drafting, engineering, police work, firefighting, or the military. If inclined toward medicine, he will be a surgeon. The person has strong blood and will be muscular or in good physical shape all his life. His constitution is solid and he combats illnesses well. He excels in sports and may become a professional athlete.

The person is hard-working and extroverted. He does not take his desires lightly and is unrelenting when committed to an issue. He is opinionated. The person is highly sexed, though such experiences may be more important to his ego than his senses. The Sun-Mars aspect is, in most ways, more conducive to quantity than quality or depth. Unless there are contrary aspects in the birthchart, the person may tend toward superficiality. He will lack self-reflection or introspective ability. The person may be rash, impatient, and highly impulsive. He may be a great fighter of crusades and may be a ruler or commander. He loves to give orders or boss people around. A man or woman with this aspect is proud and has strong masculine energy. The person must beware of accidents and fires. He should exercise daily to keep his energy flowing smoothly. Otherwise, there is a chance of occasionally attracting violence or aggressiveness from others. The person is likely to have high standards and good moral strength. He does not surrender or compromise.

The person lives with internal fire or anger that comes and goes, but never completely disappears. It is a physical, constitutionally induced condition, and is not due to any particular psychological cause. There is potentially a very hot temper. The person is alert, sharp, and decisive. He is entirely action-oriented. He may be susceptible to fevers or blood poisons, but only if the rest of the birthchart indicates health problems. Most importantly the person must learn concern for others when fulfilling his own needs. A woman with this placement is likely to have roughness in her marriage. She attracts Mars-type men who are overly physical, aggressive, and argumentative. There may be a constant battle over who will dominate the other.

David Bowie and Bruce Dern have the Sun-Mars conjunction within one and two degrees respectively. Metaphysician Elbert Benjamin (pen named C.C. Zain) and Upton Sinclair, the impassioned muckraker writer, had the Sun-Mars conjunction within one degree.

"People are always blaming their circumstances for what they are. I don't believe in circumstances. The people who get on in this world are the people who get up and look for the circumstances they want, and if they can't find them, make them."

GEORGE BERNARD SHAW

If the Sun is square or opposite Mars, the person misuses his energy and aggressiveness. His desire nature is too connected to his ego, and there is very little objectivity in the realm of compromise and social interaction. The person sees competition everywhere and feels it is his duty to win in every situation. The energy is entirely outward-directed. Introspection and self-reflection are almost impossible unless the person is alone, with no one to debate or quarrel against. Despite the definite negative tendencies of hard Sun-Mars aspects, the person is not, in most cases, purposefully mean or bad. He is simply oblivious to his true nature. He does not know that he is particularly self-centered and antagonistic. Because he is driven by his ego, he feels it is correct and proper to assert himself and get his way. He is often blinded to the feelings of others unless they match how he would react under the same circumstances. He does not empathize with other points of view and feels he is a good, upstanding person. Al Capone, the great gangster, had the opposition aspect, within a two-degree orb. Two individuals with the Sun-Mars square are Lucille Ball and Muhammad Ali.

The person is bold, strong, and forceful. He generally gets what he wants and is likely to be successful in his field. He may, of course, make enemies along the way. He is intensely ambitious and his desires are deeply rooted. He takes big risks and rushes impulsively towards his goal. There are strong sexual urges and the person is more concerned with quantity than quality. His conquests bolster his ego. The person may be seriously impatient, and there is much frustration during the life. Though accomplishments are favored and abundant, the person is rarely satisfied. He considers himself the leader, and best amongst men, and until he reaches the highest peak of success he does not rest easy. There is a possibility of high stress, strain, and overwork. Furthermore, the person may live with a continual sense of anger, bitterness, and heat in the body.

The person suffers on account of his father. There may be a history of violence, hatred, and cruelty in this realm. Females with the Sun-Mars square or opposition are in danger of being sexually abused or violated by the father and men in general. They are attracted to lovers who are aggressive, physical, highly-sexed, mean, and/or violent. For these reasons, women especially should beware of an early marriage based upon passion, lust, and sexual chemistry. Females with the Sun-Mars aspect also generally have a more difficult time socially, since their brashness and opinionated natures are more conspicuous.

The person is courageous, proud, and action-oriented. He is an individualist and does not yield to pressure. He stands up for what he considers right. There is a strong constitution and the health is robust. Problems may occur in the heart, but only if the aspect is extremely close by degree. The person enjoys a challenge and is an especially good soldier to have on one's side in times of combat and competition. There is a need for tact, diplomacy, and sensitivity to others. The person must, at some point, learn to acknowledge his stubborn, defensive, and obstinate character or he will miss out on much of the joy and sweetness of life. He should also work on the task of listening to others and separating his ego from his wants and needs. His judgement in the higher, more refined matters of life is seriously impaired by his overdeveloped ego. He does well, however, in mundane areas as he well understands the cause and effect of things. He is good mechanically and in the use of his hands.

The person has a powerful temper. He wastes far too much time and energy arguing. He is more accident prone than most and should beware of gaining power by force. He is a natural fighter and thinks compromise and settlement mean losing. There may be a self-destructiveness about the person. More than anything, he should consider the possibility that, because of his intense ego, he never really hears other points of view.

The Sun-Mars opposition generates significantly more friction and difficulties in personal relationships than the square.

If the Sun is trine or sextile Mars, the person has developed efficiency of action. He has a balanced ego, and knows how to use his aggressive energy in a controlled, healthy, and successful way. There is excellent courage and the person is adventurous. He is confident, enthusiastic, and vigorous. The health is strong and vitality is abundant. There is an enterprising nature and plenty of ambition. The person is self-motivated.

There are benefits from the father and men in general. A woman with this aspect attracts men with ease and obtains the love partner she desires. The person is extremely well-integrated in the healthy and skillful way he handles challenge, adversity, and his work in the world. He is consistent and of great endurance. He has learned or inherited exceptional masculine energy. The person is a natural leader and is respected by others in lower positions. He does not abuse his power or authority. He does well in competition, is unaffected by his fears, and loves a good challenge.

Sexual experiences are favored and the person is virile. He is patient, has command over his will, and is occasionally heroic. He is creative, decisive, and gets the job done with minimal fuss. There is a definite independent nature. The person initiates action. He is honest, stable, organized, and focused. He is assertive in a controlled, non-threatening way. He wins often, but is not a braggart. He is practical, authoritative, and hard-working. He achieves plenty of success and rewards in his lifetime, yet does not live for his ego.

The Sun-Mars trine is significantly more powerful than the sextile. The sextile indicates the opportunity to make the above characteristics a reality.

If the Sun is conjunct Jupiter, the person is divinely blessed. He lives a life of luxury and wealth. The person is protected from accidents, violence, and harm. He is optimistic, cheerful, and happy. He expects the best from life, and rightfully so. The person is innately religious. He has a strong, natural faith in God. However, in terms of activity, the life is more connected to pursuing material and worldly pleasures than religious or spiritual ideals. The person is kind, sympathetic, and warm-hearted. He has high moral standards and likes to support charitable causes. He becomes more and more benevolent as he becomes older and wealthier.

The person is strong, extremely healthy, and of the most vital spirit. He is vibrant and vigorous in a very gentle, peaceful way. The person is honest, direct, and above-board. He hides nothing. He is loved by everyone. The person is thrilled with life and meets with abundant opportunities. Because he exudes optimism, he is the best salesperson. He can sell anything for the highest possible price. There is natural leadership and teaching ability. People enjoy following and being around the person because of his enthusiasm. The person may benefit through foreigners or business dealings with foreign countries. He loves to travel and his greatest concern is to expand his knowledge and life experience. He wants to see and know everything that life has to offer. The person may be a travel agent. He may be involved in law, philosophy, invest-ments, or publishing. He has exceedingly good judgement and may even become a judge.

The negative features of the Sun-Jupiter aspect are that the person may have excessive regard for himself. He may be conceited. He is also occasionally careless, too extravagant, or indulgent. There is a need for discipline, moderation, and a sense of thrift. The person may be too materialistic or, in certain respects, superficial. He is highly ambitious and will gain more and more success as time goes by. Indeed, he is a social creature and desires to better himself and climb the social ladder. He is lucky in final outcomes and is generally spared the harsher side of life. He is generous and never petty or small-minded. He is powerfully attracted to money and may choose a career in banking or any financial field. The person profits from his father, who may be powerful, wealthy, special, and long-lived. A woman with this aspect gains tremendous material benefits from the men in her life. She gets a wealthy, loving spouse. Because of her brightness, positivity, and cheerfulness, men find her extremely desirable.

Although the health is strong, there is the distinct possibility of liver and allergy problems. This is because Jupiter, which governs the liver, is "combust" or burned by the rays of the hot Sun. The closer the aspect, the worse the ailments may be. In terms of religion and spirituality, the person has no desire for, or understanding of, the austere path (i.e., meditation, fasting, chanting, etc.). Poet Carl Sandburg had the Sun-Jupiter conjunction within one degree.

"I have not the shadow of a doubt that any man or woman can achieve what I have, if he or she would make the same effort and cultivate the same hope and faith. What is faith worth if it is not translated into action?"

MAHATMA GHANDI

If the Sun is square or opposite Jupiter, the person is indulgent and unduly confident. He has an excessively high opinion of himself and believes he deserves status and benefits without having to work for them. He expects, without any justification, a life of pleasure, personal gratification, and preferential treatment. He is neglectful, procrastinating, and in the final analysis just plain lazy. Unless Saturn is strong in the birthchart and the person develops discipline, seriousness, and a sense of priority he may live a shallow and superficial life. The person is excited, enthusiastic, and does things in a big way. He is attached to appearances and loves to make a big show of himself. Unfortunately, he rarely delivers on his promises. He exaggerates and wants too much, too fast. In severe cases the person makes an art form of pretense.

The person is kind and sympathetic. His intentions are good. He wants everyone to enjoy and does not wish to hurt others. There is a philosophical nature and a deep interest in religion and spiritual techniques. However, there may be little inclination to practice arduous austerities or disciplined regimens on a regular basis. Because of his propensity to exaggerate and embellish, the person excels on stage or in front of crowds. In this realm he is also aided by his expanded ego, overly optimistic personality, and fanciful imagination. The person is charming, magnetic, and charismatic.

There is a distinct danger of arrogance and conceit. The person suffers from poor judgement, unrealistic expectations, and foolish optimism. He is likely to demand too much from others. He does not finish what he begins, and then finds himself frustrated when he does not achieve his goals. There is too much emphasis on pleasure and sense gratification. The person should especially guard against engaging in shortcuts and "get-rich-quick" schemes. He must develop a sense of urgency, and beware of living life as a perpetual child. The person is restless, and he travels a lot. He wants to experience everything life has to offer. There are abundant opportunities which may, unfortunately, be taken for granted. Fidel Castro has the Sun-Jupiter opposition within two and one half degrees.

The person is proud and highly opinionated. He may have liver problems or allergies. Rich and oily foods should be avoided. The heart is strong, vitality is good, and longevity is favored. The person is likely to experience a divine protection from danger, or a "guardian angel" influence. He is adventurous and he absolutely loves freedom. He does not want to be restricted in any way. There is a need for maturity, seriousness, depth, and discipline. Extravagance, wastefulness, and the tendency towards scattered energies must be curbed. Further, the person should learn to embrace responsibility rather than avoid it.

There is a love of gambling and all kinds of speculation. Because the Sun is aspected by Jupiter, the person feels a definite sense of good luck. However, since Jupiter is afflicted by the hot Sun, luck is not as favored as it seems. There may be difficulties with the law, authority figures, the father, and religious or spiritual teachers. Also, if selfishness and hedonism become too extreme the person pays the price of a bad reputation.

"All of us, whether or not we are warriors, has a cubic centimeter of chance that pops up in front of our eyes from time to time. The difference between the average man and a warrior is that the warrior is aware of this, and one of his tasks is to be alert, deliberately waiting so that when his cubic centimeter pops out, he has the necessary speed, the prowess to pick it up."

CARLOS CASTENEDA, JOURNEY TO IXTLAN

If the Sun is trine or sextile Jupiter, the person is exceedingly blessed. He is happy with his life no matter what the circumstances. He has unwavering faith in the divine and is optimistic, cheerful, and content. There is generosity of spirit and a philosophical outlook. The person is psychologically healthy, and success in life is favored. There is leadership ability and the person may do well in politics. He is respected, honored, and liked by all. Evangelist Billy Graham has the Sun Trine Jupiter aspect within one and one half degrees. Karl Marx had the aspect within one degree.

Though the harmonious Sun-Jupiter aspects are quite positive, the person will not realize the full benefits mentioned unless there are strong ambitions, aspirations, and struggles otherwise indicated in the birthchart. The Sun-Jupiter trine, especially, is so indicative of ease, poise, and grace that the person may be lazy or too complacent unless Mars is significantly placed or there is significant friction exhibited elsewhere. The person is intuitive and lucky. He is protected throughout life and his needs will always be taken care of. Money is definitely favored. Compared to others, the person succeeds in his endeavors with little effort.

There are high morals and a strong sense of devotion. The person is traditional and conventional by nature. He travels a lot and always gains through foreigners and other countries. Imagination is strong and the intellect is sound. There is a balanced ego and the person knows how to exercise authority. He is kind, compassionate, and tolerant. There are abundant benefits from the father, men in general, and individuals in powerful, authoritative positions. A woman with this aspect gets a pure-hearted, special husband. If the man is not wealthy at the time of marriage he will likely become so in due course of time. The person has excellent experiences with religious figures, and may be the favorite of his chosen guru. There will be more and more material comforts as life progresses.

The person is refined and cultured. He excels in law, publishing, religious or consciousness-raising work, and theatre. He is of a visionary nature, has high ideals, and is not afraid to take a risk. Opportunities are plentiful and the person is privileged because of positive and charitable actions undertaken in past lives. Health is good and the person is happy and at peace. The Sun-Jupiter trine is significantly more powerful than the sextile. The sextile indicates the opportunity to make the above characteristics a reality.

"When all the knots in the heart are unloosened, then even here in this human life, the mortal becomes immortal. This is the whole teaching of the scriptures."

UPANISHADS

If the Sun is conjunct Saturn, the person will be conservative, cautious, and hard-working. He is wise, profound in his judgements, and never rash in action. The person is intensely responsible in always "doing the right thing." He is well-meaning, constructive, and wants to aid his community. However, he is much too hard on himself. He lives a life of <u>concentrated experience</u>, a life of incessant pressure. Because of his early years with a cold, distant, rigid, or overly-restrictive father, he lacks any sense of optimism or confidence regarding self-expression. He is powerfully inhibited and suffers from guilt, fear of rejection, and feelings of inadequacy. The two most typical responses to the Sun-Saturn conjunction are: 1) the person uses his conservative, controlled energy to become highly successful in business, politics, or leadership, or 2) he holds himself back and becomes a dismal, depressive failure. What actually occurs depends upon the evolution of the soul, other aspects of the birthchart, the free will factor and the level of adversity the person grew up with.

The person's greatest ability is organizing. He is very ambitious, although this may not be apparent because the person is extremely reserved and restrained in appearance. However, the person (even the one who falls into failure) has strong desires to make his way to the top. He does so slowly, systematically, and responsibly through diligence and persistence. He will become an authority figure. He has no interest in the easy route or "quick scheme to riches." The person's values and morals are exceptionally laudable. There is one serious potential drawback, though: the person may be highly selfish, greedy, or self-centered. While the person may be working for justice, fairness, and the benefit of the greater whole, he may still exhibit baser qualities at the same time. However, no matter what the person's behavior, he is keenly aware that his life is karmic. He knows that above all, he is here to learn lessons. Should this person ever commit wrongdoings or negative actions, he fully expects to pay the price —with interest. In any case, the person lives cautiously, ever considering and contemplating the worst possible results of each action.

If the rest of the chart indicates a religious or devotional nature, the person with the Sun-Saturn aspect may be, spiritually, the greatest of the greats. In Hindu astrology Saturn represents Lord Shiva, the God of austerities and destroyer of ignorance. This aspect therefore may reveal an ascetic of the highest order. The person may have no attachments to anyone or anything in the material world. He may have integrated perfectly all spiritual qualities so that they are absolutely part of him even though they do not show. Even he may not acknowledge his evolutionary attributes as significant. The person is, in a way, quite humble. However, at the same time, he is very proud. He clearly has a strong personality type. And he knows the value of his well-earned accomplishments. At any rate, the person evolves spiritually through meditation, fasting, avoidance of the senses, and other austere disciplines. Guru Maharaji, the youthful guru and founder of the "Divine Light Mission," has the Sun-Saturn conjunction within one degree.

The person may be overly rigid, short on humor, and depressed in spirit. His worst quality is the tendency to censor himself. He is, physically, too rigid and must beware of arthritis or paralysis. He should avoid salt, hard cheese, eggs, and meat. He may have difficulties with the teeth, bones, lower back or spine, and the heart. There is a need for calcium. Life is distinctly more successful and enjoyable as the person grows older. Due to his serious and responsible nature, the person may have missed out on childhood and the spirit of youth. However, having matured so young, the person finds in adulthood that he is far ahead of others in handling the struggles of life. The person was raised with great restriction and therefore knows how to make the most of opportunities. He is thrifty, knows no waste, and is exceedingly good at driving a hard bargain. He almost never overpays and is rarely taken advantage of. He may be attracted to real estate or construction. The person understands form and structure better than anyone. He knows how to put a plan into action and make it work. He is adept at distinguishing and dealing with public perception and the powers that be.

The person is down-to-earth and hard to fool. He may be skeptical to a fault. Psychologically, the person must transform the "scarcity consciousness" of his childhood into "prosperity consciousness." As with any strong Saturn aspect, the person finds it difficult to let go of old fears, past hurts, psychological complexes, etc. Since the Sun represents men, a woman with this aspect may find herself in a difficult marriage with too much responsibility. She is attracted to older, conservative men, or authority figures. The father may have been too prominent in the formative years and this may have resulted in a lifelong scar or complex concerning men. The person attempts to create a life of meaning and security. Traditional astrological texts indicate that the person's life is filled with a disproportionate amount of isolation, sorrows, burdens, losses, depression, and other gloomy features.

If the Sun is square or opposite Saturn the person experiences restrictiveness of spirit and an inferiority complex. He is restrained, inhibited, and lacking confidence. There may have been suffering on account of a cold, distant, or rigid father. The father may have been strict, severe, cruel, or (especially with the opposition aspect) absent. Thus, the person did not receive the positive masculine energy base necessary for self-assuredness and a sense of conquest. He approaches life too seriously and from an intrinsic sense of scarcity. Optimism, enthusiasm, and humor should definitely be cultivated. There is a pervasive sense of guilt, and the person does not feel he deserves an easy life with abundant pleasures and comforts. His most plaguing trait is the tendency to censor himself and suppress his self-expression.

On the positive side, the person is moral, upright, and always wanting to do the right thing. He is extremely responsible, although this quality is generally warped in the sense that the person does right by everyone but himself. Nevertheless, he can certainly be trusted to keep his word and fulfill his commitments, no matter how extenuating the circumstances. There is a powerful sense of humility and the person embodies all the Saturnian characteristics. He is thrifty, abhors waste, and does not overpay. He is disciplined, and his spiritual evolution comes from austerities such as meditation, fasting, and other such controlled regimens. He may worship Lord Shiva, be a supreme ascetic, and experience a profound sense of detachment to ego and material life.

There may be difficulties with government and men in general. The person feels especially vulnerable around bosses, wealthy people, or anyone in a position of power and control. He is likely to have a deep-seated distrust of, or hatred for, authority figures. A woman with the Sun-Saturn square or opposition experiences trouble in her love life. She is attracted to strict, austere, older, or authoritarian-type men like her father. Therefore, she is well-advised to marry later (late twenties or early thirties), after she has learned to confront her inherent fears and insecurities. Otherwise, she chooses a mate based on her feelings of scarcity, obligation, and duty.

The person must beware of rigidity. He is too dogmatic, biased, and fixed in his opinions. There is a need for tolerance, acceptance, and compassion. Health-wise the teeth, bones, heart, lower back, and spine are all vulnerable. Also, as with all Saturn afflictions, arthritis or paralysis is a possibility. The person needs plenty of rest and calcium. He should avoid contractive, crystallizing foods such as salt, meat, hard cheese, etc. He should beware of the tendency to overwork himself or strain his resources by involvement in intense, self-sacrificing situations. Some with hard Sun-Saturn aspects feel obliged to serve others to an excessive degree, while others are extremely selfish and can hardly tolerate the thought of service. Those in the first category are often acting out of a sense of guilt, while the miserly types are at the mercy of their interminable feelings of scarcity. At any rate, one of the person's major tasks in life is to develop a balanced sense of responsibility. He will only succeed, of course, when he creates a healthy experience of self-love and self-worth.

The person is conservative, traditional, and orthodox. He is of strong character. He feels a constant sense of pressure and must learn to be easy with, and less critical and demanding of, himself. There is talent in carpentry, construction, and/or real estate. The person is a realist and does well with form and structure. If the Sun-Saturn aspect is too strong, by degree, there may be chronic health problems and a slower-than-normal ability to heal. There are serious fears of rejection and it is of supreme importance that the person choose friends and associates who are supportive and encouraging. The person is a hard worker and finds it difficult to seek recognition and acknowledgement. There may be indecision and lack of spontaneity.

Hard Saturn aspects to the Sun or Moon can, in certain cases, have a devastating effect on the entire life. Even if the rest of the birthchart is powerfully well-disposed, the person may not achieve anywhere near his potential. He must learn, through therapy or spiritual disciplines, how to disregard the critical, self-censoring voice he always hears in his head.

If the Sun is trine or sextile Saturn, the person is disciplined, mature, and practical. His willpower is strong, he is patient, and he fulfills his goals steadily. He is focused and concentrated, and does not waste energy. He is reliable. There is good mental and physical health, and the person is balanced. He is responsible and always knows to do the right thing.

The person gains from his father, the government, and men in general. A woman with a harmonious Sun-Saturn aspect receives benefits from her lovers and attracts solid, secure men. The person is of good character and moral fiber. He is developed and knowledgeable from an early age. He is loyal, trustworthy, and stable. His work is consistent and of high quality. He does well in politics and positions of authority. There is humility, and the person does not let his ego get out of hand. He is poised, and his masculine energy is abundant yet controlled. The person is proud, strong, and confident. He has integrity and keeps his word. He is extremely adept at distinguishing his purpose and organizing his life. Louis Pasteur had the Sun Trine Saturn aspect within two degrees.

The trine aspect is significantly more powerful than the sextile. The sextile indicates the opportunity to make the above characteristics a reality.

If the Sun is conjunct Uranus, the person lives a life of excitement and insatiable zest. He is independent and individualistic. He is strong-willed to the extreme, at times to his own detriment. The person lives life by his own impulses and inclinations, and gives little weight to the traditions of the day. Personal freedom and self-sufficiency are the most important features of his life, and he does whatever it takes to maintain them. Uranus is the higher octave of the mental planet, Mercury. When placed near the Sun, Uranus gives intellectual brilliance, intuitive flashes, and genius. The nervous system is highly charged. The person has little patience for routine, discipline, and system. He detests "nine to five" jobs. The person is highly developed spiritually. He is attached to no one and nothing (except freedom and independence). Therefore he is relieved of the "materialistic" or object-oriented suffering of the common person. He cuts his losses, recovers quickly, and moves on. The person lives absolutely in the present and is not troubled by guilt, regret, and other such debilitating complexes. However, self-reflection, and consideration of the effects of his actions upon others, may be somewhat lacking. The person is irresistibly drawn to the occult and the hidden forces of nature; he may choose a career along such lines. He will be interested in astrology, aviation, computers, space travel, or any profession ahead of the times.

The person is decisive and dynamic. He is powerfully magnetic, and people are awed by his enthusiasm and enormous self-integrity. The person is extraordinarily original and creative. Because he gives no credence to rules, regulations, and other man-made limitations, the person is an inventor par excellence. He is innovative in his chosen profession. He is gifted in science, technical fields, and any research endeavors. Talent (creative aptitude) is absolutely guaranteed. The person is a <u>natural humanitarian</u>. In addition to his innate desire to aid humankind, he accepts as valid each individuals' viewpoints, morals, and concerns. He himself is likely to be rather amoral; his actions are dictated by the objective needs of each particular circumstance, rather than any one religion or philosophy. The person is loathe to judge anyone or anything as "right" or "wrong," or "good" or "bad." He sees each action as the cause of a particular effect. One of the greatest attributes of the person is that his knowledge is "structured in consciousness," not structured in the intellect. This is because he bases his life on experience and keen personal perception, rather than theory and the philosophies of others. The person is honest and direct. His intuition occurs as sudden flashes and is especially accurate. The person is a reformer and feels a continual urge to change and better the circumstances. He may experience considerably more paths, lifestyles, and careers than most people.

At times the person may be overpowering or explosive in order to get his way. The temper will definitely show. The most harmful feature of the Sun-Uranus conjunction is that the person may be too radical, rebellious, self-centered, or childish in demanding his own way. Although open-minded, he may be extremely opinionated in feeling that his ideas are the best and only the best. He may thus appear stubborn, obstinately persistent, and set in his ways (all of which are vital qualities for inventors and reformers). The person is restless and impatient. He craves excitement. On occasion he is erratic, unpredictable, and easily frustrated. He does not, by any means, react well to force. The person may have had an erratic or "up-and-down" relationship with his father. Or the father may have been independent, changeable, eccentric, or volatile. The father also may have also been a genius. A woman with the Sun-Uranus aspect may attract men with the same qualities. She may also attract men who are unstable or incapable of commitment. She will experience many separations from men.

As with all Uranus aspects, the ability to trust, in any significant (or even healthy) way, may be lacking. In this case the deficiency may stem from the formative years, during which the person quickly learned not to rely on his unusual or irregular father. Thus, in his compulsive self-sufficiency, the person may miss out on an important element of closeness and love — both in his friendships and intimate relationships. The person is aware from the start of life that he is "different." He loves the color white and often wears white clothing. He may appear youthful all his life. Jerry Lewis and Baba Ram Dass both have exact Sun-Uranus conjunctions. Joel Grey has the aspect within two and one half degrees, and Sigmund Freud had the aspect within four and one half degrees.

If the Sun is square or opposite Uranus, the person is independent, rebellious, and self-willed. He has powerful convictions and does not compromise. He is intensely experience-oriented and does only what he wants. There is a dislike of authority, routine, and system. If the person feels pushed in a certain direction by others, he is likely to take a diametrically opposite course. There is a progressive and revolutionary nature, and a large ego. The person hates boredom and needs lots of stimulation. He is extremely proud and does not allow anyone to control him. Relationships are difficult, especially with the Sun opposition Uranus aspect, and the person has to work on trusting others. Otherwise he spends entirely too much time and energy defending himself. He is hypersensitive in certain ways and should not mistake feedback for criticism. In his love life the person may have problems with give-and-take. He feels that EITHER he gives OR he receives. Balance may somehow be missing.

During childhood there are likely to be problems with the father, who may be unstable, weird, strange, occultish, undependable, or an eccentric-type genius. Because the father represents a woman's primary role model for love, a woman with this aspect experiences difficulties in her intimate relationships with men. She may attract men who are erratic, inconstant, unpredictable, and incapable of commitment. There are many separations from men, or intense relationships which start and end suddenly. Because of his all-encompassing need for self-sufficiency, caused by the inconsistent father, the person may be unable to trust even his closest loved ones with any depth or profundity.

Although intuition is remarkable, the person must beware of making rash, impulsive decisions. There will be plenty of occasions for regret, and the person needs to develop respect for the wisdom of his elders. The person may have problems with government and authority figures. He must resolutely guard against arrogance, obstinacy, and the attitude that he is always right. The person is dramatic and dynamic. He does things in a big way. If Saturn is strong in the birthchart and the person learns discipline, consistency, and endurance then he can go far in his achievements. His best characteristic is his courage, decisiveness, and ability to take big risks. He is a great pioneer and is never afraid to buck the system. He is inventive, original, and creative. He is open, honest, and sincere. There may be an abrupt personality or a directness that is hard for others to bear. Sentimentality is never a problem.

The person may be egocentric and stubborn. He enjoys controversy and likes to stir things up. Bette Davis, Vanessa Redgrave, and Judy Garland all have (or had) this square aspect in their charts. The person goes through radical changes in his lifetime. Traditional astrological texts declare that when such happenings occur, the person feels a need to completely, and ruthlessly, sever himself from his past. There is a strong desire for acceptance and recognition. This, however, is never very apparent, since the last thing the person wants is to reveal his need for anything outside himself. The person may occasionally be dogmatic or intolerant. He does not function well in groups or any endeavor where compromise and negotiation is necessary. He is, however, very concerned with truth and justice. He lives in the present and is not interested in ventures which mature too far into the future. The person is occult-minded and always open to new concepts. He is not given to criticizing others or passing judgement. Astrologer Grant Lewi and spiritual leader Jeddu Krishnamurti both had Sun-Uranus oppositions within three degrees.

Psychologically speaking, life may be quite rough until the person gains a significant degree of maturity, tolerance, and discipline. There is simply too much tension and disruption in his force field. There is also too much unnecessary resistance and juvenile behavior. Above all else the person must learn to be responsible for his individuality. Because his independent nature was not at all appreciated during the formative years, he developed a defensiveness about his ideas and convictions. By force of habit, he expects to be attacked whenever he goes against the norm. What he must realize is that childhood is over and he is now entitled to think and live any way likes, as long as he is willing to bear the results.

If the Sun is trine or sextile Uranus, the person is inspired, spirited, and ahead of the times. He is flexible, adaptable, and versatile. There is talent in science, the occult arts, aviation, and computer work. The person is individualistic and greatly enjoys the fact. He is charming, magnetic, and popular. He gains benefits from men, his father, government, and authority figures. A woman with this aspect easily attracts brilliant, unconventional, and highly creative men. Marriage is favored and her relationship brings deep stimulation. Life is experience-oriented and the person's knowledge is structured in consciousness rather than theory or dogma.

There is a constant and profound open-mindedness, and the person is never fooled into following rules and regulations for their own sake. Physical energy is plentiful and the person is excited to be alive. Intuition is excellent and the person makes a particularly fine astrologer, counselor, or therapist. There may be flashes of genius. The person is of a humanitarian nature and wants the best for everyone. He is a good leader, more concerned with altruism than his own ego. Life will be fascinating, with many varied and interesting experiences, and the person always enjoys new adventures. He is as progressive as they come and is extremely interested in enlightenment. His capacity for self-improvement is acute and he recognizes truth, fairness, and authenticity immediately. Cheiro, the renowned palmist, had an exact Sun-Uranus trine. Astrologer/author C.E.O. Carter had the aspect within one degree.

There is strong willpower and the person finds creative solutions to problems. He does well in his friendships and is never bigoted or prejudiced. He does not pass judgement on others. He is optimistic, pleasant, and on the move. Unlike the other aspects from Uranus, the person is tolerant and knows very well how to get what he wants from leaders, bosses, and authoritarians. The person is original, inventive, and never hemmed in by tradition and convention. The trine aspect is significantly more powerful than the sextile. The sextile indicates the opportunity to make the above characteristics a reality.

If the sun is conjunct Neptune, the person is a mystic in the truest sense. He is concerned with, and connected to, the mysteries of existence. The person is powerfully, often divinely, inspired. He loves contemplation and meditation, and it is likely that he will take to the spiritual path. The person enjoys the most profound sense of devotion, and his greatest evolution and fulfillment comes through discipleship to any guru, mentor, or hero. On different occasions he will experience a merging, on an emotional or feeling level, with God or universal consciousness. The person is a visionary and lives life as if no boundaries exist other than the false ones inflicted by humanity. The person is an idealist of the highest order and barely knows the meaning of compromise.

Of all astrological aspects the Sun-Neptune conjunction is one of the best in terms of accomplishing one's most far-reaching dreams and visions. Dreams and visions are this person's *reality.* There is, of course, the possibility that the person becomes mired in a life of self-delusion and fantasies, but that occurs only if the rest of the birthchart is badly afflicted or the person's evolutionary level is low. There will be a significant degree of illusion, daydreaming, self-importance, and gullibility in any person with this aspect, but these traits are commingled with the more beneficial effects already mentioned. The person will often appear *spaced-out,* as if he lives in his own secluded world. His most crucial experience of life occurs internally, in his ideas, perceptions, and deeply sensitive feelings. The person is delicate and refined. Genius, especially mental brilliance, is a typical feature.

Because Neptune is the higher octave or vibration of Venus, the person will be extraordinarily gentle, compassionate, sensitive, and sympathetic. The person experiences a profound and constant sense of love for others. He is a humanitarian with strong desires to serve and please. In close personal relationships, the person enjoys the most sublime experience of love. He easily can make others happy. The person is talented in the arts, especially music, drama, film, and photography. Even if he is not a professional musician, the person may be constantly humming tunes or hearing them in his mind. He also adores movies and magic. There is a great affinity for the ocean and other bodies of water, near which the person will want to reside.

78   The Sun-Neptune conjunction indicates a frail constitution. The person will be especially susceptible to illnesses resulting from stress, emotional strife, and overwork. The person must heal himself through natural means, as he is extremely sensitive to drugs and medications. The person is quite delicate and abhors fighting, hard physical work, getting his hands dirty, aggressiveness, and other *lower* characteristics of life. He is adverse to routine and is not thrilled with the concept of discipline. There is great feminine energy. The person is decidedly psychic. His intuition comes from a heightened or superfine level of feeling. His intuition is a somewhat natural and logical process, distinctly different from the "*Uranian*" intuition which occurs in sudden unpredictable flashes.

     The Sun-Neptune person must always trust his feelings, as they are seldom off the mark. And in any case, it is only when he ignores his feelings that he has occasion for regret. The person is open to the spiritual and astral realms, and is extremely receptive to the hidden forces of life. He has no need to touch, taste, smell, see, or hear something in order to affirm its existence. He need only sense or intuit its reality. No concept is too far-fetched for this person to consider. According to the great British astrologer, C. E. O. Carter, the Sun-Neptune conjunction is the most common aspect of astrologers, "*especially of those interested in the predictive art.*"

     The most difficult feature of the Sun-Neptune conjunction is that the person will not have a clear, objective, or accurate self-image. Neptune symbolizes a *watery* type of influence which erodes and dissolves its associations. In this case, the Sun (which represents confidence, the power to be, and father) is subject to such erosion. The person intellectually may learn how capable, lovable, and special he is, but lack emotional and visceral self-confidence. This is largely due to the abnormal relationship with the father during the early, formative years. The person idealized his father, who unfortunately was not *there* for him. The father may have been an elusive character emotionally, or may have simply been physically absent. The father may have been weird or mysterious in a major way, or he may have been an alcoholic or drug user. On the other hand, the father may have been a highly religious, refined, spiritual, or devotional type. However, most importantly, the father was useless in providing the person with the masculine energy base necessary for self-esteem and real inner confidence.

     The Sun Neptune-conjunction may be more difficult for a female, since the father represents her essential model for love relationships. Aside from attracting men who may be deceptive, elusive, alcoholic, *spaced-out*, or highly devotional types, the woman may find it difficult to secure a partner who can live up to her idealistic (and perhaps unrealistic) expectations. This aspect may also be more disruptive to self-esteem in women than in men. This is because as men mature, they are more likely to associate confidence with doing (i.e., accomplishments), while women, being closer to nature, are more involved in their *beingness.* Thus, the intellectual path to confidence, the main one available to the Sun-Neptune person, may be slower and less accessible for a woman.

The person will be extremely appreciative and have good taste in all facets of life. He will have great imagination. He may be attracted to careers involving gas, oil, drugs, and the sea. The person, detesting pettiness and inconsequentials, is essentially an escapist from the mundane world. He is attracted to the spiritual plane as well as drugs or alcohol. However, the latter should be avoided at all costs, as addictions would be easily formed. The person may occasionally have difficulties facing the truth, especially about himself. He may tend to overly dramatize situations and thereby lose or confuse himself. Because of his deep inspiration the person is likely to be self-motivated. He may be an inspired politician or consumed with God.

Emotionally, the person is like a sponge. He keenly feels positive and negative energies. He must leave negative environments immediately or suffer debilitating consequences. The person is sensitive to heat and cold, and is sensuous. Because the Sun-Neptune person is compassionate, sympathetic, and emotionally giving, he will need habitual periods of restful seclusion to recoup his energy. For this reason, the person is better suited to project-oriented work where energies are concentrated in spurts. Louis Pasteur had an exact Sun-Neptune conjunction. Edmund Rostand, author of "Cyrano de Bergerac," and William Jennings Bryan had the aspect within two and one half degrees. And Carrie Fisher has the aspect within three degrees.

If the Sun is square or opposite Neptune, the person has a weak or diffused self-image. There may have been difficulties with a father who was ineffectual, alcoholic, strange, or simply emotionally or physically absent. Thus the person lacks a strong masculine energy base and the confidence needed to function powerfully in life. He cannot see himself clearly and does not, viscerally, know how good he is. He holds back his power and intensity due to imaginary fears and psychological complexes. The person is decidedly psychic and receptive to spiritual realms closed to the ordinary person. He is significantly affected by dreams, visions, and the subconscious mind. There is an openness to astrology, mysticism, and all paradigms leading to enlightenment. The person feels a yearning for perfection deep in his soul. He is an escapist from the mundane world. Drugs and alcohol should be avoided at all costs, as addictions are too easily formed. If the person is able to abstain from such harmful indulgences, he is likely to eventually find his way to a devotional or spiritual path.

The person is sensitive, delicate, and fragile. He is like a sponge and has difficulty shielding himself from surrounding vibrations. Illnesses come easily and are especially due to anxiety, pressure, overwork, and emotional tension. Harsh and negative individuals should be averted, as should long-term stressful situations. Caution should be taken regarding poisons or spoiled foods. The person is impressionable, gullible, and easily deceived. He is overly emotional and lacks a sense of objectivity. Problems come especially from men, government, and authority figures. A woman with this aspect may have big troubles in married life. She may marry someone like her father who is undependable, spaced-out, sickly, unrealistic, or emotionally deficient. She should be particularly careful not to involve herself with love partners who take drugs or alcohol. Instead, she must find someone whose Neptunian qualities manifest as idealism, devotion, or spirituality.

In some cases there is an inclination to deceitfulness and dishonesty. Motives are of extreme importance and the person should not engage in subtle or sophisticated methods of trickery. There may be delusions of grandeur and exaggerated mental fantasy. Expectations are too high and there is an over-developed sense of idealism. Therefore, the person suffers a disproportionate amount of disappointment and disillusionment during his lifetime. Being emotional as he is, there is great vulnerability to pain and sorrow. The person is easily seduced and he often feels like a helpless victim. There is artistic talent and a great imagination. The person is romantic and has a limitless capacity for empathy and compassion. He enjoys films, magic, and the sea.

The person may be dreamy and he may experience trouble with boundaries. He may be confused and unwilling to take absolute responsibility for his being. There is continual self-doubt and the person must beware of compulsive or obsessive behavior arising out of a distorted perception of reality. He is also too often dissatisfied. Traditional astrological texts say that the person is prone to scandals and secretive activity.

> "To risk is to risk appearing the fool. To weep is to risk appearing sentimental. To expose feelings is to risk exposing our true self. To place your ideas, your dreams, before the crowd is to risk loss. To love is to risk not being loved in return. To live is to risk dying. To try at all is to risk failure. But to risk we must. Because the greatest hazard in life is to risk nothing. The man, the woman, who risks nothing, does nothing, has nothing, is nothing."
>
> *EMERSON*

If the Sun is trine or sextile Neptune, the person lives from his heart. He is gentle, sensitive, and feeling. He is always aware of his relationship to God and he is a natural mystic. The consciousness is open and receptive, and the person's inner vision is acute. He may have special abilities with any or all of the five senses. The person is drawn to the arts and excels in music, drama, film, photography, etc. He also enjoys the ocean and other bodies of water. There is a humanitarian nature or at least great concern for the feelings of others. The person is kind and compassionate. Because of such fine characteristics he is well-loved by all.

Benefits come especially from men, government, and a father who is loving, tender, and caring. The person is refined and cultured, and has good taste. He is creative and has an excellent imagination. He is not overly bound by rules, regulations, and traditions. There may be a need for discipline, urgency, and structure if the rest of the birthchart does not indicate significant struggle, desire, or friction. In such cases, the person must beware of a pervasive sense of laziness and complacency. The person is inspired, optimistic, and enthusiastic. He is poetic and has great feminine energy. There are high expectations and yet the person is patient and tolerant. Indeed, he has tremendous faith in the divine order of nature. There is a dreamlike quality about the person as well as a subtle sensuality. The person is vulnerable and should avoid crude people and discordant surroundings.

Because awareness of God is so keen and ingrained, the person finds his spiritual path early on in life. Furthermore, he never (or at least very rarely) wavers in this realm. There is talent in astrology, tarot, secretive affairs, and any occult subject. There is plenty of intuition and psychic ability. The person knows he is here to work on his enlightenment, and he does this by emotionally merging with Universal consciousness. The trine aspect is significantly more powerful than the sextile. The sextile indicates the opportunity to make the above characteristics a reality.

If the Sun is conjunct Pluto, the person experiences all of life in an emotionally concentrated way. This is because Pluto is the higher octave or higher vibration of the Moon (not of Mars, as is commonly thought). However, the emotional feature of Pluto, sensitive though it is, expresses itself as a masculine, "yang," forceful response rather than as a feminine, soft, or flowing energy. The person will be intense, instinctive, and determined. He will be extraordinarily sensitive, especially to criticism, and will live a life of psychological transformation. This transformation occurs as a continual process of ego death-and-rebirth. The person will go through many major life changes. He has the ability to heal others through the warmth of his touch. There is also tremendous regenerative energy to heal or improve himself in any way desired. Recovery is swift and smooth. The person is resourceful to the extreme and knows himself to be a survivor. The ego is expanded and there is a strong drive for fame and recognition. The person is compulsive about finding significance in all undertakings. He is a leader, desires power, and has no apprehensions about influencing the lives of others and taking responsibility for all his actions. The person lives life to the fullest and demands the same from others. Therefore, the person's relationships (especially with loved ones) will be taxed to the limit. Relationships may suffer on this account. The person may be stubborn, possessive, and occasionally jealous. He may wish to remold others.

The person continually looks for hidden meanings and considers life to be extremely "fated." He lives with a profound sense of destiny. In his great ambition for power or recognition, the person is potentially ruthless about obtaining his objectives. Because of his inordinate sensitivity, he may be a great loner. However, there is an almost compulsive desire to merge or absorb oneself with something (anything) in the outer world. The sex act is extremely important to the person, because it facilitates just this experience in the most intense and complete way. The sex drive is strong and the person is sexually powerful. He may be orgiastic. Because the person lives life on such a concentrated emotional level, he will consider each and every occurrence to be significant, lasting, and real. For this reason, perspective may be lacking in his personal life. Too much weight and significance is accorded to passing fancies. The person is very spiritual, talented in the mystical arts, and is greatly concerned with universal welfare. He may be a healer or spiritual leader. He will be psychic, intuitive, and impressionable. Evolutionary growth is of utmost importance to the person. He will have great magnetism. One of his greatest attributes is the ability to let go of any features of his life which suddenly become unacceptable or life-damaging. This includes partnerships, careers, loved ones, habit patterns, etc. The person may permanently relinquish such affairs in an instant.

There is magnificent willpower and the person's creative potential is unlimited. Due to his sensitive nature, the person is secretive and private in response. However, at times he also opens up and reveals the deepest intimacies of his existence, in order to purge himself and evolve to higher states of consciousness. It is likely that as a child there were intense or difficult experiences with the father, who himself may be a compulsive type given to extremes. The father may have been manipulative, domineering, powerful, famous, or extremely special in some way; or the father may have disappeared during the person's youth, with no explanation. In any case, the person may have some psychological scar or complex about his father. In a woman's chart this feature may be especially troublesome, since a woman's association with the father is the basis for her future love relationships. Since the Sun rules men in general, a female with the Sun-Pluto conjunction will seek a husband who exhibits all the above-listed "Plutonion" characteristics (i.e., someone who is intense, powerful, domineering, spiritual, etc.). The person is an inspiration and catalyst for other people's growth and transformation.

If the Sun is square or opposite Pluto, the person tries to control all of life. He is vulnerable, intense, and potentially manipulative. He is sensitive to criticism and experiences continual episodes of ego death-and-rebirth. Desires are keenly felt, and certain individuals with this aspect are ruthless or devious (in a subtle way) in pursuing goals. The person is likely to have been dominated (whether openly, subtly, or covertly) by a strong, obsessive, or overzealous father. As a result, he does not feel safe to express himself. He is secretive, hidden, and very serious about his feelings. There is also the possibility that the father died or disappeared from home without a word. In any case, the person was strongly influenced by the affairs in this realm. There is enormous willpower and the person has to learn how to manage his intensely powerful nature. He must beware of intimidating others with force or trying to bend people to his will. As with all Pluto afflictions, the person resists change and tries to control experience in order to escape his vulnerability to emotional pain.

The person is earthy, possessive, and possibly jealous. He may be occasionally tyrannical or angry. There is a fascination with power and the person is unconsciously stubborn. He must guard against overconfidence as he is, by nature, willing to affect other peoples' lives in any way he deems fitting. There may be struggles with government, authority figures, or any other individual competing for command. The person is somewhat compulsive, and does things in a very big way. He enjoys having great impact on the world or anyone in his presence. He has a strong sense of destiny.

Relationships are strenuous because the person may be demanding, forceful, or critical. He is also sexual, erotic, passionate, and libidinous. A woman with the Sun-Pluto square or opposition should be careful not to unconsciously marry a man of her father's temperament. In such cases the husband could be oppressive or dictatorial, or in extreme cases cruel-hearted. He would also be jealous and possessive. There will be significant periodic crises, and the person goes through much transformation in his lifetime. Though these experiences are arduous and stressful the person is, fortunately, a survivor. He is resourceful, creative, and ingenious.

The person may be interested in metaphysics. He is psychic, has great thirst for knowledge, and wants to get to the root of things. He has a powerful presence and a large ego. There is strong ambition and a desire for fame and recognition that, in certain instances, may be the outcome of childhood insecurity or a poor self-image. Health-wise the person may be susceptible to cancer, depending upon how fervent and rigid he is in his controlling and resistant behavior, defensiveness, and repressed emotionality. In severe cases the hard Sun-Pluto aspects indicate tendencies towards violence, criminal activities, Mafia association, and indulgences in any anti-social or forbidden endeavors. The person also may have been a victim of incest or sexual abuse. Above all, he should let go of his attachments, learn to trust the universe, and stop trying to change or remold his loved ones. Most individuals with hard Sun-Pluto aspects are woefully unconscious of their oppressive or controlling behavior. They are just as often unaware of their father's manipulative demeanor.

"Great spirits have always encountered violent opposition from mediocre minds."

ALBERT EINSTEIN

If the Sun is trine or sextile Pluto, the person has the greatest ability to improve himself, raise his consciousness, and transform any psychological complex he possesses. There is remarkable willpower, and an interest in all metaphysical or spiritual development techniques. The person immerses himself one hundred percent in any endeavor he undertakes. His concentration is impeccable and he sees activities through to their successful end. There will be many major changes in life which the person accepts, indeed embraces, as part of his maturing process. Nobody enjoys growth, or gains more actual evolution in life, than he.

The person is powerful, confident, and believes in his personal calling. He is extremely resourceful, and knows how to use his energy wisely and well. There is leadership, organizational talent, and flair to inspire others. The person is individualistic, innovative, pioneering, and unafraid. He is determined, firm, and almost certain to succeed. He is intuitive, psychic, and interested in meditation. He is open to all kinds of different religions and philosophies, and is seldom dogmatic or narrow. The person excels in occult sciences or any research field. He is a natural humanitarian and is always concerned with universal welfare. There is good healing ability, and talent in counseling or any form of psychotherapy.

The person benefits from men in general, and government or authority figures. A woman with this aspect gets a spiritual, philosophical, or religious husband. The husband may be powerful, famous, charismatic, or extraordinary. The Sun-Pluto harmonious aspects indicate strong procreative and regenerative tendencies. The person is sexual, virile, and energetic. He is a hard worker and may even be "driven." He is wonderfully responsible, and brings his concentrated intensity to every situation he encounters. He is noticeably flexible, versatile, and adaptable. He lives in the present, lets go of the past, and never looks back. He is a survivor. The person influences others naturally, by virtue of his remarkable integrity and spiritual wholeness. He is magnetic, dynamic, and appealing. There is no obstacle too extreme and no hurdle too high for the person to overcome if the spirit moves him. Diana Ross has an exact Sun-Pluto trine. Albert Schweitzer had the aspect within four degrees.

The Sun-Pluto trine is significantly more powerful than the sextile. The sextile indicates the opportunity to make the above characteristics a reality.

Churchill wrote, "As I went to bed at about 3 A.M. I was conscious of a profound sense of relief. At last I had the authority to give directions over the whole scene. I felt as if I were walking with destiny, and that all my past life had been but a preparation for this hour and for this trial." And his secretary reported that he was sobbing like a child when he dictated the peroration of one of his most famous speeches in the dark days of World War II. "We shall not flag or fail. We shall go on to the end. We shall fight in France, we will fight on the seas and oceans, we shall fight with growing confidence and growing strength in the air. We shall defend our island, whatever the cost may be. We shall fight on the beaches. We shall fight on the landing grounds. We shall fight in the fields and in the streets. We shall fight in the hills. We shall never surrender."

FROM "LEADERS" BY RICHARD NIXON

If the Moon is conjunct Mercury, the person is emotionally expressive. He is aware of his feelings and lets them be precisely known. Mercury rules the intellect, while the Moon governs memory and common sense. Thus, the person is the most intellectual and self-expressive of all beings. He is the consummate and eternal thinker. Excited by concepts and theories, he lives for knowledge. The person is prolific. He has great creative aptitude, and the richest imagination. If other aspects of the birth chart point to a literary or education-oriented life, the person may be the most brilliant writer or scholar. His mind is versatile, flexible, and unrestricted. He may have a tireless capacity for detail work. He may be an inventor. The person is practical, street-smart, and has the best common sense. He is straightforward with everyone, and unabashedly blunt around wishful thinkers, sweet-talkers, and idealists.

Despite the person's special mental abilities, there are some very distinct problems caused by the Moon-Mercury conjunction. Whenever two extremely personal influences come close together in the same sign, there is intrinsic "double" perception of all individual issues. While double is not necessarily bad, it is decidedly different from the rest of the world (whose intellectual and emotional faculties are allowed to separately analyze life). The person is self-centered and overly subjective. Because his opinions are the combined result of feeling and mind, he is intense about his judgements. He may be stubborn in his ideas and truly suffer when others do not see things his way. The person may be restless, nervous, excitable, and of a wandering mind, especially if there are planetary afflictions to the conjunction. The person needs to cultivate patience and tolerance for others. He must learn that just because his perceptions are stronger, more personal, and occasionally more accurate than everyone else's, they carry no inherent privilege of acceptance or respect. Otherwise, the person may become angry or bitter.

The person may choose a career in counseling, psychology, or any communicative art. He loves languages and learns them with ease. He is intrigued by puzzles and the deciphering of symbols. He may be a great translator, interpreter, teacher, or writer. The person is talkative, witty, and humorous. He is keen and insightful. He is adept in dealing with the subconscious mind and is powerfully drawn to hypnotism or any mental technique delving below the mind's surface. The person appreciates music, poetry, and the arts. He loves libraries, museums, and intellectual institutions. The person is a capable merchant, and is aided by his earthy common sense. Because of his expressiveness, the person may be an excellent salesperson. He may be concerned with diet, medicine, and other healing methods, since Mercury is the ruler of Virgo.

The person may be constantly busy. He craves change, excitement, and a variety of experiences. He is sensitive, articulate, and emotionally and physically demonstrative. He learns kinesthetically (through his feelings). The person's mother may have an intellectual nature. A man with this aspect may get a wife who is intelligent, youthful, eloquent, and communicative. She may also be fickle or changeable. Lyndon Johnson, our ceaselessly detail-oriented president and school teacher (he taught speech and debate), had the Moon-Mercury conjunction within two degrees. So did Muhammed Ali, the most verbal and poetic boxer of the times. Michelangelo had the aspect within four degrees, and Robert Redford has it within one degree.

"Not so easy to find the balance, for if one does not have wild dreams of achievement, there is no spur even to get the dishes washed. One must think like a hero to behave like a merely decent human being."

MAY SARTON

If the Moon is square or opposite Mercury, the person struggles to find the balance between his feelings and his intellect. Because his emotions are connected to his mind, he has little perspective and is always searching for definitive answers. He seeks advice and counsel from others. The person is particularly affected by his subconscious. He has trouble concentrating and may be habitually confused, unfocused, or daydreaming. For some with the hard Moon-Mercury aspects, especially the opposition, there is a tendency to irritate others with incessant talking. The person asks too many questions, and even after his curiosity has been satisfied he may return a day or two later with the exact same inquiries.

The person is very mental. He is inquisitive and desires to understand the workings and motivations of the human spirit. Because of his particularly subjective nature he is especially vulnerable to criticism. He may be nervous, moody, or hypersensitive. He is high-strung and requires a lot of attention in close relationships. He worries too much and has a difficult time making decisions. There is a caring, feeling, and compassionate nature. The person is always willing to help friends and loved ones. He is witty, humorous, and has a fertile imagination. He is clever, sarcastic, and the best satirist. Robert De Niro has the Moon-Mercury opposition within four degrees. Alexander Graham Bell had the aspect within the exact degree.

The person may be interested in hypnosis. He is emotionally excitable and has trouble letting go of the past. He is an independent thinker and is extremely passionate about his beliefs. He takes life very personally and may, therefore, occasionally appear biased or prejudiced in certain realms. The person suffers on account of his mother. There are significant disagreements in the relationship, and the person feels misunderstood by her. He is erratic and needs to work on his inordinate self-doubt. There may be a deep shyness or feeling of mental inadequacy. The person may feel notably different from others. Because the Moon rules females, and is afflicted with Mercury, the person may get a wife who is argumentative, unstable, weak, or greatly lacking in confidence. She may also be fickle and overly picky.

In the ancient system of Hindu astrology, Mercury represents Lord Vishnu, God of the intellect. Therefore, in this lifetime major growth and spiritual evolution come through Zen, astrology, psychology, or any technique which dispels "the mistake of the intellect." However, in some cases (especially those with tight Moon-Mercury oppositions) the person cannot see the forest for the trees. He is so immersed in the mind that he over-intellectualizes all of life. Self-improvement and enlightenment become nearly impossible, because the person will not let go of his attachment to the thinking process. He wins the individual debates and battles, but horrendously loses the war.

"Nurture great thoughts, for you will never go higher than you think."

DISRAELI

If the Moon is trine or sextile Mercury, the person is articulate, optimistic, and of great mental dexterity. He is psychologically healthy and has a balanced, well-reasoning mind. The person is a natural communicator and excels in writing, languages, and the deciphering of symbols. He loves music, poetry, and the arts. He speaks sweetly and is the best storyteller. People love listening to him. He is receptive, and extraordinarily sensitive to his own feelings as well as the feelings of those around him. He is diplomatic, compassionate, and especially personable. Sally Field, one of the most expressive of all actors, has an exact Moon-Mercury trine. The great guru, Yogananda, had the aspect within two and one half degrees.

The person is curious and has great passion for knowledge. He is restless and craves adventure, excitement, and new experiences. The Moon and Mercury are both fast-moving planets. Therefore, in order to make the most of this aspect, the person must have significant depth and stability exhibited elsewhere in the birthchart. Otherwise, he may be too fickle, flighty, or frivolous. There is good common sense and practical judgement. The mind is quick, sharp, and alert. The person is bright and has a great sense of humor. He is witty, intelligent, and perceptive. He is generally happy.

The person is picky, analytical, and critical. He is a perfectionest. His mind is stimulated by information which is emotional, intimate, and personal. Thus, there may be a tendency to gossip. The person is loved by the public and he succeeds in affairs dealing with the masses. He feels no resistance to putting his ideas into action. The memory is good and the person retains what he learns. He is compatible with his mother and gains value and benefits from her, as well as from females in general. A man with this aspect gets a youthful, communicative, and fun-loving spouse. Experiences in the home are favored. The person is honest and direct. He is good in commerce. He is particularly lucid and writes likes he talks. The Moon trine Mercury is significantly more powerful than the sextile. The sextile indicates the opportunity to make the above characteristics a reality.

If the Moon is conjunct Venus, the person is sensual. He is pleasant, smiling, and always craving physical pleasures. The person is beautiful and charmed. His greatest concern is with physical beauty, comforts, and luxuries. He is attracted to the arts and has excellent taste. He is gentle, soft, and eager to please others. The person is romantic and demonstrative. He loves parties, events, and gatherings. He has no interest in difficult, tedious, or energy-consuming jobs. The person excels as a social (or party) director, talent scout, artistic agent, or any job where he puts his great sensual judgement to work.

The person benefits greatly from his mother and all females. There will be many female friends. A man with this aspect has a gentle, rather feminine, free-flowing emotional nature which disarms women. They will feel entirely open and comfortable around him. They want to please him. Either a man or a woman with this aspect will be exceptionally attractive to the opposite sex. The person gets a great deal of sexual pleasure and enjoys many purely sensual love affairs. Since the Moon rules females and is conjunct Venus, a man with this aspect gets a beautiful, artistic, or youthful wife. The person is irresistibly drawn to money, which he may spend with ease. He may be overly indulgent or a lush. He must beware of his vanity. Unless the rest of the chart indicates depth of character the person may be shallow and superficial. Because the person is absorbed in his positive and pleasant feelings, he is easily fooled or taken advantage of. However, there is almost no possibility of being harmed in a major way because of the optimistic nature, charm, and sheer luck which pervades the person's life.

The person is passionate. He loves sex and has no trouble obtaining partners. Since Venus rules the love life, a woman with this aspect gets a "Moon-type" man. The husband may be emotional, sensitive, nurturing, lazy, or lethargic. He may also be brilliant and special. The Moon-Venus woman has the most wonderful feminine energy of all. She may also have a beautiful, sexy, and soothing voice.

Childhood is generally fortunate and the person lives in nice homes all his life. He is an excellent decorator and is inclined towards interior design as a career. Although the person is entirely motivated by his

96

senses, he is admirably loyal, devoted, and loving to his partner. The person should avoid drugs and alcohol since he is too enthralled by them. He may be lazy and a major procrastinator. He may not do well with credit cards. The person lives for love and is masterfully affectionate. He can be the best actor or model, and is adored by the public. He may work with sweets, flowers, jewelry, beautiful clothing, etc. The person has beautiful skin and likes the color yellow. He is compassionate, sensitive to hardship, and cannot bear to say "no."

> "The Great Spirit doesn't smile on those who dampen others and take the stars out of happy eyes."
>
> *WHITE EAGLE*

If the Moon is square or opposite Venus, the person is a sensualist. Because he did not receive the affection and emotional nourishment he desired from his mother, he spends the rest of his life pursuing the needs of the heart. The person feels somewhat unlovable and is therefore indiscriminate in love matters. He craves affection and acceptance, and needs to learn detachment in this realm. Otherwise, he picks inferior partners and then goes overboard in trying to compromise and adapt to his mate's wishes. The person is the best of lovers. He is skilled in the art of sexual pleasures and greatly pleases his mate. He is libidinous, seductive, and erotic. He lives for love. John F. Kennedy, our allegedly lustful president, had the Moon square Venus aspect within one degree. Jeddu Krishnamurti had the opposition aspect within three and one half degrees.

The person is artistic. He loves homes and excels in interior design or any area where he puts his aesthetic talents to work. There is an abundance of feminine energy and the person feels a vital need to be surrounded by beauty. He is luscious and tremendous fun to be around. He gets more physical delight from God's creation than anyone. He has good taste and enjoys luxuries and all of the finer things in life. Unfortunately, there is also hedonism and an overindulgence in pleasures. The person may be lazy, tend to procrastinate, and lack any sense of urgency. He may have problems with vanity. He eats too many sweets or rich foods, and is susceptible to overweight. He is romantic and sentimental. He experiences major disappointment from unrealized expectations. Because of his impulsiveness and lack of self-control, the person spends too much. Finances are, therefore, not favored.

The person takes life personally and suffers from emotional excess. He is vulnerable and feels constantly exposed. He is amorous, passionate, and requires a lot of attention in love relationships. The person immerses himself fully in his endeavors and may thus have less perspective than the norm. It is clearly a lifetime of desire and sense gratification. Discipline is sorely needed. The hard Moon-Venus aspects are particularly troublesome for females in their teenage years, since there is a tendency to engage in indiscriminate sexual love affairs. The person is easily exploited, due to his intense need for approval and acceptance. As with all significant Venus aspects, there is a major concern with fairness and justice.

The person is pleasant, grateful, and often praises others. He wants peace and harmony, and may find it difficult to confront stress, strain, and adversity. The person may be moody or insecure in a deep way. He is flirtatious. He is especially attracted to artistic, beautiful, refined partners. Traditional astrological texts report that their are social difficulties, unpopularity, and problems with females in general. More than anything, the person must work on self-love and self-acceptance. He must learn to distinguish real love from sexual advances. He must also develop restraint, discipline, and self-control.

"Nothing splendid has ever been achieved except by those who dared believe that something inside them was superior to circumstances."

BRUCE BARTON

If the Moon is trine or sextile Venus, the person is sweet and charming. Most importantly, he is emotionally blessed. He is happy, appreciative, and thankful. He is grateful just to be alive. There is artistic talent and the person excels in music, poetry, and drama. He is refined and cultured, and may have a very pleasing voice. The person is popular and he climbs the social ladder with ease. There is a soft nature and plenty of positive feminine energy. The person gains benefits through females and his mother. He is especially loved by the fair sex for his grace, sensitivity, and appreciation of female energy. He values women for their highest qualities, and is affectionate and caring. The person charms his prospective mate with little effort. A man or woman with the aspect gets a devoted, tender-hearted spouse.

The person is warm, affectionate, and sensual. He is an excellent lover and knows how to please his mate. There is an acute sense of fairness and justice. The person can forgive anyone and he is not given to passing judgement or holding grudges. He loves beauty, pleasure, and fun. Early home life, especially with the mother, is favored. The person has a good heart and looks for the best in everyone. He gets nice homes and cars. He is warm, friendly, and very diplomatic. Author Hermann Hesse had the Moon trine Venus aspect within two degrees.

The person is elegant and has good taste. He has an attractive appearance and does well in any career dealing with the public. Success comes more easily than normal, and the person is lucky with money. Traditional astrological texts warn of laziness and an unwillingness to confront adversity. As always with aspects between fast-moving planets, too much significance should not be assumed unless the aspect is extremely close by degree or there are other corresponding birthchart factors. The trine aspect is significantly more powerful than the sextile. The sextile indicates the opportunity to make the above characteristics a reality.

If the Moon is conjunct Mars, the person will be brave, bold, and energetic. He is strong and healthy, and is action-oriented. His blood is pure and he has a firm and muscular body. The person is competitive, highly motivated, and makes an excellent career executive. He is positive, outgoing, and talented in sports. There is strong passion and sexuality, and the person is very attractive to the opposite sex. Because Mars is the planet of personal desires, the person is adept at putting his concerns and goals above those of others. He is successful and (usually) gets what he wants. Evangelist Billy Graham and sex writer Henry Miller both have (or had) the Moon-Mars conjunction within one and one half degrees.

The person may be aggressive and impulsive. He is self-centered, always considering his own needs first. He is extroverted and has little or no natural introspective ability. The person incites strong reactions in others, and few take him lightly. He is opinionated and bluntly lets his feelings be known. He is aided in life by his spontaneity but hindered by rash, hasty, or extreme behavior. Independence is certain. The person has a sharp mind, is a quick thinker, and has good common sense. There is a strong desire to reach the top and the person may be a gifted ruler or commander. He enjoys bossing others around.

The person has a hot temper, fiery emotions, and experiences continual heat in the body. He may be irritable or easily frustrated. The person is dynamic, never backs down from a challenge, and is the best fighter. He may be a champion of causes. He is constructive and enthusiastic, and knows how to stir the masses. The person loves excitement and variety. He dislikes routine and discipline, and prefers to "direct the scene."

Despite the many benefits of the Moon-Mars conjunction, the aspect is essentially a difficult one due to the distinctly different natures of the two planets. The Moon rules comfortableness, emotional nurturing, femininity, feelings, and the subconscious being. Mars rules desires, sex, war, fighting, aggressiveness, etc. Therefore, the person may miss out on the more refined side of life. He may be unable to appreciate the sensitive and gentle qualities of others. There is a strong likelihood that

the person was denied tenderness and emotional nurturing from his
mother. He may thus have no access to such qualities himself. The
humane elements of life, such as forgiveness, mercy, humility, and
charity, may hold precious little meaning. The person may have headaches. There is an innate pressure to perform and prove oneself, which
never subsides. The Moon-Mars conjunction is decidedly more detrimental for females whose competitiveness, enjoyment of conflict, and
intermittent brazenness is surely unappreciated.

A man with the aspect may get an angry, aggressive, or selfish wife.
However, she may also be strong, sexual, and passionate. Such features
are extremely important to the person, as he is himself especially
libidinous. The person is prone to argument or strife with his wife and
mother. The mother may be an outgoing, unsubtle, "Mars" type, and be
lacking in maternalness. The person is honest and straightforward. He
is not bothered by debilitating psychological complexes. However, he
may forever hold onto past transgressions as a means of focus for his
unabating, constitutionally-induced anger. A man or woman with the
aspect may have excellent mechanical or technical ability. The person is
attracted to the military, sports, architecture, engineering, or drafting.
He may be involved in police work, ammunitions, physical therapy, or
surgery. The person has good willpower and is always ready to take a
risk. He should exercise regularly to keep his energy flowing smoothly.
He must guard against accidents and fires. If the Moon-Mars conjunction is afflicted by negative aspects from other planets, there may be
problems with the breast, brain, and menstrual cycle. There could also
be impurity or diseases of the blood. The person is successful but needs
to develop sensitivity, concern for others, and generosity of spirit. Mass
murderer Ted Bundy had the Moon-Mars conjunction within four and
one half degrees.

If the Moon is square or opposite Mars, the person is selfish. He thinks of himself before anyone else. He has trouble with his mother, who may be aggressive, pushy, and domineering. There are difficulties with females in general, and a man with this aspect attracts an argumentative or angry spouse. There will be fighting and a battle of wills in the domestic sphere. Though the person effortlessly charms the women he desires, he has little real respect or reverence for them. He is very sexual, ego-oriented, and uses females for his own pleasure. A woman with this aspect attracts an assertive, arrogant, or macho-type husband who may lack tenderness. She must beware of violence or physical abuse. In terms of love relationships, the opposition aspect is more blatantly detrimental than the square.

The person may be angry and possess a big temper. He enjoys arguing and feels it is his job to win. He is proud, defensive, and often a braggart. He may be arrogant and over-confident. There is heat in the body and the person suffers mental unrest. (In Hindu astrology, the Moon represents the common sense part of the mind.) The person may have headaches, especially if Mercury is also afflicted. There is strong independence and major stubbornness. The person does not respond at all to force. He is a good fighter and never surrenders. He is fervent in his beliefs and emotionally engrossed in life. Though it is not at all apparent, there is a good chance that self-love is seriously lacking. On some level, the person knows his selfish response to life is inadequate to fulfill the great opportunity of human existence. Because his emotions are inextricably tied to his ego, however, he feels absolutely incapable of influencing the situation. He sacrifices the softer, more subtle and profound enjoyment of existence for the gross, quantitative benefits.

The person is practical and down-to-earth. He is skeptical and not easily fooled. There is plenty of emotional excitement, impatience, and impulsiveness. Introspection and sensitivity may be lacking and the person is capable of genuine meanness. He requires much emotional support from others, and though he receives it he is unappreciative and takes favors and benevolence for granted. He is demanding and enjoys bossing others. He is direct, blunt, and unafraid. He is highly sexed and may equate fighting with passion. He may therefore habitually provoke

104   his spouse or loved one. The person is headstrong, overactive, and must beware of fevers and accidents. Moshe Dayan, Israeli general, had the Moon square Mars aspect within two and one half degrees. Astrologer Cyril Fagan had the opposition aspect within one degree.

The person is fascinating and magnetic because of his emotional intensity. He does well in gaining homes and landed property. He is mechanical and talented in technical fields. He needs to develop a sense of detachment from his ego and broaden his perspective of life. He generally considers life a win-lose adventure.

"We may not know what is right, but we always know what is wrong."

MAHARISHI MAHESH YOGI

If the Moon is trine or sextile Mars, the person thrives on activity. He is joyous about his work and is never lazy, lethargic, or idle. He is emotionally expressive and his enthusiasm is infectious. He is confident, purposeful, and enterprising as well as creative and ambitious. There is excellent courage, vitality, and leadership ability. The person is effective and success is very much favored. The person does well in dealings with the public. He stands up for his beliefs and is good at fighting for causes. He is constructive and strong-willed. There is charm and charisma, and the person has no trouble gaining the affections of his heart's desire. He is virile and potent, yet laudably controlled. He is a passionate and skilled lover.

The person is robust, healthy, and good in sports. He benefits from his mother, who supports him in living an active, independent, and unconstrained life. The person loves freedom and travel. He abhors restriction and restraint. There is a strong mind and the person is honest and direct. He is practical and hard-working. There is mechanical ability, and the person may enjoy building his own home. He is emotionally inspired in his endeavors. In the event of illness there is excellent recuperative ability. There is a certain poise and steadiness about the person because his desires and aggressions work harmoniously with his feelings. Feminist Gloria Steinem has the Moon-Mars trine within one and one half degrees. Sir Laurence Olivier had the aspect within two degrees.

The emotions are expressed best through touch, massage, sex, and other physical manifestations. The person is consciously directed about his feelings, and he can move others to action in the blink of an eye. He is sensual, inspired, and profoundly stimulated. The Moon trine Mars is significantly more powerful than the sextile. The sextile indicates the opportunity to make the above characteristics a reality.

If the Moon is conjunct Jupiter, the person is emotionally buoyant. He is happy and recovers almost immediately from depressing or negative experiences. The person is generous, pleasant, and of the kindest nature. He is well-loved by all. It is important to note the house placement where the conjunction takes place, for that area of life will prosper immensely by these two benefics. The person is a great optimist, hopeful through even the worst of times. Though he may occasionally seem a dreamer because of his positive outlook, his judgment is uncommonly accurate. Insight comes from both astute common sense and an ability to emotionally sense the nature and outcome of things. The person loves to speculate, gamble, and put forth his prophesy. Because of his charm, powerful intuition, and sheer luck he is protected from accident, violence, and danger. He appears to have a guardian angel. The childhood is an extremely happy one.

The Moon conjunct Jupiter, above all other astrological aspects, indicates a life of fun, amusement, and pleasure. The person's emotions flow with ease. A man with this aspect charms women in an instant. They trust him implicitly and want to please him. They especially want to be around him for his humor, lightheartedness, and contagious love of life. The person is good in sports. He likes outdoor activities, exploration and travel, and wants to experience everything that the world has to offer. He is, more than anyone, physically and psychologically healthy. He does not carry the past with him and expects only the best to occur in the future. Since the Moon rules females, the person benefits from his wife, mother, and all women. He gets a wife who is beautiful, wealthy, and special. She may also be spiritual, pure-hearted, and devotional. The person is especially lucky with money, which shows up (as if by divine grace) whenever it is needed. He also gets nice homes, cars, jewelry, and whatever else are the toys and luxuries of the day.

There are very few negative features to the Moon-Jupiter conjunction. However, the person must beware of pride or conceit. If he believes that he is fundamentally better than others he will, of course, eventually suffer on such account. Furthermore, he must avoid the tendency to take people's favors and good will for granted. He should never forget that the absolute grace he receives (compared to the rest of the world) is in large part due to positive actions taken in past lives. Otherwise, the **107** person unwittingly develops habits of laziness, indulgence, and superficiality. As it is, he blatantly gets away with deeds for which others would be quickly reprimanded, ridiculed, or punished. Lastly, there will be times when the person brings problems on himself because of his optimism and hopefulness. On the rare occasions when he finds himself involved in failing enterprises, he may ignore the signs of doom and wait far too long to cut his losses.

The person is compassionate, sympathetic, and has no desire to hurt anyone. Indeed, he is benevolent, charitable, and happy to share his wealth and good fortune. He is social, extroverted, and easy to talk to. He is honest, loyal, and devoted. He is very soft-natured and has a fertile imagination. He may have the greatest memory. The person is a supreme salesperson. He obtains the highest price for any item by wonderfully conveying the most beneficial features of a product. Because of the Jupiter influence, the person is innately religious, pure, and righteous. He has the deepest faith in God. While this aspect indicates more inclination to spiritual life than the Sun-Jupiter conjunction, there is still much greater appreciation of the physical and material pleasures of life. If, however, other aspects of the chart reveal a spiritual or religious nature, then this person experiences the most sublime surrender and devotion to God. He would also be a clear favorite of his guru or mentor.

The person is drawn to sales, drama, and any career involving money. He is also attracted to law, publishing, travel, or religious work. The person is adored by the public. He gains favors from people more easily than anyone. He may put on weight slowly but surely, a few pounds per year, during adulthood. The person perceives life as an opportunity for enjoyment. Johnny Carson has the Moon-Jupiter conjunction within approximately two degrees. Copernicus, the father of modern astronomy, had the aspect within one degree.

If the Moon is square or opposite Jupiter, the person is emotionally excessive. He may have been raised by a mother who was too theatrical or melodramatic. He therefore did not gain a sense of balanced emotional response. He goes overboard in his likes and dislikes. His judgement is marred by his feelings and he is often overly sentimental. The home space is very important and the person craves a luxurious home beyond his means. He desires an easy life without much hard work. He is extravagant, indulgent, and too attached to sensual pleasures. He may be lazy and tend to procrastinate. Certain individuals with the hard Moon-Jupiter aspects are conceited, proud, and profoundly arrogant. They lack any sense of awe and reverence for the talent, greatness, and hard work of unique individuals. Such persons often possess no particular talent and have achieved no significant accomplishments. Nonetheless they FEEL that they are as good (if not better) than any other human. They are, in a very meaningful way, blind to earthly reality. Appreciation, born of humility, may be completely absent.

The person is extremely devotional. Once he has pledged his allegiance to someone, he never wavers. He is obsessive in the realm of religion and philosophy. However, it is anyone's guess as to whether he will be a devout mystic or an atheist. He will have very definite and specific philosophical notions. He may give new meaning to the concept of religious fanaticism. The person is warm and sympathetic. He is well-meaning, and loved by all. He spreads his perpetual sense of enthusiasm and abundance wherever he goes. He must, however, be careful not to spend too much money and overextend his resources. He may be too grandiose in his plans and schemes. He should watch his diet, especially with sweets and oils. There may be allergies or liver ailments.

Jupiter afflictions, in Western astrology, manifest as lack of moderation and excessive behavior. When configured with the all-important luminary, the Moon, the person is in danger of major imbalances in perception. His experience is simply too affected by his heart. He should do his best to try and understand others' viewpoints, even if they are at definite odds with his own feelings. His life is disproportionately based on emotional conditioning that was developed early. Furthermore, he is at the mercy of rigidly-fixed habit patterns, whether he is conscious of these habit patterns or not. Though there is a likelihood of great intelligence, the person does not rate high on the scale of common sense or balanced choices. Discipline and self-control may be much lacking. The person should embrace responsibility and follow through on his promises. He must learn, as soon as he can, not to make spur-of-the-moment agreements that are based on emotional enthusiasm.

There is plenty of energy and excitement. Because the emotions run high, the person is susceptible to disappointment and discouragement. He needs to set priorities, and develop a sense of urgency and consistency. He should beware of sloppy work and wastefulness. Though he feels happy-go-lucky and blessed, he should not gamble. Most of all, he is well-advised to let go of his emotional certainties, consider deeply the special qualities of those around him, and try to develop some appreciation and humility. Robert Bly has the Moon-Jupiter opposition within three and one half degrees. Astrologer C.E.O. Carter had the opposition within two degrees.

If the Moon is trine or sextile Jupiter, the person is emotionally blessed. He is optimistic, hopeful, and cheery. He knows he is here to enjoy, and therefore never takes the game of life too seriously. He has unshakeable faith in God and nature. He is lucky, favored, and protected from harm as if by a guardian angel. The person is popular, kind, and pleasant. He is supremely warm and compassionate. His presence alone is enough to uplift others.

The person benefits through his mother and all females. He is sensitive, caring, and has wonderful feminine energy. He is refined, gentle, and wants happiness for everyone. There is a profound love of religion, philosophy, and higher knowledge. The person is intuitive and spiritual. He is mentally healthy and has the best inner harmony and peace of mind. He is sympathetic and forgiving. There is a rich and fertile imagination. The person does well with the public. He lives in nice homes and domestic life is favored. Happiness comes from consistently practicing the golden rule.

The person is a fine human being. He is honest, loyal, and sincere. He has integrity and can be trusted to refrain from cruelty, revenge, and other base behavior. Theatrical work is favored, as is any career where the person spreads his sense of hope and faith to the common person. There is abundant humor, happiness, and contentment. If the rest of the chart indicates too much ease or complacency, the person will have to beware of laziness, indulgence, or hedonism.

Health is good and the person benefits from foreigners, travel, and activities in other countries. He is tolerant, non-judgemental, and protective. There is an excellent sense of devotion. Life is spirited, inspiring, and fun. The person is appreciative and lets his gratefulness be known. He does not mind praising others. Karl Marx, James Dean, and astrologer Dane Rudhyar all had strong Moon-Jupiter trines. The Moon trine Jupiter is significantly more powerful than the sextile. The sextile indicates the opportunity to make the above characteristics a reality.

If the Moon is conjunct Saturn, the person is emotionally inhibited. He is serious, shy, timid, and reserved. The person is easily hurt as a child and the pain may be so great that he builds a permanent wall of defense through which no one may penetrate. The person may be deeply selfish and thereby miss out on the greatest joy of life. He does not know how to trust and is suspicious of being taken advantage of. It is hard for him to give. He may find it almost impossible to share his feelings, for he does not wish to open himself up to possible rejection. Furthermore, his emotions may be so repressed that they are unclear even to him.

The person is the most practical and down-to-earth of all beings. He has phenomenal endurance and staying power. His tolerance to pain is unlimited. He is unfazed by pressure, and does not know the meaning of the word "quit." Except for certain actions caused by his excessive commitment to self-protection and personal security, his morals are high. He is acutely aware of right and wrong, and wants to do the right thing. His greatest quality is his sense of responsibility. However, as one's highest attribute is always his greatest potential liability, the person may go overboard in his sense of duty. He may also deny himself the sweet pleasures of life, due to a pervasive sense of guilt. The person is thrifty and abhors waste. He is austere. He drives a very hard bargain, is an excellent buyer, and easily gets the better of others. He rarely overpays.

Because of his tremendous self-control, the person appears extremely confident. But in fact, there is likely to be a firmly-planted inferiority complex carried over from his sensitive childhood. The person does not flow emotionally, and he is therefore at the mercy of all past disturbances. The last thing he wants to do is take a risk. Emotional vulnerability is his greatest fear, and counseling may be required if the person wants to change the situation. The person is good with facts and figures. He is simple, unembellishing, and to the point. He has great common sense and can easily size up a situation in terms of what he stands to gain. He is objective in analysis and allows no space for his feelings to affect his judgement. However, his viewpoint is ultimately too narrow. Though he wins most battles he may lose the war. For he may gain wealth, security, and success, but come nowhere near happiness.

The person may have been denied emotional nurturing from his mother. She may have been strict, rigid, cold, or physically absent. She may have lived a life of suffering. If the person was denied maternal tenderness as a child he may consider himself unlovable or unworthy, even though this attitude is not apparent on the surface. The person is conservative and never gambles. He is extremely adept at routine and discipline. He does not procrastinate. The person rarely praises others. However, he may be an excellent provider. He is conscientious and does not run away. He expresses his love through loyalty, commitment, and action rather than words or touch. The person is likely to suffer on account of females or his wife. Marriage may entail hardship and obligation. The person is prone to marry someone who becomes ill or worse. A woman with the Moon-Saturn conjunction may have problems with frigidity.

The person may experience periods of self-imposed isolation. He is somber, tends toward depression, and needs to cultivate joy and optimism. The person is ambitious and has fine organizational ability. He is good in business and carefully considers the potential downside of each and every action. He may have experienced poverty or other deprivations during childhood. He is thin, rugged, and tougher for having survived adversity. There may be difficulties with the breast, brain, and (for a woman) menstrual cycle. The person may be hard-hearted, yet it is unlikely that there is malicious intent unless other birthchart afflictions exist. Bob Dylan has the Moon conjunct Saturn aspect within two degrees.

If the Moon is square or opposite Saturn, it is an emotionally karmic lifetime. The person is raised by a reserved, formal, or stern mother. There is an insufficient amount of warmth and nurturing during childhood, and the person is greatly affected by this. He may deduce that he is unlovable or inadequate, and live with irrational fears and complexes the rest of his life. He is self-denying and too hard on himself. There is an imbalanced or distorted sense of responsibility. The person does good for everyone but himself. He should beware of creating, or unconsciously attracting, restrictive circumstances where he cannot achieve happiness and fulfillment. He should work on self-love and self-acknowledgement. Above all, he must surround himself with supportive people who are approving, appreciative, and praising.

The person may lack confidence or suffer from an inferiority complex. He may create troubles for himself in love relationships by choosing a partner who cannot meet his needs. The person suffers on account of females. A man with this aspect may get a wife who becomes ill or worse. There are rigidly-fixed habit patterns, and the person is inordinately affected by his subconscious mind. He has difficulty letting go of the past. He is too crystallized and should avoid salt, eggs, meat, and hard cheeses. Physical ailments may come from arthritis or paralysis. The person is extremely conservative and should structure regular fun and recreation in his life. He fears rejection and must allow himself to take more risks. He is a strong soul, stable and persistent. He can endure any adversity.

The person is sensitive and vulnerable. He feels the pain of others acutely. He is reflective and contemplating. Unfortunately, he blames himself unduly. He lives with chronic feelings of guilt that are exacerbated by selfishness. His greed is likely to be strong and caused by a pervasive sense of scarcity. Since the Moon represents nurturing, there may be health problems as a child, but the health may improve as life advances. The person's mother may live a difficult life or die early. The person must guard against taking life too severely. He should cultivate joy, humor, and cheerfulness. He should especially make a conscious effort to enjoy life and participate in the endeavors he loves the most.

The person may be too easily discouraged and thus appear lazy. He is defensive and always fearing the worst. He is serious, shy, and often feels undeserving. He believes that burden and hardship is perfectly normal. There may be a cold or detached nature, since the emotions are not warm and flowing. Jack Nicholson, the master of aloofness and dispassionate feelings, has the Moon opposite Saturn within one degree. The person should work on flexibility and emotional expression. Psychodrama is one good way for the person to get in touch with his feelings and break down walls of defense.

With hard Saturn aspects to either the Sun or Moon, the success of the entire life very much depends upon how well the person learns to disregard the automatic, self-censoring voice in his head. Even if the rest of the birthchart is extraordinarily powerful, the person may never realize his potential unless he is rigorous in his resolve.

"After the final no, there comes a "yes." And on that "yes," the future of the world depends."

WALLACE STEVENS

If the Moon is trine or sextile Saturn, the person is emotionally mature. He is practical, realistic, and stable in his feelings. He has an excellent sense of duty and is the most reliable of all beings. He can always be counted on to take the human qualities of mercy, fairness, and justice into consideration. He is compassionate, caring, and ever empathetic. The person is traditional, and he values family life above all else. He is calm, composed, and tranquil under the most stressful circumstances. He is emotionally wise and is not distracted by petty or inconsequential occurrences.

The person loves his mother, and benefits from her and other females. He is protective and nurturing. Domestic harmony is very favored. Discipline is well-ingrained and the person is a fine worker. He is organized and controlled. He can become a master of his field because of his patience, depth, and endurance. He has good common sense and learns well from his experience. Success comes slowly but surely, and the person is honored for his exceptional attitude. Once he recognizes his goals, he strives valiantly to achieve them. The person may be, in certain ways, too reserved and restrained. He needs to take more risks and enjoy the excitement of life. He may also be too reticent to let his emotions, desires, and aspirations be known.

A man with this aspect gets a pragmatic and sensible wife. There is plenty of respect for elders and superiors. The person is honest and trustworthy. He is cautious and powerfully discriminating. The person's logic is profound and he has high standards. He is loved by all for his charitable, responsive, and loving nature. The person does well with the public. He gains from land, homes, and real estate. He is good in business and may be talented in carpentry. The Moon-Saturn trine is significantly more powerful than the sextile. The sextile indicates the opportunity to make the above characteristics a reality.

If the Moon is conjunct Uranus, the person is emotionally high-strung. He is restless, impatient, and active. He craves excitement. Above all he wants freedom from restraint. He will sacrifice anything to maintain his independence. With this aspect, it is crucial to note if Saturn is strong in the chart or whether there are other indications of responsibility, depth, and discipline. If there are not, then the Moon-Uranus conjunction is powerfully disruptive and difficult to deal with. The person may be erratic, unstable, and fickle. He abhors monotony and routine, and is quick to make changes or arouse others if he is not receiving his required stimulation. The person may be extremely moody, not in a depressive way but in "running hot and cold." He is seriously impulsive, and more than anyone else, at the mercy of his ever-changing, unpredictable emotions.

The person is magnificently intuitive. He may have sudden flashes of genius. He is creative, talented, and original. Concentration and endurance, however, may be lacking. The person's greatest attribute is his ability to live entirely in the moment. He is capable of making strikingly accurate or appropriate judgements on the spot. He is spiritual and is unfazed by guilt, insecurity, and other such debilitating complexes. He is unconcerned with the past and the future. The person is experience-oriented and is unaffected by dogma, doctrine, and theoretical knowledge. He is highly perceptive, yet does not sit in judgement of others. He is happy that he is "different" from the rest of the world, and feels completely detached from societal and religious moral codes. Indeed, he gains pleasure and excitement from engaging in any forbidden or frowned-upon social behavior.

Uranus is the higher octave of Mercury. The Moon-Uranus aspect therefore indicates a high-strung nervous system. The person may feel perpetual emotional tension. He is subject to spasms or muscular contractions. The person is extremely magnetic. He is inspiring, youthful, and stimulating. For these reasons, the person easily attracts the opposite sex. However, there are likely to be significant difficulties in the love life. The person is extremely self-centered. Furthermore, he is ruled by his feelings and may be especially unwilling to compromise or listen to reason. He will be unpredictable, and flagrantly insensitive to the other person's needs if they interfere with his freedom. He does not equate emotions with attachment and commitment. Although he desires emotional nourishment as much as anyone, he may run like the devil when he feels himself merging any aspect of his identity with another. This may play havoc with his lover, who must have the strongest ego and sense of detachment if the relationship is to have a chance.

In some cases, the opposite of all that has just been said is true. It may be the love partner that exhibits the "Uranian" qualities. If this is true and the person continually attracts partners incapable of commitment and dependability, then he must consider whether he is unconsciously choosing such individuals in order to ensure a life of independence. Since the person craves a life of emotional freedom, his relationships are unorthodox and unconventional. In some cases, there may be a lack of genuine intimacy and depth. This occurs because the person is so self-reliant that he does not know how to trust. The person may have had an up-and-down relationship with an inconsistent or unreliable mother and consequently learned not to count upon others. As the Moon rules females, a man with the Moon-Uranus conjunction may get a wife who is exciting, free-spirited, and spiritually- or metaphysically-oriented. She may be eccentric, ever changing, and erratic. She may be unfaithful or undependable. The Moon-Uranus person loves anything new and different. He is drawn to science, research, computers, aviation, astrology, or any pursuit that is ahead of the times. He may experience many major life changes and more different paths or lifestyles than the common person. The person may be a reformer who is interested in social change. He may be somewhat radical or rebellious.

The person is determined, even relentless, when gripped by strong emotional desires. At times, he is the most irrational and inflexible of all beings. Others may have great difficulty in understanding or empathizing with the person. His interests are decidedly out of the ordinary, and he likes to surround himself with nonconformists or odd characters. His childhood was untraditional. The person's greatest attribute is his tremendous and magnetic spirit. He is an infectious lover of life. Orson Welles and the famous Danish astronomer Tycho Brahe both had the Moon-Uranus conjunction within three and one half degrees. Paul Cezanne had the aspect within two degrees.

If the Moon is square or opposite Uranus, the person is an individu-alist. He lives by instinct and impulse, and is egocentric and rebellious. Above all, he is emotionally independent. He cares little about the opinions of others and does not respond to force or manipulation. He receives immense pleasure from breaking the rules and watching everyone's reaction. The person may have been raised by a mother who was inconsistent, unreliable, or undependable. Thus, he has no emo-tional footing upon which to trust others in a deep way. He feels entirely self-reliant and is in danger of missing out on the profound joy of deep human intimacy. During childhood, there may have been too many residence changes or other forms of domestic instability. The person is stubborn, obstinate, and powerfully self-willed. Moon-Uranus aspects are especially difficult because the emotions are subject to such intense upheaval. Therefore, it is extremely important to note how strong the aspect is by degree. In severe cases the person is childish, petulant, and demanding. He expects the people around him to satisfy his every wish. He may throw fits of rage or emotional tantrums on an unpredictable, yet semi-regular, basis.

The person is creative, inventive, and progressive. He is incredibly intuitive and may have flashes of genius. There is great emotional tension, and the person may be acutely high-strung. He is unpredict-able, erratic, and craves excitement. He loves being different, and may have anti-social leanings. He is a revolutionary with little respect for tradition. He has no regard for rules, regulations, and moral or philo-sophical codes. He is entirely experience-oriented. The person is very perceptive, trusts his own judgement implicitly, and is never fooled by authority figures or pomp and circumstance. There is a desire for absolute, unconditional freedom. Therefore, the person may take to the spiritual path, with his eye firmly set on final liberation.

Relationships are difficult. Although the person desperately wants and needs emotional intimacy and tenderness, he is very afraid of getting too close to someone and thereby losing his independence and freedom. Also, there is such an aversion to routine and monotony (not to mention a potentially fickle nature), that the person is probably wiser to marry after the late twenties or early thirties. Since the Moon rules females, the person experiences discord with his mother and women in general. There is a serious need for discipline, maturity, and consistency. The person must learn patience, tolerance, and how to keep his word when the spirit to do so does not particularly move him. Some individuals with this aspect are inconsiderate, habitually late, and blatantly insensitive to the concerns of others. They give new meaning to the concepts of irresponsibility and thoughtlessness.

There may be an interest in the occult, computers, aviation, or any endeavor which is ahead of the times. A woman with the aspect may find motherhood much too limiting on her freedom and need for excitement and stimulation. The person may be moody or volatile. He loves to experiment with sex and all kinds of unusual emotional responses. He is the most active, dynamic, and energetic of beings. Of course he may also be nervous, irritable, or frenetic. The person is sensitive to criticism. He needs more emotional support than others, despite the fact that he appears indifferent and detached. He loves eccentric, occultish, and spiritual friends.

As with all significant Uranus afflictions, the person may be defensive. He expects to be reprimanded (as he always was in childhood) for his independent, individualistic nature. He must come to realize that all human beings (whether they choose to lead, follow, or accept domination) are exercising their own God-given choice. Traditional astrological texts say that there are intense, radical changes throughout life, and that the person feels an inordinate need to break away from his past. Entertainer Tommy Smothers and Princess Diana both have the Moon opposition Uranus aspect within two degrees. J. Edgar Hoover had the Moon square Uranus aspect within four degrees.

If the Moon is trine or sextile Uranus, the person is emotionally free. He is quite enlightened, and is spared the burden of living life to satisfy the opinions and reactions of the crowd. He is magnetic, charismatic, and sparkling. He is adored by the public and is colorful, stimulating, and fun to be around. The person is open-minded and always ready to enjoy the changes of life. He goes with the flow, and experiences unique and exceptional opportunities during his entire stay on earth. There is excellent judgement caused by detachment and emotional objectivity, and the person trusts his perception unconditionally. He is expressive and thrilled with life.

Benefits come from the mother and females, and the person has many women friends. A man with the aspect is especially appreciated by the fair sex for his lack of possessiveness, jealousy, and egotistical needs. He loves women and attracts the most exciting, stimulating, and independent types. The person is rarely threatened by anyone or anything, because he is experimental and always looking to develop new, more liberated ways of dealing with his feelings. He is mystical, occult-minded, and devotional. He is creative, inspired, and progressive. The person is unaffected by rules, regulations, dogma, and rhetoric. He is a natural humanitarian and does not pass judgement on others. He excels in science, advanced or progressive healing methods, and any new-age endeavor. He is very concerned with fairness and justice.

As with nearly all trines and free-flowing aspects, there is potential laziness. In order to make the most of positive Moon-Uranus aspects, there should be some significant friction, discord, or struggle elsewhere in the birthchart. The person craves freedom and stimulation. He does not want to be tied down, and therefore may have trouble making commitments. The mind is highly alert and the person has excellent reflexes. The person is strong-willed and there is potential genius. He has an interesting and favorable domestic life, and may do well with land and homes. He is sensitive and responsive, and has great ability to excite the masses. There may be special abilities with any of the five senses.

The person is psychologically healthy and does not carry troubles from the past with him. He is tolerant of others. He has a distinctive and unique personality. He may be restless and move around a lot. He particularly enjoys new beginnings, even if he has to start over from scratch. He has good friends and greatly enjoys them. The trine aspect is significantly more powerfully than the sextile. The sextile indicates the opportunity to make the above characteristics a reality.

"If there are only two available options, choose the third."

ANCIENT JEWISH PROVERB

If the Moon is conjunct Neptune, the person lives in his feelings. He is the most sensitive and impressionable of all beings. He is powerfully affected by outside stimuli. He feels as if he does not belong on the earth, because it is so gross. The person is mystical, intuitive, and open to the spiritual realm. He longs for perfection and may be involved in astrology, metaphysics, or any human-potential endeavor. The person is highly idealistic. But his idealism is an internal, <u>emotional</u> process that does not lend itself to being brought out into the world of form and structure. Therefore, the person may suffer disappointment and disillusionment caused by his lack of achievement. He may occasionally experience powerful bouts of depression due to unfulfilled expectations. The person is extremely refined and considers the higher qualities of life (such as honesty, integrity, kindness, humility, etc.) as the bare minimum of human behavior. The world around him seems quite base, and is a source of pain and bewilderment.

The person is magnificently compassionate. He is tolerant, patient, and entirely accepting of others. His greatest concern is to help. The person is understanding, empathetic, and looks for the best in others. People feel at ease and set their defenses aside when around him. Emotionally, the person lives an unbounded existence. Therefore, he is rather Aquarian in nature. He is extremely open and is slow to judge or condemn anyone. He is not bound by the world's standard moral code. He takes experiences for what they are, and has no desire to categorize, or place restrictive demands on, relationships. He gives people the benefit of the doubt, takes them at their word, and expects the same in return. He is exceedingly careful not to hurt anyone's feelings. Because Neptune is the higher aspect of Venus, and is conjunct the Moon, the person is the greatest lover of the arts. He is creative in music, drama, photography, film, and magic. He is excited by sounds, smells, textures, and colors. It is crucial to note that the person is more an <u>appreciator</u> of life than a doer. Therefore, career-wise he functions better as one who discovers, displays, and promotes the arts (or anything else) rather than being someone who actually produces the work. His job is to inspire others.

124   The person is refined and cultured, and should try to create a life of ease for himself. He does not handle stress, long hours, and hard physical labor well. He is emotionally giving and needs periods of seclusion to recoup his energies. He may find city life difficult. Although the person is physically very delicate, he is not likely to be thin. He will appear solid and may put on weight as a protective layer from the coarseness of the world. Regarding the inordinate sensitivity to life's friction, the Moon-Neptune aspect is easier for a man than for a woman. While a man with this aspect is certainly vulnerable, emotional, and sensitive, yet he is aided by his masculine gender. Thus the struggle to handle daily life is not nearly as acute as it is for a female. In love relationships, however, this aspect is harder for a man. He is forever seeking the absolute perfect woman, an ideal that may not exist. Furthermore, as a child he craved his mother's affection, of which no amount was enough. In his adult life with females, the same pattern continues.

A woman with this aspect also has an intense need for emotional nourishment. But this need is not necessarily as inextricably connected to the primary love relationship. Because the Moon rules females, and is conjunct Neptune, a man with the aspect may get a wife who is ungrounded, emotionally unstable, or attracted to drugs or alcohol. She may also be mystical or highly devotional. The person's mother may also have been strange, weird, or unstable. Or she may have been useless as a provider of emotional support. In the case of females for whom this is true, the effects are especially devastating. This means the woman had no role model as a child and was forced to fend for herself. Her confidence in herself as a capable and loveable person, may suffer throughout all of life.

Since the Moon rules the mother and is conjunct Neptune, it is expected that the person would idealize the mother. Although this is very often true, there are plenty of cases where the father is revered instead. As sensitive as the Moon-Neptune person is, he does not wear his feelings on his sleeve. He is quiet, contemplative, and slow to respond. This is not, by any means, from lack of intelligence. It is due to his habit of consulting his feelings first. The person is inspired and has great imagination. He loves to help people who are down and out. He is gullible, unsuspecting, and bothered by his tendency to be taken advantage of. He is seriously moody. The constitution is frail, and the person should avoid drugs and alcohol. Illnesses are due to stress and upset emotions, and the person can only heal himself with rest, proper diet, and other natural remedies. To outsiders who are unaware of the person's sensitivity, the person may appear to be a hypochondriac. There is a subtleness or dreamlike quality about the person that he especially may use to his advantage on the theatrical stage. Dustin Hoffman has the Moon-Neptune conjunction within one degree. Humanitarian Albert Schweitzer had the aspect within three degrees.

The person experiences the most powerful emotional merging with the universal force. However, because of this he is acutely aware of the imperfection and limitations of mortality. Thus he is, as they say, "divinely discontented." The person's home environment is of utmost importance. He is loyal and devoted. Most importantly, he should choose his associations carefully and create a protected environment for himself.

"I don't know what your destiny will be, but I do know that the only ones among you who will be truly happy are those who have sought and found a way to serve."

ALBERT SCHWEITZER

If the Moon is square or opposite Neptune, the person suffers on account of emotional deception and disillusionment. The first experience occurs in the home space with a mother who may, unfortunately, be unstable, weak, or ineffectual. She may have been physically or emotionally absent, or addicted to drugs or alcohol. The person is at the mercy of an idealistic, romantic nature and he cannot clearly perceive who should or should not be trusted. Although the Moon rules females and therefore indicates trouble in a man's marriage, a woman also is subject to marital difficulties. The nurturing element during childhood may simply not have been stable and secure enough to provide the person with a solid basis from which to choose a suitable, loving partner. The self-image is weak, fuzzy, or distorted, and there may be deep insecurity. The person feels a yearning in his soul for contentment and fulfillment. More than anything, he craves support and emotional nourishment. He wants to be loved in the most personal, intimate way and taken care of unconditionally (something which did not properly occur in the formative years).

The person idealizes either, or both, of his parents. He is the warmest, most compassionate being. He is spiritual or mystical, and is open to realms closed to the average mortal. He believes in astrology, higher consciousness, the astral world, and other intangibles. There is great intuition. The person is sensitive and enormously vulnerable. There may be a lifetime of emotionally painful experiences due to overpowering or uncontrollable feelings. The person is extremely impressionable, and if the rest of the birthchart reveals mental difficulties, psychosis may result. The problem results from the combination of a great imagination and fantasy life along with a very real, and accurate, psychic nature. The person may be moody or depressive. His goals and ambitions are large, and he is subject to delusions of grandeur as well as serious disappointment.

Career-wise, there is talent in magic, film, photography, and especially theatrical work. Artistic, aesthetic, and cultural endeavors are definitely favored. The person is a dreamer. He follows his heart, not his mind. This is advantageous in certain respects, but there is, in most hard Moon-Neptune cases, a need for discrimination, clarity, and practicality.

The person must learn to distinguish the real from the fanciful. He is an escapist. He craves perfection, and should pursue spiritual methods rather than drugs or alcohol. The latter would be dangerous and detrimental. Habits and addictions would, in this case, be very easily formed. As always with Moon afflictions (because the Moon rules nurturing), there may be health problems during childhood.

The person experiences too much confusion. It may be a lifelong goal for him to learn how to separate his feelings from his intellect. He must beware of lying or deceiving others. A man or woman with the aspect may choose a Neptunian mate: one who is illusive, deceptive, mystical, confused, or highly emotional. During adulthood a tranquil, stable home space is an absolute must. The person may experience the greatest devotion and merging with God or Universal consciousness. Traditional astrological texts always mention the likelihood of major scandal at some point in the life. Werner Erhard, founder of the EST training, has the Moon square Neptune within one degree.

If the Moon is trine or sextile Neptune, the person is kind-hearted and emotionally inspired. He lives for the romance, beauty, and passion of life. He is the greatest poet, musician, or artist. There is acute sensitivity and the person is cultured and refined. He is delicate, gentle, and subtle. Because he was nourished so well during childhood, he is magnificently sympathetic and compassionate. He wants goodness and happiness for all. The relationship with mother and females in general is favored. A man with the aspect gets a tender, well-bred, beautiful wife. She may be sensuous, artistic, ethereal, and spiritual. The person is highly idealistic and devotional. He is powerfully psychic and open to mystical realms. He has unwavering faith in God.

There is a wonderful and prolific imagination. The person loves beauty, luxury, opulence, and style. He surrounds himself with elegance and wants to create heaven on earth. The home space is especially beneficial and the person excels in interior design. He is warm, friendly, and altruistic. He does exceedingly well in any benevolent, charitable, or service-oriented work. There is, of course, a danger of laziness, unless other aspects of the birthchart indicate maturity, discipline, and depth. Also, there may be a tendency towards indulgences or escapism even with the harmonious Moon-Neptune aspects.

The person feels things deeply and must shield himself from negative vibrations and harsh surroundings. He may want to avoid cruel and blunt individuals. There is a dreamy nature and fine acting ability. Film, photography, and theatrical work are all favored. The person is optimistic. He expects good things to happen and is easygoing about life. He is sensual, soft, and receptive. There may be an interest in occult subjects. Bo Derek has the Moon-Neptune trine within two and one half degrees. The trine aspect is significantly more powerful than the sextile. The sextile indicates the opportunity to make the above characteristics a reality.

If the Moon is conjunct Pluto, the person lives a life of emotional compulsion. He is swayed by cravings and desires. However, no one enjoys the profundity and depth of feeling as much as he. It is clearly a life of personality transformation. The person is here to learn a sense of balance and detachment. He will do this through a perpetual process of attachment and forced relinquishment. He will experience death and rebirth of the emotions. There will be, at the very least, one dramatically "fated" relationship in which the person is consumed with desire for his partner. He will want to own the other person, but control, in the final outcome, will be out of his hands. The person wants to lose his personal identity by becoming totally absorbed in experience. He merges himself with his love partner, and all other objects of desire, as completely as is humanly possible.

The person is psychologically sensitive. He is psychic and effortlessly understands the inner workings of others. Therefore, he is an excellent psychologist, counselor, or therapist. Because Pluto is the higher vibration of the Moon (not Mars) the conjunction of the two influences indicates a "super lunar" type. This means that each and every function ruled by the Moon may be both experienced and expressed in an excessive way. The person is tenacious to an extreme. He clings to people and situations long after they have outlived their usefulness. He is tremendously maternal and nurturing. His body exudes the warmest healing energy. However, the person must resolutely guard against an overbearing or domineering nature, especially with his loved ones. He must also release his over-protectiveness with his children.

The person is faced with the difficult task of managing his fiercely raw emotionality. In this sphere, he feels naked, insecure, and oppressively vulnerable. His typical reaction is to control and manipulate his surroundings and associates. Of course, in the long run, such actions merely invite disaster in the person's intimate life. Control and manipulation may also lead to health problems — cancer and ulcers especially. The person may tend toward jealousy, revenge, lust, or any obsessive behavior. The extent to which this is true depends on many factors, especially the person's evolutionary level. Fortunately, the Moon-Pluto conjunction indicates strong spiritual development and a phenomenal capacity for self-discipline. The person intermittently uses these abilities to completely remake and remold himself. He has powerful energy to regenerate his cellular structure and improve himself in any area of life. He is a walking mass of human potential.

The Moon represents passive and receptive (yin) energy. However, Pluto, the higher Moon, is a "yang" and active force (extreme "yin" always becomes "yang," and vice-versa). Thus, the person is creative, expressive, and dynamic. He is often quite "driven." He is attracted to psychology, spiritualism, massage therapy, or any of the healing arts. He is a proponent of universal welfare. He has, from the beginning of his days, a desire to get to the core of existence. He loves the earth, gardening, archeology, and farming. The person may have an uncommon or broken childhood. His mother is likely to be smothering, too intense, or over-protective. There is a psychic bond with the mother that lasts throughout the entire life. In the event of accident or danger, the person's mother will sense the problem even if she lives on the other side of the earth. The person may have a similar connection to his own children.

A man with the Moon-Pluto conjunction may get an intense, powerful, or manipulative wife. She may be spiritual, psychic, compulsive, or famous. Relationships during the early part of life may entail phenomenal closeness, intensity, pain, loss, and separation. In some cases, the partner may suddenly disappear or die. The person is fascinated with power. He is incredibly resourceful and is concerned with preservation of the self and species. He may perceive himself as a universal protector. A female may consider herself a cosmic mother. The person is serious and does not wish to be taken lightly. He may be practically insatiable regarding desires and emotional fulfillment. Traditional astrological texts report that there are periods of emotional turmoil, outbursts, or upset, and that the person leaves home at an early age. This may be one way for the person to experience his lessons and emotional initiations as quickly as possible. Health-wise, the breast, brain, and menstrual cycle may be delicate. There is a need to learn objectivity and emotional moderation. The person must develop tolerance and allow others to learn their life lessons for themselves, at their own pace.

The impassioned composer Wolfgang Mozart had an exact Moon-Pluto conjunction. David Bowie has the aspect within one degree.

If the Moon is square or opposite Pluto, the person lives a cathartic, emotional life. His desires run deep, and he is at the mercy of an inordinately sensitive and vulnerable nature. He is greatly affected by his early childhood years, with a mother who may have been too intense, powerful, smothering, or devouring. There was not enough balanced, stable nurturing at home, and the person seeks emotional security for the rest of his days. There may be great secretiveness, and, as Isabel Hickey put it, a "lone-wolf type" personality. The person is very "Scorpionic" and cannot bear to be humiliated, laughed at, or teased. He feels things intensely and takes life very personally.

The person experiences a daily death and rebirth of the emotions. He avoids people and situations where he may be criticized or embarrassed. Rejection is, of course, his worst nightmare. The person suffers most on account of his mother and females in general. If Venus is also afflicted in the birthchart, the person may be paying off enormous love debts from past lives. Now he is learning the lesson of tender human emotion and the heartache that results from violating peoples' feelings and vulnerability. The person should beware of domineering, overbearing women. The spouse may be a controlling, manipulative, "Plutonian" type, especially in the case of a man with the aspect. Some men with hard Moon-Pluto aspects scare females away with their brooding intensity and volatile emotions.

Because the person so wants control, he is extraordinarily demanding in love relationships. He may be selfish, jealous, and possessive. And, if his feelings are transgressed, he may certainly seek revenge. He is powerful and creative. He wants to get to the core of existence and understand himself completely. He may be willing to do anything to transform, or transcend, his psychological limitations. He thrives on self-improvement, and is more than content to shed his old, turbulent personality for a newer, more liberated one. There are major, periodic crises in the life, and the person moves on without ever looking back. He is stubborn, independent, and does things his own way. He may occasionally win the grand prize for obstinacy.

There is healing ability, and the person is warm, compassionate, and nurturing. He may be well-liked for his caring and fervent nature. He excels in psychology, counseling, metaphysics, or any occult or research field. He expresses himself strongly and well. However, he must take care not to manipulate, smother, or overpower others. Some individuals, especially during childhood, have so little control over their feelings that they are given to tantrums or fits of rage. Their behavior is obsessive and compulsive, and they make fanatical demands of others. The person needs a calm and peaceful home space, where he feels safe and in complete control.

The person loves deeply and passionately. His entire being is absorbed in his loved one. He is psychic, creative, and remarkably self-disciplined. Health-wise, there is a danger of ulcers or cancer if the person does not learn to let go of his excessive control of life. He needs to develop emotional flexibility and confront the causes behind his consuming obsessions, fixations, and attachments. Fortunately, the person is a survivor. He may be successful as a result of the need to satisfy his intense inner struggles and complexes. He is also aided by his natural habit of connecting emotions to images, thus imbuing his thoughts with creative power. The person does not respond well to force. In his natural concerned and counseling way, he may be a catalyst for others to release their repressed or unresolved emotions.

Johnny Carson has the Moon opposition Pluto aspect within one and one half degrees. Martin Luther had the aspect within two degrees. J. Edgar Hoover had the Moon-Pluto square within one degree.

If the Moon is trine or sextile Pluto, the person is blessed in the art of living. Though his feelings are deep and profound, he is emotionally resilient. He is courageous and consistently willing to take risks. In the case of failure he confronts his pain. He is not one of the "walking wounded." Because of his extreme emotional potential and psychological well-being, he is incredibly versatile. He can play in more areas of life than anyone. He is self-motivated and thrilled to try new endeavors. There is excellent confidence, and success is very much favored due to the person's fine attitude. President Jimmy Carter has an exact Moon-Pluto trine. Hugh Hefner has the aspect within one degree, and Francis Ford Coppola has the aspect within three and one half degrees.

The person is interested in the occult, metaphysics, and spiritual disciplines. He is very concerned with growth, transformation, and enlightenment. There is talent in the healing arts and the person excels as a counselor or psychologist. He is warm and compassionate, and acts as a catalyst for others to express their feelings and unresolved complexes. Dealings with the public are favored, and the person inspires others for his reverence and understanding of the human condition. The person provides sustenance and nurturing to those around him. A woman with this aspect has the greatest mothering ability.

The person is considerate and cooperative. He is very gentle and careful not to hurt anyone's feelings. Though he is expressive and excited to be alive, his emotions are under control. He is flexible and adaptable. The person is tenacious and practical. He is a survivor. He manifests his desires easily because his thoughts are imbued with emotional force. There may be extreme psychic talent. The person is determined, and makes a great deal of soul progress in his lifetime. His greatest love is self-improvement. As always with harmonious aspects, there needs to be significant friction or struggle elsewhere in the birthchart in order for the person to take optimum advantage of this aspect. As always, the trine aspect is significantly more powerful than the sextile. The sextile indicates the opportunity to make the above characteristics a reality.

If Mercury is conjunct Venus, the person lives a life of refinement and culture. He is delicate, sensitive, and mentally blessed. He is bright and cheerful, optimistic and humorous. Above all other astrological aspects, this conjunction indicates musical and poetic talent. The person is expressive and his greatest fulfillment comes from sharing his wonderful mental harmony with others. He is eloquent, intelligent, and often brilliant. There is a marked dexterity to the person's intellect. His mind is in a state of restful alertness, ever ready to feel out, or objectively analyze, a situation. Once he does this, he is then able to generate the most precise and appropriate response. Like Paul Newman and Robert De Niro, who have the conjunction within two or three degrees, the person can charm anyone. He knows which words cause what effects in whom.

The person is drawn to all of the arts. He is graceful, agreeable, and lighthearted. However, he is also a creature of comfort. He craves luxuries and the good life. Unless Saturn is strong in the birthchart, the person has no patience for discipline and responsibility. He detests hard work, struggle, and dirty hands. He may be lazy, shallow, and indulgent. He is powerfully discriminating, and knows art and beauty better than anyone. He is appreciative. However, the person expects to receive pleasure and be treated well. He avoids difficult or challenging people as well as stressful situations. He has no use for austerities, the rugged life, or any variation of "roughing it." The person may, at times, frustrate friends and loved ones with his near-hedonism and unwillingness to confront adversity. In this regard, the person may be selfish and self-centered.

The person is kind, sympathetic, and fun to be around. He is tactful and diplomatic. Women feel immediately at ease with him. As Venus rules the love life, the person gets an intelligent, communicative spouse, one who is youthful and beautiful. Unfortunately, the partner may be fickle or emotionally detached in the relationship. The person is very social. He wears nice clothing and has a youthful appearance his entire life. He may be somewhat effeminate due to his grace and sensitivity. He may also be accused of vanity. Aside from music and all arts, he is attracted to jewelry, fashion or design, drawing, and writing (but not the

136   tedious sort). If the conjunction is extremely close by degree, the nerves will be too delicate and the person suffers mentally. In nearly all cases, there is an occasional, but profound, stubbornness because the person is so enamored with his own logical and mental process.

"True teaching is even more difficult than learning. We know that; but we rarely think about it. And why is teaching more difficult than learning? Not because the teacher must have a larger store of information, and always have it ready. Teaching is more difficult than learning because what teaching calls for is this: TO LET LEARN. The real teacher, in fact, lets nothing else be learned than learning. His conduct, therefore, often produces the impression that we properly learn nothing from him, if by "learning" we now suddenly understand merely the procurement of useful information. The teacher is ahead of his apprentices in this alone, that he still has far more to learn than they. He has to learn to let them learn. The teacher must be capable of being more teachable than the apprentices. The teacher is far less assured of his ground than those who learn are of theirs, if the relation between the teacher and the taught is genuine. Therefore, there is never a place in it for the authority of the know-it-all or the authoritative sway of the official."

MARTIN HEIDEGGER

If Mercury is conjunct Mars, the person is mentally aggressive. He is direct, outspoken, and enjoys a good argument. The person is talented in mechanics and has great manual dexterity. He is attracted to all technical fields such as architecture, engineering, drafting, etc. He is the best trouble-shooter and problem-solver. The person is competitive and nothing but goal-oriented. He is successful, and does whatever it takes to obtain desired results. The person is ingenious and easily solves puzzles. He is a perfectionist and a great detail worker. His mind is sharp and alert; he learns at lightning speed. There is a magnificent practicality to the person. He understands cause and effect better than anyone, and may be a genius at manipulating circumstances to get what he wants.

However, the person is too selfish and self-centered. His thoughts are only directed toward fulfillment of personal desires. Though he succeeds in getting his way, he has little chance for happiness because he has left no room in life for sentiment, generosity of spirit, idealism, and other refined sensibilities. He is keenly perceptive, but in a base way. He knows human nature but sees selfishness and self-serving motives everywhere. This is because awareness of his own intentions makes him skeptical, suspicious, and on his guard. It is also as if the person was deceived early in childhood and never overcame the hurt. Like Richard Nixon and Lyndon Johnson, who have the Mercury-Mars conjunction within one or two degrees, the person may spend the rest of life beating an invisible enemy. There is a tendency to live as if the end justifies the means. The person must stop his very natural inclination to lie or insignificantly "shade the truth."

The Mars-Mercury conjunction is a fascinating one. Aggressive Mars benefits greatly from association with intellectual and sensitive Mercury, while Mercury is burnt by they fiery nature of Mars. The person's peace of mind is definitely disturbed. He may have a hot temper or be on the angry side. The person will have powerful "pet peeves," minor issues that truly infuriate him. He can retain his anger at a person or particular situation for a lifetime without a thought of forgiveness. The person may be blunt, aggressive, and argumentative. He is extremely witty and incisive. He is good at satire and sarcasm. He excels at public speaking, debate, and politics. He loves to talk, stir up controversy, and challenge

138   others. He makes an excellent lawyer and is drawn to the profession at an early age. The person is a natural boss, and it is interesting to note that many leaders and presidents have the aspect. The person does not mince words. He says what is on his mind and evokes powerful reactions in others. He is capable of tact and diplomacy, but uses them infrequently, or only when it serves his purpose.

The person does not lack for courage and never backs down from others. He is impulsive and goes after what he wants. He is high-strung. There is a need for patience, tolerance, and consistency. The person may start many quickly-conceived projects which he does not finish, for his mind exceeds his actions. He is good with his fingers and excels at sleight of hand. If the conjunction is not too close by degree or if the rest of the chart indicates good discipline and patience, then the person makes an excellent teacher. He is an independent thinker. Although the person is brave and assertive, his confidence may be weak. This is because the nervous system, which is ruled by Mercury, is under constant pressure. The person should practice meditation or, if he cannot sit still that long, hatha yoga. He must also eat well to avoid problems with the lungs and intestines.

The person is excitable and has powerful desires. He has a healthy sex drive. There may be an indecisiveness caused by his wavering confidence. Because Mars rules sexual passion and is conjunct Mercury, the person is fascinated by intellectual, communicative lovers. He (or she) may also be extremely taken by youthful, fickle types. The person is strong-willed and has powerful blood. He is adventurous and active. The person is too conscious of the coarse and base aspects of life. He must focus on joy and sweetness by actively looking for the good in others. Otherwise he will resign himself early on to a discontented, even though successful, existence. Dean Martin had the Mercury-Mars conjunction within two degrees, and metaphysician Elbert Benjamin (C.C. Zain) had the aspect within two and one half degrees.

If Mercury is square or opposite Mars, the person is a professional critic. He is perceptive and sees peoples' flaws and imperfections without the slightest effort. His mind is sharp and analytical, and works too rapidly for his own good. There is great impatience and nervousness. The person may be irritable and have a short, hot temper. He may have problems during childhood with hyperactivity or tantrums. The person is a great problem-solver. Unfortunately, his morals are not the best, as he considers life a win-lose game where "the good guy finishes last." He is fairly selfish, and his first task in life is learning how to beat the system. His greatest pleasure comes from circumventing or bypassing the rules. The person may lie regularly or fail to keep his word. He believes the end justifies the means and is not particularly concerned with integrity. In extreme cases, there may be stealing, shoplifting, or criminal activity.

The person is direct and blunt. He often speaks before thinking and may thereby offend others. He has the most energetic mind and is witty, sarcastic, and humorous. The person is as practical as can be and he learns very quickly. He is curious and adventurous. He is not, however, likely to be a scholar since he is impatient and wants his answers quickly. He does not like school and is bored with the slowness of others. There is excellent mechanical ability and the person loves a good mental puzzle. He is like a detective in deciphering peoples' motives. However, he is too skeptical and suspicious, and generally projects his own greed and selfishness onto the world.

The person must beware of headaches as well as problems with the lungs, intestines, and nervous system. Most importantly, he needs to learn to separate his mind from his ego, and open up to the advice, counsel, and support of friends and loved ones. Many individuals with hard Mercury-Mars aspects are stubborn to the extreme. They equate winning with following their own impressions, and losing with listening to others. They do not understand surrender or compromise, and may have a "corner on the market" when it comes to being arrogant.

Because Mercury is the natural ruler of the third house, there is a strong chance of difficulties with siblings. There may be too much rivalry, jealousy, or some other problem. The person may be argumentative or

140   quarrelsome. He loves to debate. He is excitable and suffers from mental strain. Because he finds fault with everyone else so easily, he may be conceited in a major way. He may also be opinionated. The person is spontaneous and impulsive. He enjoys life a lot and is always ready to secure the moment. He is courageous in speech and asks for what he wants. He is street-wise and rarely fooled or taken advantage of. He must guard against lying, however, or his reputation will eventually become tainted. Some individuals with this aspect are sloppy, careless, and unreliable.

If Mercury is trine or sextile Mars, the person is intelligent, incisive, and of the best attitude. He is optimistic, enthusiastic, and determined. He loves knowledge and is an independent thinker. He will never be pushed to deny his own perceptions. There is literary talent and excellent communication skills. The person is expressive and lets his feelings be known. He is direct and to the point. He excels in mechanical ability, architecture, engineering, or drafting. He has great common sense.

The nervous system is solid and the person is confident. He is resilient and recovers quickly from failure. He is alert, clever, witty, and humorous. He loves life and is active and adventurous. The person is competent, and success is favored. He is well-organized and readily accomplishes his goals and intentions. He is practical and skeptical, and learns things on the first try. He is sarcastic and satirical. He enjoys a friendly argument and wins in debate.

There is a danger of selfishness and a strong temper. The person is creative and curious and always open to new concepts. He may be an excellent speaker. His mind is positive and outgoing, and he rarely gets caught in depression. F. Scott Fitzgerald had Mercury trine Mars aspect. Because Mercury and Mars are both fast-moving planets, this aspect should not be accorded too much significance unless it is very tight by degree, or other birthchart factors concur. The trine aspect is significantly more powerful than the sextile. The sextile indicates the opportunity to make the above characteristics a reality.

If Mercury is sextile Venus, the person has artistic potential. He is graceful, expressive, and charming. There is interest in music, drama, photography, or any aesthetic endeavor. The person has fine taste. He may be a good speaker with a nice voice. There is talent in literature or poetry. The person is refined, cultured, and well-liked. He is never cruel, coarse, or mean. There is a pleasant sense of humor and a balanced, idealistic nature.

Other than the conjunction, the sextile between Mercury and Venus is the only aspect possible between these two planets. Being the gentle aspect that it is, not much importance should be accorded to it unless it is corroborated by other birthchart factors.

"The reasonable man adapts himself to the circumstances that surround him...The unreasonable man adapts the surrounding circumstances to himself...All progress depends on the unreasonable man."

GEORGE BERNARD SHAW

If Mercury is conjunct Jupiter, the person is mentally exuberant. He is excited, enthusiastic, and wonderfully expressive. He is broad-minded and open to new concepts. The person loves words and excels in any secretarial, literary, or communications career. There is an expansive quality to the person's mind and he is constantly coming up with creative ideas. He makes the best advertising agent or publicist. He absolutely lives in the moment and takes care of letters, phone calls, and other organizational details without any apparent loss of energy. The person is optimistic, hopeful, and does not get caught up in depression or negative thinking. He is easygoing, cheerful, and ever looking to spread the good word. He is generous in spirit and wants everyone to enjoy the brightness of life as he does. He is compassionate and caring, and makes others feel genuinely uplifted. His greatest happiness may come from supporting other peoples' projects. He is popular, well-liked, and may be the life of parties.

Unfortunately, the person may be lazy. Because of his certainty that all will be well, he may procrastinate or fail to see urgency when it exists. He will pass up opportunities because he lacks ambition and incentive. He is not at all fond of discipline, routine, or painstaking, time-consuming endeavors. He is admirably spiritual in his thinking and openness. However, his enlightenment must come through either devotion to God (evolution via Jupiter) or dispelling the mistake of the intellect (evolution via Mercury). Like most Jupitarian types, the person has no desire to practice austerities, arduous meditation techniques, etc. He loves law and philosophy. He wants to travel and experience everything. He may be an editor or publisher. The person makes a great teacher, and is extremely content to spread knowledge in any way he can. The longer he lives, the more his interests expand and the more knowledge he collects. He is, mentally, the healthiest of all people. He is always present, never preoccupied with the past or future. He has nothing to hide. He is amongst the rare few who enjoy public speaking from early childhood. Shirley Temple has Mercury conjunct Jupiter within three degrees.

In certain cases, especially if the conjunction is very close by degree, the person may have nervous difficulties. This can be due to an expanded nervous system, excessive mental activity, too much analyzing, etc. He may suffer from overwork and having his hands in too many projects at the same time. Much as he dislikes routine, he must follow a regular system of rest and recreation. The person may have an exceedingly high opinion of himself, and he must guard against conceit. He should also be more careful and precise in his job. Although he is a tireless detail worker, his ultra-positive mind may see no fault in second- or third-rate results. He lacks perfectionism and discrimination. The person is honest and straightforward. His morals are high. However, his mental expression is entirely outward, and he may therefore lack introspection, depth, and subtlety.

The person is tenderhearted and merciful. He is well-read and loves universities and all higher knowledge. He is tolerant and patient with others. Traditional astrological texts indicate that there may be a distinct stubbornness or conceit, and that the person may always think he is right.

If Mercury is square or opposite Jupiter, the person has no sense of mental proportion. His thinking is too expansive or exaggerated, and his judgement may be distorted. He may give poor advice to others. In his great optimism, he is too certain of his opinions and does not consider all the facts and particulars. He is blinded in his beliefs and stuck in his convictions. He has a rich imagination and fantasy life, and thinks in grandiose terms. He may have his hands in too many projects at the same time. Some individuals with the hard Mercury-Jupiter aspects are fuzzy in their communications and amazingly unable to come to the point.

The person is warm, generous, and sympathetic. He is good-natured and wants everyone to enjoy. He is charming and loves to party and indulge in the senses. Arnold Schwarzenegger has the Mercury opposition Jupiter aspect within one degree. The person relishes art, music, drama, and all cultural endeavors. There may, unfortunately, be a tendency toward extravagance or waste. The person talks a lot and his greatest pleasure in life may be gossip or long, idle conversations. The person is curious and loves new knowledge. He is open to metaphysics and all kinds of different philosophies. However, he needs to learn focus, and to pay attention to details. He is so fixed on broad outlooks that he fails to ever master anything, or to truly grasp the practical functioning of a chore. The person may be careless, forgetful, and unreliable. His work may be haphazard.

Because of his expansive viewpoint, the person does not mind lying. He tells small fibs or white lies constantly, whenever they serve his interest without hurting anyone else. Travel is favored, and the person gets great pleasure from experiencing all that life has to offer. He is an idea person and his mind never stops. He has big expectations and is therefore susceptible to disappointment. He may promise too much and then fail to keep his word. Public relations, or any other occupation which supports the work of others, is a good career choice so long as the person is involved in creative activities, and not administration or management.

146   The nervous system is expanded and the person may be restless and easily excitable. He may also be gullible and superstitious. The person must beware of impulsive decisions. Evolution-wise, Zen or any reasoning technique which dispels "the mistake of the intellect" may be used to great advantage. In certain cases, if the aspect is too strong by degree, the person may be profoundly conceited and arrogant. His seeming "belief" in himself is an abomination.

"It is remarkable how much mediocrity we live with, surrounding ourselves with daily reminders that the average is acceptable. Our world suffers from terminal normality. Take a moment to assess all of the things around you that promote your being "average." These are the things keep you powerless to go beyond a "limit" you arbitrarily set for yourself. The first step to having what you really want is the removal of everything in your environment that represents mediocrity, removing those things that are limiting. One way is to surround yourself with friends who ask more of you than you do."

STEWART EMERY

If Mercury is trine or sextile Jupiter, the person is the best learner. He is clear-thinking and has great intellectual dexterity. He excels in writing, languages, and the deciphering of symbols. He is eloquent and expresses himself with charm and precision. He is versatile, and succeeds in life through his ability to make the best use of the knowledge and information which comes his way. Others may be envious of the person, for he appears to be exceedingly lucky. In fact, his fortune is caused by an optimistic attitude in which he always expects things to turn out in his favor. And because thought is the creative power of the universe, he does get his way remarkably often.

The person is tolerant, patient, and broad-minded. He is never given to prejudice or bigotry. He is kind, compassionate, and sympathetic. There is exceptional mental health and psychological balance. The person has a wonderful and bright sense of humor, and he is rarely found in a depressive mood. He is philosophical and has unwavering faith in God. He has good religious experiences and is able to pardon any imperfections or flaws in the doctrine of his choice, or in its teachers and leaders. There is great honesty and integrity. The person is refined and cultured, and he climbs the social ladder with ease. He is extremely flexible and adaptable, and can play in any area of life, or with any social group.

The person is adept in business and commerce. He has an outgoing nature which charms those who come in contact with him. He is constructive, well-meaning, and ultra-positive. He loves school and makes an excellent teacher. His memory serves him favorably, and he has fine powers of concentration and observation. Accordingly, his judgement is accurate more often than not. Traditional astrological texts mention that travel is much favored. The trine aspect is significantly more powerful than the sextile. The sextile indicates the opportunity to make the above traits a reality.

If Mercury is conjunct Saturn, the person lives a life of concentrated thought. His mind is slow, but deep. There is great logic and reasoning power. The person is cautious and serious. In the beginning of life his communicative ability is significantly inhibited. He may even have a speech defect, lisp, or stutter. As a result, the person is shy and self-conscious, and he works diligently to correct any imperfections he feels he has. He may be a slow learner in school and find himself behind his peers. However, he patiently applies himself and in the end may surpass all others. He is exacting and very careful to avoid mistakes. As he gains in maturity he is likely to become an authority in his field. If the rest of the chart indicates a creative and intellectual life, the person may be profoundly perceptive. Two notable examples of this are Albert Einstein and Edgar Cayce, who had the aspect within one and two degrees respectively.

The person is practical and down-to-earth. He is not easily fooled. He is adept in math and science, and enjoys facts and figures. He is objective, rational, and detached in his thinking. He is methodical and systematic, disciplined and responsible. Indeed, all the significations ruled by Saturn flourish. There is humility, tolerance, dignity, etc. The person honors his commitments and his word is ironclad. He knows thought to be the substance of existence and the essence of life. His greatest talent is the ability to turn ideas and concepts into physical realities. Because Saturn is the ruler of Capricorn (the career sign) and is conjunct Mercury, the person is attracted to any mental career. He has phenomenal endurance with details and research. He is contemplative, reflective, and gains in wisdom with each passing day.

Because Mercury rules the nervous system, and is so harmed by Saturn, the person may have nervous problems or suffer the most intense lack of confidence. He may be fearful and have tremendous difficulty improving or overcoming psychological complexes. Health-wise, he must take care of his lungs, intestines, and nervous system. He must especially cultivate joy and optimism, and learn to stop worrying. He should schedule regular vacations and recreational activities. Otherwise, there is a chance that the person gets stuck in habitual depressions. There is a marked tendency to overwork that may be resented by the person's family or loved ones. If the conjunction is not too close by degree, the person may be an excellent writer. He knows how to use words for their truest meaning and best effects. The person is a good organizer. He takes his time and is rarely impulsive. However, he may be moody, selfish, and self-centered. He may lack spontaneity and seem old before his time.

In his slowness of mind the person may experience mental blocks. This may be due to his having decided early in life that he is unintelligent. The person is hard on himself and should guard against feelings of guilt. He must also beware of rigidity and narrow-mindedness. He is master- fully critical and makes a fine teacher. He is thoughtful, tactful, and diplomatic. He is strong-willed. Although most people with this aspect think very carefully before they speak, some individuals are talkative to the point of annoyance. If the rest of the chart is weak (in planetary aspects, etc.) or if laziness and indulgence are indicated, then the Mercury-Saturn aspect may indicate that the person is dull, unimaginative, and pessimistic.

If Mercury is square or opposite Saturn, the nervous system is under continual pressure and the confidence is adversely affected. There may be a deep-rooted inferiority complex or a sober and solemn personality. Early childhood may have brought difficulties which conditioned the person to expect things to turn out badly during his entire life. There is a great fear of failure and criticism, and the person may find it impossible to take risks. On the positive side, if the rest of the birthchart is powerful and indicates ambition, the person may be very disciplined and well-organized. He may be capable of excellent logic, and precision in his work.

Because Mercury is the natural ruler of the third house, there will be problems or discord with siblings or relatives. Some individuals with hard Mercury-Saturn aspects are slow in thought and have trouble learning. In nearly all cases, there is a danger of narrow-mindedness and an unwillingness or inability to open up to the support of others. The person is extremely sensitive and vulnerable, and finds it hard to acknowledge his limitations and deal with them in a constructive way. He is strict and rigid in his thinking, and unconsciously pessimistic about change and transformation, especially in psychological or emotional areas. He would do well to culture a sense of experimentation, without attachment to the outcome. If he is not careful he may become a living example of denial.

The person is cautious and introspective. He needs to cultivate humor, fun, and excitement. Many individuals experience speech defects and difficulties expressing themselves. The latter is, by no means, due to lack of intelligence. It is a result of too much self-criticism and censorship. Also, whenever there is pressure from the outside (which adds to the strain he experiences naturally), the person may feel mentally blocked. Traditional astrological texts report that the person may be a worrier who is lonely, depressive, suspicious, or defensive. They also say that there will be obstruction in educational endeavors. Above all else, the person should learn to listen to his friends and loved ones, who could be of great help because of their objectivity. Otherwise, the person is at the mercy of a very confining perspective which dampens every aspect of his enjoyment and potential achievement in life. Health-wise, there may be nervous disorders or mental problems. The lungs and intestines are also at risk. Author Hermann Hesse, who was plagued by depression and suicidal thoughts, had the Mercury-Saturn square aspect within two and one half degrees.

Lost his job in 1832. Defeated for the legislature in 1832. Failed in business in 1833. Elected to legislature in 1834. Sweetheart died in 1835. Had nervous breakdown in 1836. Defeated for speaker in 1838. Defeated for nomination for congress in 1846. Lost renomination in 1848. Rejected for land office in 1849. Defeated for the Senate in 1854. Defeated for nomination for Vice President in 1856. Again defeated for senate in 1858.

But...in 1860 Abraham Lincoln was elected President of the United States of America.

If Mercury is trine or sextile Saturn, the person is the most consci-entious of all people. He is patient, precise, and trustworthy. He thinks everything through thoroughly before acting. He is practical, purposeful, and performs his job with great accuracy. There is a genetic or intuitive feeling of insecurity or inferiority, and the person uses knowledge and efficiency as a means to prove himself. He is serious by nature and does not praise or compliment others easily. For one thing, he is very analytical and sees flaws in others immediately. For another, he consid-ers perfection to be the order of the day. He is, more than anyone else, willing to pay his dues. And he expects the same from the rest of the world.

The person loves to learn. He bases his existence and self-value on knowledge. He may therefore feel petrified when he is mentally unpre-pared. He is a lifelong student and wants direct, definitive answers. He does not much appreciate abstractions unless they support some practical purpose. The person is the most rational and reasonable of all beings. He is like a detective, and solves puzzles and mysteries easily. He is honest, responsible, and moral. He has great integrity. Concentration is good and traditional astrological texts report that the memory is excellent. The nervous system is strong. Thus, the person is resilient and unaffected by long hours of tedious detail work. Aside from possible shyness and a lack of self-esteem and desire for recognition, the person is mentally quite healthy. There is, of course, a very traditional and conservative mentality, and the person should beware of rigid, narrow-minded thinking.

If the person is spiritually inclined he may be the best meditator. He is capable of great focus, observation, and contemplation. There may be talent in math or science, and the person generally does very well on tests. He is an excellent secretary, organizer, or planner. Teaching is a possible profession, as is writing or any communications activity. However, Mercury-Saturn aspects do not particularly indicate joyous-ness in such endeavors, just great efficiency. There is abundant common sense and the person is cautious. He rises slowly in status and does not have much ambition for "name and fame." Reasoning power is great and the thinking is deep. The person may be witty, sarcastic, and satirical. He is persistent and works hard.

If Mercury is conjunct Uranus, the person lives a life of independent thinking. He is original, inventive, and highly alert. The mind works at lightning speed and there are continual flashes of intuition. The person may be brilliant or a genius. He will be talented in astrology or any occult art. He may be drawn to math or science. Astronomer Johannes Kepler and the great French painter Renoir both had the Mercury conjunct Uranus aspect. The person is open-minded and anything but traditional or dogmatic. He is honest, direct, and free in his speech. He is clear-thinking and may be helpful in guiding others to find their way. Unfortunately, he does not possess the same objectivity in dealing with his own life.

The person may be high-strung and easily excitable. He has difficulty appreciating rules, regulations, and the sluggish pace of ordinary life. He is greatly annoyed by slow thinkers. The person lives a life of incessant activity, and his body will eventually pay the price unless he learns intelligent restraint and the importance of taking care of himself. His mind may exceed his capabilities. The person is experimental and entirely unafraid of new endeavors. He may be inspired, shrewd, and insightful. He is also potentially stubborn, self-willed, and infatuated with his own mind. He occasionally may seem fanatical.

There is a need for patience, discipline, tolerance, and humility. The mind is dynamic, positive, and outgoing. Any techniques the person may practice to develop self-reflection will be extremely useful. The person may use his spiritual and intellectual perception to help others, yet ignore his own growth and well-being. He may be too detached about his own life. He is good at finding solutions and living in the moment. He values the truth. He is experience-oriented and does not get bogged down in philosophy. The person should schedule regular periods of rest and recreation, and develop methods to quiet the incessant activity of his mind. There is great talent and potential genius if the person learns to harness his energy.

If Mercury is square or opposite Uranus, the person is a revolutionary thinker. He is eccentric, perceptive, and extraordinarily experimental. He loves to arouse, incite, and shock those around him. He always wants to try the new and fascinating. The person does not enjoy rules, regulations, traditions, and convention. And he is a thorn in the side of the powers that be. Most certainly, he will not be told what to do or think. The mind works too fast and the person is as mentally impatient as they come. He needs a great deal of stimulation and is easily bored. He may often speak without due forethought and thereby offend others. However, his spontaneity is essential to his creativity and inventiveness. Friedrich Nietzsche, the great philosopher, had the Mercury opposition Uranus aspect within one degree.

The person is intuitive and lives by instinct. He is impulsive and unpredictable. He is too restless and may suffer from nervousness and irritability. Above all, he must take responsibility for his independent nature, and stop defending himself — a tendency he may have developed during rebellious childhood years. There is a definite openness to metaphysics and the occult. The person is nothing if not adventurous and progressive-minded. However, he does not slow down long enough to hear exactly what others are saying. He may be touchy, high-strung, overly sensitive, and in extreme cases just plain paranoid. Trust is a much needed commodity.

There is, most likely, great intelligence or genius. But the person may be only too aware of the fact. He may fancy himself a gift to the world, and make a pest of himself to others. If he does not learn responsibility, discipline, maturity, and order, his talents and liberating concepts go entirely wasted and unused. The person identifies with his mind, and lives an essentially mental life. His greatest concern is the advancement and promotion of truth and freedom. He loves to change the status quo. He is highly principled and will never compromise his ideals or buckle under pressure. He is proud, rebellious, willful, and obstinate. He is temperamental and stubborn-minded.

The person is inspirational and exciting. He is honest and direct. However, he may also be outspoken, blunt, and tactless. He learns

156 things fast, but may be too quick in his judgements. He may not take advice from others well. He is of radical and extreme opinion but is rarely, if ever, bigoted or prejudiced. He enjoys taking the side of the underdog or downtrodden. He excels in inventions, astrology, or any mental endeavor that is ahead of the times. There may also be talent in math or science. In certain cases, the person may be foolish or lacking in common sense. He may also be mischievous. He supports alternative methods and new-age procedures. Traditional astrological texts report that the person has a keen memory, but should be careful in signing documents.

"Let a man live so that at the closing of each day he may say "I have not wasted this day."

THE ZOHAR

If Mercury is trine or sextile Uranus, the person is an inspired, experimental thinker. He is magnificently intuitive, and excels in dealing with abstract concepts. He is talented in astrology, the occult, or any subject that is ahead of the times. The person is resourceful, and courageous in his ability to live in the moment. He is imaginative and always open to new ideas. There is a keen mind and great mental dexterity. The person is honest, direct, and concerned with truth. He is an excellent communicator and gets straight to the point. He may write with fine clarity. Abraham Lincoln had the Mercury-Uranus trine aspect within one degree.

The mind works quickly and there may be flashes of genius. Careers involving science and math are favored, and the person may be capable of new inventions. He is original, creative, and able to separate the ego from his thought process. He is rarely jealous or possessive, and does not pass judgement on others. He looks for alternative methods to solve problems. The person is spontaneous and adventurous. He does not hold onto the past and is ever willing to take a risk. He may be brilliant and have a good memory.

The person is independent and progressive. He does not get carried away with tradition and convention. The harmonious Mercury-Uranus aspects indicate extreme intelligence, but there must be significant ambition or struggle indicated elsewhere in the birthchart, or this aspect may go relatively unused in terms of actual achievement. The person is certainly advanced, witty, and clever, but discipline and responsibility are needed to make the most of his significant mental talents. The person is clever, and can do anything he wants if he puts his mind to the task. The Mercury-Uranus trine is significantly more powerful than the sextile. The sextile indicates the opportunity to make the above characteristics a reality.

If Mercury is conjunct Neptune, the person is the most imaginative of all people. His reality is entirely conceptual and he lives in his visions and inspirations. He is a dreamer in both the best and worst sense. There are no boundaries to his mind and he is comfortable with the mystical side of life. He is intuitive in a profound way and gets his information from sources that are hidden even from his own understanding. The person is sensitive, delicate, and especially artistic. He excels in music and poetry. He is drawn to sounds, colors, smells, etc. He is the best writer of fiction and fantasy. There may be difficulty with concentration, as the person's mind chases pleasure as a bee follows honey. The person makes an excellent actor, photographer, or painter. He may avoid dealing with facts, figures, and sciences. He is not enthusiastic about discipline and restriction.

The person suffers in his personal life because of an inability to distinguish objective reality from wishful thinking. He is powerfully idealistic about his ideas and concepts, and clings to them in the face of any opposition. The person may absolutely, even if quietly, disregard the wishes of others in order to follow the dictates of his own mind. He may lie and regularly fail to keep his word; however, there is no malicious, or even purposeful, intent in such actions. The person simply has difficulty associating form and structure with the thought process. He forgets his promises and commitments because he lives in a world of mental unboundedness, and there is little connecting thread from moment to moment. However, if he wishes to live a life of integrity, he must consciously and rigorously dedicate himself to honesty and responsible communications. This means especially rooting out <u>subtle</u> forms of deceit, a potential art form to the Mercury-Neptune person. Unfortunately, the person receives almost no incentive from outside for his attempts to reform, since his optimistic and uplifting mind evokes immediate forgiveness from friends and acquaintances. He pays the price of his flawed behavior in family relationships and important business dealings.

The person is refined and cultured. His thinking is sublime and transcendental, and his consciousness moves unfettered through different realms of existence. He loves meditation or any discipline which makes use of his limitless perception. Astrology, occult subjects, and spiritual endeavors may all be vital features of the person's life. He is an excellent disciple, thrives on devotion, and easily surrenders to his chosen guru. He understands prayer better than anyone. He may be religious and receive divine guidance or inspiration. Martin Luther had the Mercury Neptune conjunction within one degree. Robert Redford has the aspect within three degrees.

The nervous system is delicate and easily disturbed. The person needs plenty of rest and should avoid drugs, alcohol, overwork, and stressful surroundings. He must differentiate his own reality (which is based on dreams and ideals, etc.) from that of the rest of the world. The person is romantic and impressionable. His energy often may be diffused or foggy. This causes confusion, absent-mindedness, and sloppy work. Like all Neptunians, he may suffer disappointment due to his idealism. He must strive for consistency. He appreciates beauty and does well with film, magic, and stage productions. If the conjunction is extremely close and the person is too *spaced-out* or "otherworldly," others may have difficulty communicating with him.

If Mercury is square or opposite Neptune, the person is mentally unfocused. His thinking is clouded by his feelings, and he is often confused, scattered, or diffusive. He lives by psychic impression, not rational thought. He does not create enough mental boundaries for himself and is therefore an easy target of deception. He loves gossip and other emotionally stimulating diversions. He is concerned with sensations and abstractions rather than details, facts, and figures. There is a rich and vivid imagination, and the person may live a fantasy or dreamlike existence. There is a need for practicality and realistic vision.

The person lacks confidence in a major way and may be powerfully self-deluded. He may ignore, or totally deny, troublesome aspects of his existence which he is afraid to confront. He may flagrantly lie to himself as well as others, though not purposefully or out of harmful intent. Decision-making may be a complex source of struggle. The judgement is marred because the person does not perceive things from an earthly perspective. Some individuals with hard Mercury-Neptune aspects are seriously unreliable and unable to keep their commitments. Drugs and alcohol should be avoided at all costs.

The person is metaphysically-oriented and open to the occult. He believes in astrology, the psychic world, and all phenomenon of a non-physical reality. Art, music, poetry, and other sensual or cultural pursuits are highly favored. The nervous system is delicate and the person must avoid overwork and stressful situations. He may be prone to such illnesses as epilepsy, asthma, etc. There may be a deep, irrational fearfulness. The person has a hard time concentrating. His greatest task in life may be to learn how to communicate clearly and effectively. He is sensitive and idealistic, and should try to distinguish the difference between practical reality and his own desire-based version of the truth.

If Mercury is trine or sextile Neptune, the person is of an acutely sensitive and delicate mind. He is psychic, intuitive, and gains knowledge from realms closed to the average mortal. The person is warm, kind-hearted, and generous. He wants happiness and pleasure for all. He is an eternal optimist and always looks for the best in others. Unfortunately, he is also impressionable and gullible, and occasionally taken advantage of. There is a passion for the occult or metaphysical sciences. Art, music, poetry, and creative writing are all very much favored. The person is cultured and refined. He has the best sense of humor.

The nervous system is sensitive, and the person should avoid harsh people and stressful situations. He is easily hurt or offended because he expects only good intentions from others. The mind is dreamlike, idealistic, and as flexible as can be. The person may be a great visionary. He is always open to new ideas. He is compassionate and sympathetic. There is great ability to affect others with tactful or praising communications. The person expresses himself from the heart.

There is an excellent imagination and a good memory. The person is broad-minded and has breadth of perspective. William F. Buckley has the Mercury-Neptune trine aspect within one degree. The person likes to daydream. His thinking transcends the ordinary process of logic. He is not enthusiastic about facts and figures, or math and science. There is a distinct subtleness about the person, and he is tender, sublime, and spiritual. Because of his mental sensitivity, he is prone to depression, but this passes in the course of time. There may be many prophetic dreams throughout the life. The trine aspect is significantly more powerful than the sextile. The sextile indicates the opportunity to make the above characteristics a reality.

If Mercury is conjunct Pluto, the person lives a life of probing and observing. He is as a detective; he is curious, discriminating, and determined. Nothing escapes his eye. He is the best analyst and psychologist, and often makes accurate judgments which come far more quickly than they should. The person loves knowledge, and is compulsive in his desire to know and learn; this acquiring knowledge is a major purpose of his life. He has a deep, penetrating mind and wants to get to the core of all matters. He may be particularly relentless when pursuing an issue. Galileo had the Mercury-Pluto conjunction within one degree. Abraham Lincoln had the aspect within three and one half degrees.

There is a spirituality, or profound wholeness, to the person's thinking. His blending of acute perception and abundant knowledge leads to great mental dexterity and resourcefulness. He does well with meditation, Zen, astrology, and any evolutionary technique which dispels "the mistake of the intellect." He may be talented in the healing arts, especially those which deal with hidden causes or difficult-to-diagnose illnesses. He favors natural remedies. The person is an excellent problem solver. However, he may occasionally evoke bitterness or anger from others, due to his direct, incisive, or piercing manner.

The person is capable of profound concentration. He may have easy access to his unconscious mind. It is crucial that the person be extra sensitive to the effects of his mentality and expressions. His thoughts carry enormous psychic power and his words have great impact on peoples' lives. He can gain more from affirmations, positive thinking, and creative visualization than anyone. He is persuasive and may live to disseminate knowledge. Being aware of the human conditions of laziness and superficiality, he is naturally suspicious and always careful about ferreting out the truth. He is a free thinker and abhors dogma or any form of restrictive thinking. He loves to delve into every subject, especially those considered taboo or off-limits. He is fascinated by languages, puzzles, interpreting, and deciphering. He is drawn to the sciences and research endeavors.

On the negative side, the person should beware of the tendency toward manipulative or overbearing communications. If other aspects of

164 the birthchart indicate desires for power or a dictatorial nature, then the person may use his mind and communicative skills to dominate or overwhelm others. The person is intense in his thinking and may be opinionated or stubborn-minded. If the Mercury-Pluto conjunction is too close by degree, there may be an overly-delicate nervous system or other related problems.

"Every now and then I think about my own death, and I think about my own funeral...I don't want a long funeral. And if you get somebody to deliver the eulogy, tell them not to talk too long...Tell them not to mention that I have a Nobel Peace Prize...Tell them not to mention that I have three or four hundred other awards...I'd like somebody to mention that day, that Martin Luther King Jr., tried to give his life serving others. I'd like for somebody to say that day that Martin Luther King, Jr. tried to love somebody...

"Say that I was a drum major for justice. Say that I was a drum major for peace. That I was a drum major for righteousness. And all of the other shallow things will not matter. I won't have any money to leave behind. But I just want to leave a committed life behind."

DR. MARTIN LUTHER KING, JR.

If Mercury is square or opposite Pluto, the person is too intense and subjective in his thinking. The mind is attached to the ego and the emotions, and the person is stubborn and opinionated. There is a possibility of prejudice, bigotry, and deep-rooted arrogance. During childhood the person was manipulated and dominated in his ideas, concepts, and personal philosophy. Because he was criticized and made to feel incompetent or ineffectual at such an early age, there may be a lifelong psychological complex which is difficult to eliminate. The nervous system is delicate and there may be great fearfulness. The person is highly secretive, as criticism or disapproval from others is his worst anxiety. At the same time, he is highly critical and judgemental of others. Furthermore, he is likely to continue the same domineering manner of expression that was perpetrated upon himself. He must beware of communicating in an overbearing, forceful way that evokes resistance, conflict, and excessive reactions from others. General George Patton had the Mercury opposition Pluto aspect within three degrees.

The person is direct and blunt. He chooses his words carefully, and knows exactly how to verbally affect others. He is capable of extreme sarcasm and ridicule. Because the nervous system is adversely affected, there may be restlessness and impatience. Illnesses are caused by stress, strain, and overwork. The lungs and intestines are vulnerable, and there is susceptibility to asthma, epilepsy, and other nervous ailments. The mind is analytical and penetrating. The person is acutely aware of peoples' flaws and weaknesses. He is quick-witted, wonderfully curious, and interested in secretive or occult knowledge. He wants to learn everything he can in life and get to the core of all matters. Unfortunately, he may not be open and trusting enough to benefit from the wisdom of his peers and elders.

Thought, or consciousness, is the basis for all of life. Consequently, the Mercury-Pluto square or opposition can be considered (in a certain sense) one of the most difficult of all astrological aspects. When one's thought process is subject to such concentrated focus, pressure, and scrutiny, a unique situation certainly exists. Also, when Pluto — the planet of unbridled power — is configured with Mercury, this gives such resourcefulness and potency to the intellect that if the person adopts any negative or life-damaging perspective, the results can be devastating; the person is psychologically constructed in such a way that he trusts his own opinions implicitly. Therefore, he becomes hopelessly stuck in his own convictions. If he has not resolved his anger or hurt at having been intellectually manipulated as a child, he will possess an unhealthy or destructive attitude which he never corrects. He may be defensive in a major way. Most importantly, however, he is closed to the support of others if their ideas differ at all from his own. The person is exceedingly skeptical and suspicious. He has decided early on that others are out to change or dominate his thinking. There may be pessimism and a profound resignation to feeling victimized. The person is guarded and occasionally paranoid. Flexibility of mind and a willingness to grow are desperately needed.

The person has tremendous oratorical ability and there is profound power in his communications. He must be very careful in what he says to others, because his words have deep impact and are not easily forgotten. The person can manifest his desires and create any reality he wants by virtue of his natural, all-powerful mastery of language and the thought process. Richard Nixon declared in his twenties that he would become president. He kept his word. He has the Mercury opposite Pluto aspect within two degrees.

The person is serious and often remains silent rather than opening himself up to possible rejection. He is excellent at research and does not miss a trick in analyzing other peoples' behavior and actions. There is great intuition or psychic ability. The person must, however, let go of his past and work on regaining his faith in others. He should also consider the spiritual teaching that, "it is only when a person fully realizes that he knows nothing that real knowledge dawns."

If Mercury is trine or sextile Pluto, the person is balanced and whole in his thinking. He is confident, stable, and psychologically healthy. The nervous system is solid and the person is secure. He excels in languages, writing, or any communications field. He enjoys deciphering symbols or puzzles. The person is direct and persuasive. His reasoning ability is acute and he influences others profoundly and with ease. There is great optimism as the person knows he can solve any dilemma through his intellectual dexterity. He is witty and humorous. He rarely, if ever, becomes depressed or negative.

The person is sharp, analytical, and critical. He does not miss a trick. Concentration is excellent and the mind is deep but flexible. The person loves all fields of knowledge and wants to learn everything he can. He is drawn to metaphysics or the occult because he is compelled to get to the root all matters. Religion, philosophy, and evolutionary techniques are a source of fascination. The person is original and creative. He is broad-minded and open to new concepts. He is an independent thinker and does not follow the crowd. He is not overly influenced by tradition and custom. He recognizes truth and justice immediately. He is strong in his beliefs and is never easily dissuaded.

The person is extremely adept at understanding the psychology of others. Therefore, he makes an excellent advisor, counselor, or thera- pist. He is logical and keenly aware that knowledge, information, and wisdom mean power. He wins enemies and rivals over to his side through diplomacy. When this is not possible he defeats them with his adroit intellect. He is an excellent communicator, speaker, and salesman. He is the best of all teachers. He must beware of stubbornness and the tendency to pass judgement. There may be talent in research and investigation. And, because Mercury rules Virgo there may be interest in medicine or healing.

The person is intuitive or psychic. His perspective is balanced and there are no limits to the capabilities of his mind. He is intellectually disciplined and moderate in temperament. Traditional astrological texts report that the person is masterful in understanding nuclear power and all kinds of energy systems. Dionne Warwick has an exact Mercury trine

168 Pluto aspect. Poet Carl Sandburg had the aspect within two and one half degrees. The trine aspect is significantly more powerful than the sextile. The sextile indicates the opportunity to make the above characteristics a reality.

"There is nothing more difficult to take in hand, more perilous to conduct, or more uncertain of its success, than to take the lead in the introduction of a new order of things."

NICHOLAI MACHIAVELLI, FROM HIS TOMBSTONE

If Venus is conjunct Mars, the person thrives on passion. He is enthusiastic, excited, and fervent in all his endeavors. He abhors boredom, complacency, and mediocrity. He is the ultimate romantic and his greatest concern is his love life. In this realm, he will experience both the best and worst of cupid's arrow. He may obtain the most beautiful, sensuous, and artistic lovers but there will certainly be difficulties to endure and consequences to bear. The person is driven by his desire nature, and has little understanding of how to distinguish love from physical attraction. He immerses himself in relationships too quickly and compulsively with little awareness of the practicality of the situation. If the love partner satisfies the person's craving for beauty, sexual ecstasy, and emotional closeness, he may immediately declare his undying love. He may even propose marriage to one he barely knows.

The person is charming, magnetic, and vibrant. He fascinates others with ease, and his personality and charisma increase with each passing year. Like Mahatma Ghandhi and Adolf Hitler (who both had very close Venus-Mars conjunctions) the person knows how to excite and inspire. There is a generous, demonstrative, and affectionate nature. Mars is the planet of rulers and commanders, and Mars benefits from the energy of benefic Venus; consequently, the person may be a leader. He enjoys bossing others and giving orders. While there is definitely strong masculine energy and aggressiveness for both men and women with this aspect, the person is also warm, loving, sensitive, and harmonious. The Venus-Mars conjunction, perhaps more than any other astrological aspect, indicates a mixture of personality extremes.

The person is creative, action-oriented, and potentially artistic. He is adventurous and fun-loving. He may also be impatient, impulsive, and very demanding. In attempts to fulfill his intense pleasure desires, he may be selfish, or blatantly use members of the opposite sex. He relishes his deeply emotional response to life, yet occasionally suffers terribly on account of it. Being at the mercy of his passions, he has to endure the most consuming crushes and infatuations. Sometimes his affections are requited, sometimes not.

Since Venus rules love and is conjunct Mars, the marriage partner is likely to be fiery, aggressive, physical, and/or arrogant. He or she may also be sexy, sensual, and red-headed. There will be arguments and fighting in the love life and the person may have a profound love-hate relationship with the spouse. This may happen because the person witnessed significant discord in his parents' marriage. If this is the case, for the rest of his life he equates friction and fighting with love and passion. The closer the conjunction is by degree, the more difficult the problem.

The person is strong, energetic, and physically fit. His blood is pure and he excels in sports. He is direct and expressive. There may be prostrate problems or other reproductive ailments. The throat is also at risk. The person is skilled in the art of sexual pleasures and is extremely attractive to the opposite sex. He will have many love affairs in his life. He may be hedonistic, oversexed, and too enamoured of physical beauty. There is heat in the body, and the person may live with a continual sense of anger. The person is significantly unhappy when he is not in a relationship. Although he wants to marry young, he would be wiser to wait.

If Venus is square or opposite Mars, the person has difficulties in relationships. His love life is significantly influenced by early childhood years, during which he witnessed too much parental discord. As a result, he equates friction and competitiveness with love and passion. Men with hard Venus-Mars aspects are prone to harsh, aggressive, insensitive behavior, while women with the aspect are more likely to be victimized by domineering, selfish men. There is, in certain of these cases, a danger of attracting cruelty or violence from the spouse or partner. Men with this aspect should resist the temptation to use females for strictly carnal pleasures.

The person is erotic and lustful. His passions and affections are too strong, and he may marry early for purely sexual reasons. Unless he is cautious, he is likely to wind up with a partner of very little compatibility or common interest. The person may experience perpetual arguments, dissension, and resistance in his marriage. He lives to satisfy romantic cravings and must beware of creating love-hate relationships. There is a charismatic, fervent, and interesting personality. The person is inventive and energetic. He is courageous and adventurous. His appetites are intense, his desires fierce.

The person hates boredom and wants to live a passionate, profound existence. There is a tendency towards impatience, impulsiveness, and forceful behavior. The person is stubborn and may try hard to change his loved ones. He is demanding, pushy, and occasionally obstinate. Healthwise, the reproductive system is at risk. Above all, the person must learn compromise, surrender, and sensitivity to the feelings of others. Otherwise, there is a good chance of numerous antagonistic relationships which end in hostility. The person is well-advised to marry later than the norm, in his late twenties or early thirties. In certain extreme cases, individuals with hard Venus-Mars aspects are crude, vulgar, and coarse. They are selfish, driven by lust, and entirely incapable of monogamy, empathy, and tenderness.

If Venus is trine or sextile Mars, the person is romantically healthy. He is confident in courtship and relates well to the opposite sex. He knows how to flirt and always gains the object of his heart's desire. The person is excited, enthusiastic, and thrilled with life. He is expressive and creative. There may be talent in art, music, or drama. The person is vibrant, lively, and spirited. There is abundant sexual energy and the person is passionate. He pleases his mate in bed and is an ardent romantic.

The person is optimistic about fulfilling his pleasure desires, and therefore succeeds in this realm more often than not. He knows intuitively when to pursue and when to retreat. He immerses himself fully in his endeavors. The person is warm, sociable, and affectionate. He compromises when necessary and gets along well with others. He is attractive and magnetic. Money and comforts are favored and the person has many friends. There is considerable personality and presence. The person is well-loved and not easily forgotten. He is fun-loving, graceful, and harmonious. He has good taste.

There is a strong, yet controlled, sex drive and the person loves deeply. Relationships begin early and the person should beware of marrying prematurely. Willie Mays has an exact Venus trine Mars aspect. The trine aspect is significantly more powerful than the sextile. The sextile indicates the opportunity to make the above characteristics a reality.

If Venus is conjunct Jupiter, the person is supremely lucky. He enjoys his life on earth as a result of good actions performed in past lives. The person is happy, excited, and enthusiastic. He is extremely popular and constantly spreads his optimism. He is witty and humorous, and tremendously entertaining. He is the best comedian. The person is affectionate, open, and friendly. Henry Winkler, with an exact Venus-Jupiter conjunction, is a typical example. His phenomenal success, as well as the wonderfully lovable television character he created, are all exemplified in this astrological aspect.

The combination of these two special benefics indicates an abundance of positive energy. The person is fortunate and protected from harm. He is adventurous and fun-loving. He loves comforts and physical beauty. However, he may be too enthralled by appearances. He may also be shallow and over indulge in the senses. Because he is so outgoing, there is a marked lack of introspection or self-reflection. Also, although the person is very loving and considerate, he must develop sensitivity to his surroundings and the desires of others. In his never-ending role as "life of the party," the person may occasionally be intrusive — he may dominate the scene when such energy is inappropriate or unwanted. For this reason, the person may be considered offensive or obnoxious by conservative types. But he will rarely, if ever, be hated.

The person may be a lush. He must be careful with sweets. Since Venus rules love, the person gets a Jupitarian mate. The spouse will be beautiful, special, wealthy, and successful. The spouse may be honest, direct, philosophical, and foreign. The person does very well in love matters and has no trouble gaining the affections of his heart's desire. Although he has little inclination toward religious or spiritual life because of his ultra-spirited enjoyment of material existence, there is a deep and powerful love of God. Further, the person is especially charitable. He has a big heart and wants happiness for everyone. The person benefits from his mother and all females. They will want to please him (or a woman with the aspect). The person is artistic and does well in films or on stage. He is talented in any area that uplifts humankind. The person may work with jewelry, sweets, paintings, clothing, movie theatres, photography, etc.

There will be plenty of wealth, and the person is always taken care of. He is physically, mentally, and emotionally healthy. He is cultured, refined, and is adverse to harshness. He loves beauty. Most importantly, the person should not overdo things in his actions or make overly grandiose plans. If other aspects of the birthchart reveal difficulties in relationships, then his most vulnerable feature will be his expansiveness in love and lack of restraint. The person is possessive. However, he is also loyal and faithful. He should beware of vanity, and work on his sense of discipline and responsibility. The house position holding the Venus-Jupiter conjunction will be an important area of extreme good fortune. John Belushi had the Venus conjunct Jupiter aspect within one and one half degrees.

If Venus is square or opposite Jupiter, the person is too indulgent in comforts and luxuries. He is lazy, extravagant, and overly concerned with his feelings. He thinks life exists merely for the enjoyment of personal appetites, and is in danger of living a shallow, superficial life. There is a serious need for discipline, as the person always takes the easy way out. He is charming, graceful, and enthusiastic. He may also be vain and conceited. Since Venus and Jupiter are both benefic planets, hard aspects between the two do not cause severe difficulty or conflict. However, many individuals with the square or opposition are so opposed to hard work that their lives suffer dramatically as the years go by. They do not achieve their goals or live up to their potential.

The person is warm-hearted, sentimental, and affectionate. He has good taste. He is optimistic and loves to have fun. He is easily excited by entertainment and recreations. Unfortunately, the person lacks a sense of priorities, depth, and values. Unless other birthchart factors indicate otherwise, he misses out on the profundity of life. He may be spoiled, and greedy for fleeting treasures. He likes attention from others. The person may be gullible due to excessive, and expansive, emotions. He needs to cultivate discretion, detachment, and intellectual objectivity.

The person is talented in artistic and aesthetic endeavors. He is spirited, buoyant, and cheery. John Denver has Venus square Jupiter within one degree, and Richard Pryor has the opposition aspect within one degree. The person is emotionally affected by religion and philosophy. He is enthusiastic about such matters, and is conscientious in sharing all the higher knowledge that comes his way. Traditional astrological texts warn of hypocrisy, especially in love matters. They also report that the person eats abundant sweets and spends too much.

If Venus is trine or sextile Jupiter, the person lives a life of abundant pleasure, opulence, and good fortune. He is graceful, charmed, and as poised as can be. The person is optimistic and knows he will be wealthy and prosperous. He has good taste and is refined and cultured. He is supremely lucky in gaining the affections of any love partner he desires. The spouse will be beautiful, devoted, wealthy, and/or special. The person is very well-liked. He is compassionate, sensitive, kind, and sympathetic. He has a great social life and is always in demand. There is talent in the arts and the person is remarkably expressive. He conveys his thoughts and feelings adroitly. He excels in music and drama. His voice is sweet and melodious, and he may be an excellent singer or songwriter. There are high morals and good ethics. The person never fails to distinguish right from wrong. He is loyal, devoted, and trustworthy. He will never purposely hurt his lover's feelings.

Experiences with religion and philosophy are favorable. The person has unwavering faith in God, and always expects the best to occur. He is happy, enthusiastic, and thrilled with life. He will make great amounts of money and is extremely fortunate in business dealings. He loves parties and all worldly pleasures. He fulfills his desires easier than anyone and is generous with his wealth. He is relaxed and does not take life in a burdensome way. There is a fine sense of tolerance for others.

The person must beware of occasionally taking his lovers for granted. Because he so easily fulfills his love desires, he may not realize how fortunate and blessed he is compared to rest of the human race. There may also be a tendency to be too enthralled by money and material comforts. In certain cases there is a possibility of laziness and indulgence. Also, the person may be so comfortable in his charmed existence that he is avoids all circumstances of potentially gloomy or melancholy vibrations.

The person may have been extremely charitable, benevolent, and generous in past lives and he now receives the rewards of his selfless efforts. He may also have been profoundly devoted and supportive of his love partners. Gloria Steinem has an exact Venus trine Jupiter aspect. Van Cliburn has the aspect within two and one half degrees. The trine aspect is significantly more powerful than the sextile. The sextile indicates the opportunity to make the above characteristics a reality.

If Venus is conjunct Saturn, the person is overly cautious in love matters. He is inhibited, shy, or repressed, and always compromising for his mate. He creates unbalanced relationships by choosing partners who are ultimately incapable of fulfilling his needs and desires. The person may feel unlovable because he was denied tender affection during childhood, most likely by his father. He approaches love from a profound sense of scarcity and may need prolonged therapy to influence the situation. Relationships are definitely karmic; the person is paying back love debts from former lives. He is at the mercy of his mate, because his overdeveloped sense of duty will not allow him to leave the relationship, no matter how extenuating the circumstances.

Despite the difficulties caused by the Venus-Saturn combination, the person is by no means doomed to a complete life of suffering. Since Saturn is the indicator of profession (because it rules Capricorn, the natural ruler of the tenth house) and is conjunct Venus, the person may have the greatest career in the arts. He has an extremely practical appreciation of beauty, and knows exactly how to produce the desired artistic results. He is patient, exacting, and applies his perfectionist tendencies to his craft. Humphrey Bogart, Venessa Redgrave, and Rudolf Nureyev are typical examples. Also, although the first part of the person's life is less joyful and buoyant, the second half promises success, accomplishment, and honor. Furthermore, the person has tremendous ability to handle adversity because he learned discipline, responsibility, and restraint during his formative years. Indeed, all of Saturn's significations flourish, because Saturn receives the benefic energy of Venus.

The person is loyal and genuine. He keeps his word and always wants to do the right thing. He is sincere and practical. He is extremely concerned with fairness. Unfortunately, he does more for others than for himself. He is self-effacing and lacking in confidence. He feels too much guilt and is constantly sacrificing himself. There may be problems in the throat, genitals, and/or reproductive system. The person is prudish, sexually repressed, or afraid of sex. He may be frigid, impotent, or unable to let loose. He may experience pain during sex. The person may be so preoccupied with his own inhibitions that he fails to please his spouse. In such cases, he unwittingly drives his mate into the arms of another.

The person will experience extended periods of celibacy. He is attracted to older, authoritarian partners. He looks for mates who will provide security and status, when he should be looking for love and affection. He needs to work on self-love, and to develop and nurture the child within.

Although the person may consider himself a victim or martyr, he should consider the extreme selfishness that perpetuates his self-deprecating activity. There may be profound stubbornness and a tremendous resistance to owning up to his real self-value. There is also a slight possibility that the Venus-Saturn person is outwardly selfish or cold. In such cases, the fears and insecurities experienced during childhood may have run extraordinarily deep. The person may be miserly and stingy due to his pervasive feelings of scarcity. Marriage opportunities are rare, or occur later in life, after the late twenties. In some cases there is a good deal of loneliness with no marriage at all, but this does not occur often. Most individuals with this aspect are busy serving a dominant, influential, or demanding mate.

Because Venus is a planet of feminine experience this aspect is, psychologically, far more difficult for females. A woman with this conjunction may feel unworthy to the core if she, or others, cannot appreciate her beauty and femininity. In ancient Hindu astrology, Venus is one of the chief indicators of happiness (along with the fourth house). Its conjunction with the great malefic Saturn may dramatically disturb the joy and sweetness of the person's life. The person must develop optimism and confront his fears of rejection. Above all, he must guard against an attitude of resignation in his unconsciously self-imposed, marital struggle. English poet Lord Byron and the famous sculptor Rodin had the Venus-Saturn conjunction within two and one half degrees.

If Venus is square or opposite Saturn, the person suffers in his love life due to harmful or abusive actions he may have committed in past lives. He has difficulties giving and receiving affection, and his relationships entail an inordinate amount of duty, sacrifice, and hardship. There may have been coldness or insufficient warmth from one of the parents, causing the person to believe he is unlovable. Thus, he approaches love with an acute sense of scarcity. He is pessimistic about his beauty, sex appeal, and ability to attract a mate who meets his standards. It is very important for the person to work on self-love and self-worth. Vincent Van Gogh had the Venus-Saturn conjunction within two and one half degrees.

The person may be selfish, greedy, and very concerned with personal security. Because he is too absorbed in his own doubts and insecurities, he may unwittingly drive his partner into the arms of another. He may be repressed, shy, or inhibited in lovemaking, and fail to provide his mate with enough stimulation, excitement, and pleasure. There is a need to cultivate a sense of abundance, and to have more fun, pleasure, and enjoyment. Health-wise, the genitals, reproductive system, and throat may be delicate. The person is a good worker, a perfectionest in his craft. He is loyal and trustworthy. He has integrity and knows right from wrong.

The person fears criticism and rejection. If the hard Venus-Saturn aspect is strong by degree, the person may feel depressed, lonely, and as if he is missing out on the sweetness of life. He believes discipline and austerity are the order of the day. His behavior in love matters is too stiff and he must work on developing more flexible, optimistic emotional responses. The person may choose an older, authoritarian-type spouse. There may be difficulties with the mother, and the mother's life may be tedious and trying, especially if the fourth house is also afflicted.

Though it is not obvious, the person may be frightened of true intimacy. He may be attracted to married or unavailable individuals. There may be money problems, and the success and happiness of the spouse is not favored. As with all Venus aspects, the person is concerned with issues of fairness. He feels pain deeply and is easily hurt. He may hold grudges and often be sad. Love relationships are decidedly karmic, and the person may wish to obtain therapy or counseling in order to stop creating situations in which he is a victim.

If Venus is trine or sextile Saturn, the person is an excellent marriage partner. He is loyal, responsible, and trustworthy. He is a product of good breeding, and is disciplined and patient. He is practical and has a fine sense of fairness and compromise. His love relationship is a priority, and he does everything he can to preserve the sweetness and success of the union. He is serious and sincere, and chooses his mate carefully. He does not experiment with many lovers. He may find his spouse early in life and never question his selection. Divorce is highly unlikely unless the seventh house or the rest of the birthchart indicates love problems. The person is known for his steady emotions and long-lasting marriage.

There is talent in at least one of the fine arts. The person is exacting, and has exceptional ability to give form and structure to his aesthetic visions. His artwork is consistent, and improves with each passing year. He is concerned with the art, not his ego. Money and investments are favored. The person does not chase after get-rich-quick schemes. Rather, he amasses wealth slowly but surely, until, in the end, he is very well-off. He is modest and conservative, and has no problems with extravagance. He is self-controlled. He may do well with real estate or any construction-type enterprise.

The person has the strongest sense of duty and fairness. He has good friends. He is refined and devoted. He is instinctive and knowledgeable where friendships and love relationships are concerned. The person may be attracted to older, successful, authoritarian-type mates. Princess Diana has the Venus trine Saturn aspect within three and one half degrees. Traditional astrological texts report that the person may be overly inhibited, reserved, or restrained. The trine aspect is significantly more powerful than the sextile. The sextile indicates the opportunity to make the above characteristics a reality.

If Venus is conjunct Uranus, the person is excited about love. He is attractive, magnetic, and stimulating. He is independent in relationships, and destined to have many love affairs. Indeed, being born into monogamous society, the person may feel like he has incarnated on the wrong planet. He is the epitome of spontaneity. Relationships come on suddenly, with bursts of intense passion and excitement. They may burn out just as quickly. There is a keen appreciation of beauty, and the person recognizes his attractions instantly. He charms and seduces the opposite sex with the greatest ease. Because Uranus represents freedom and independence, this aspect is a difficult one for bonding. The person, whether he is conscious of it or not, has little inclination toward commitment in love. He is such a delighted connoisseur of affection and mating that he instinctively feels it is absurd to bring duty and obligation into his love life. Furthermore, there is an inextricable connection between his sense of individuality and his romantic endeavors. How is he to ever impose the values of others and a binding contract (of all things!) on the joyous, free-spirited experience he knows love to be? Warren Beatty, Elizabeth Taylor, and Cher are all examples of strong Venus-Uranus conjunctions.

The person is artistically gifted. He excels in music, dance, drama, painting, photography or any other art form. His work is original, unique, and experimental. He stretches the boundaries of convention. The person has a keen (actually, ultrasensitive) eye for beauty. He is intuitive, open-minded, and uninhibited. He is sexually exciting and enjoys breaking the rules. Bisexuality is possible. The person is powerfully drawn to Uranian types. He will have affairs with astrologers, mystics, spiritualists, geniuses, eccentrics, new-agers, and other brilliant, unconventional individuals. The person is intensely strong-willed. He has little understanding of compromise and may be entirely unaware of his selfish, egocentric behavior. For all his passionate affection and genuine caring, he is ultimately detached in love matters. Also, there may be a certain lack of intimacy because the person does not give his partners the kind of deep trust that longtime companions typically experience.

182   The person needs plenty of freedom and space in his relationships. If he is unaware of such needs, he may attract partners who are married, unstable, unpredictable, or otherwise incapable of commitment. He ensures his own freedom this way, but he also guarantees loneliness and suffering. The person is wiser to acknowledge his particular requirements, and search for a mate who also wants a less traditional marriage — a marriage without constricting rules, regulations, and demands. The person may choose a spouse of a different race or religion. The spouse also may be much older or younger, or from a foreign country. A man with this aspect may marry late in life, or never; a woman with this aspect has a greater chance of marrying many times, whenever her fierce passion comes on too strong. The person experiences his love as a universal and unconditional phenomenon, and it is "nothing personal" should he decide to sever a relationship and begin a new one.

The person is social and popular, he is thrilled with life. He is sensual, high-strung, and has a sparkling, effervescent quality. He enjoys flirting. The person loves astrology or any occult science. He is honest, direct, and optimistic. He is free with his money, and his wealth may fluctuate tremendously.

Jesus said "If you bring forth what is within you, what you bring forth will save you. If you do not bring forth what is within you, what you do not bring forth will destroy you."

FROM THE INTRODUCTION OF THE MYSTIC GOSPELS,
BY ELAINE PAGELS

If Venus is square or opposite Uranus, the person is fickle or divorce-prone. He wants to do things his own way, and has little understanding of surrender and compromise. The person is magnetic and exciting, but needs to learn the art of cooperation. Most individuals with hard Venus-Uranus aspects make poor marriage partners until their late twenties or early thirties. Although they often cause their own divorce by rebellious behavior, irresponsibility, and excessive independence, their experience of separation is generally extremely painful. Through suffering, the person may eventually learn a sense of compassion and empathy for the feelings of his partners.

The person is emotionally restless. He craves freedom and excitement, especially in love matters. He cannot stand boredom and complacency, and therefore has many intense, passionate affairs. Relationships may start quickly and end abruptly. The person is experimental in love and unconventional in his sexual desires. He is not bound by typical standards, principles, and lifestyles. Bisexuality is possible. The person attains great pleasure from breaking society's rules. He is experience-oriented, and not much concerned with other peoples' opinions. There is an inordinate need for freedom to fulfill his cravings in any way he desires. The person may unconsciously choose mates who are unstable, unreliable, or incapable of commitment. In this way, he is ultimately guaranteed independence and lack of restraint. There may be unrecognized fears of intimacy and rejection. The person may avoid commitment like the plague. He may be attracted to individuals who are married, culturally different, or much older or younger. His spouse may be spiritual, occult-minded, scientific, and highly individualistic.

The person is talented in the arts. He is inventive and creates work which is innovative and ahead of the times. He is electric, charming, and very flirtatious. He obtains the love partner of his choice with ease. A hasty marriage based upon intense passion should be postponed until an appropriate amount of time has elapsed and the relationship is found to be consistent and stable. The person enjoys being different from the world, and he surrounds himself with eccentric or non-conformist friends. He is erratic, high-strung, and often ego-centric. He should beware of rigidity and inflexible attitudes towards his loved ones. He

184   must be more responsible, and learn to disagree with dignity rather than rebelliousness when his opinions differ from others. There will be many important love relationships throughout life, and the person may be promiscuous in his early years. Princess Diana has the Venus square Uranus aspect within one and one half degrees. Former Attorney General John Mitchell, who was often embarrassed by his unpredictable wife, has the Venus-Uranus opposition within one degree.

"Life cannot wait until the sciences have explained the universe. We cannot put off living until we are ready. The most salient characteristic of life is its coerciveness; it is always urgent, 'here and now' without any possible postponement. Life is fired at us point blank."

JOSE ORTEGA Y GASSETT

If Venus is trine or sextile Uranus, the person is thrilled with life and excited about love. He is vibrant, spirited, and charming. He lives an interesting, distinctive life. The person is highly artistic, and recognizes beauty immediately. He is good at flirting, courting and mating, and easily gains the affections of his heart's desire. He is attracted to Uranian-type mates. The spouse will be advanced, magnetic, individualistic, and ahead of the times. That person may also be spiritual, occult-oriented, or scientific.

The person is popular and enjoys a good social life. He is open-minded, non-judgemental, and always creating harmony with friends and acquaintances. He is creative, imaginative, and emotionally expressive. He is experimental sexually and in his love life. He gives his love generously, with no ties or strings attached. He is not fond of restrictions, limitations, and constraints. Harmonious Venus-Uranus aspects are quite fortunate for marriage and love affairs in general. However, if other aspects of the birthchart indicate love problems, there may be divorce which, even though painful, works out very much to the person's advantage.

The person is original in his likes and dislikes. He does not follow the crowd. He is stimulated and lives an impassioned existence. He abhors complacency and mediocrity, and must find an interesting spouse or he will become easily bored. He should be careful not to marry too hastily, especially since his interests and pleasures will expand with each passing year. Relationships come on suddenly and the person attracts lovers who are special or renowned. There will be many unique opportunities which arise throughout life. The person is very appreciated by females in general. Prince Albert had an exact Venus-Uranus trine aspect. The trine aspect is significantly more powerful than the sextile. The sextile indicates the opportunity to make the above characteristics a reality.

If Venus is conjunct Neptune, the person idealizes love. He is romantic and impressionable, and far too trusting. Like Shakespeare's Othello, he may love "not wisely, but too well." He is so swayed by his feelings and emotions that he does not see his partner clearly. He is likely to be deceived or victimized, in a major way, in one or more "fated" relationships. Also, because of a poor self-image or feelings of inadequacy, the person is indiscriminate in his love choices. The person is of very good character. He is innocent, and pure of heart. He cannot conceive of harming another. Unfortunately, however, because his intentions are good he sees only the positive side of people. There will be disillusionment and suffering on this account. The person is sensitive, delicate, and refined. He is compassionate and sacrificial. He enjoys service, and his ability to love and care for others knows no boundaries. The person is loyal and devoted. He is vulnerable and fascinating.

The person may be mystical and extraordinarily devotional. He is discontented with ordinary existence and feels a yearning in his soul to transcend the boundaries of earthly existence. He may lead a life of discipleship or religious ecstasy. He may be powerfully attracted to drugs or alcohol. Naturally, he would be wiser to practice meditation or other spiritual disciplines. There is a dreamlike quality, or sublime gentility, to the person. He may be inspired and artistic. He excels in music, photography, and any endeavor where he applies his acute appreciation of beauty. The person is attractive to the opposite sex for his innocence, softness, and subtle seductiveness. He is kind and sentimental. In love relationships he is likely to give more than he receives. The person is drawn to "Neptunian" mates; escapists, alcoholics, spiritualists, and devotional individuals. Therefore, he should consciously choose the "higher" types. Women with the Venus-Neptune aspect should especially resist the temptation to martyr themselves by wasting their life on an alcoholic, emotionally weak, or parasitic spouse.

The person is uncomfortable with the harsh side of life. He is greatly repulsed by ugliness, meanness, and pain. He often considers sex a too physical, coarse, or dirty means of expressing the divine emotions he feels in love. Eroticism and "earthy" sexuality may be lacking. In some cases there are sexual difficulties or a lack of interest. Some with the

Venus-Neptune conjunction choose celibacy, which they practice with ease. The person is profoundly appreciative. He is imaginative and expressive. However, he is gullible and easily taken advantage of.

There is a distinct universality to the person's love nature. Therefore, he may not be bound by the same limitations and restrictions as the rest of society in matters of affection and sex as the rest of society. Bisexuality is possible. Also, because of his cosmic manner of expressing affection, his spouse or lovers may never feel "personally" desired. If the Venus-Neptune aspect is close by degree, the person is well-advised to consult his friends and parents regarding his choice of a marriage partner. Years of suffering may thus be avoided, as his own selection may be an obvious error. More than anything, the person must learn the difference between love in its pure and perfect form, and love's general functioning in human life. He may then gain some mastery of discrimination in matters of the heart. Leonard Bernstein and Enrico Caruso had the Venus-Neptune conjunction within one degree.

If Venus is square or opposite Neptune, the person romanticizes love. Because he lives in his imagination, where passions and feelings are concerned, he is likely to be seriously deceived in one or more fated, intimate relationships. He is too emotional and trusting, and does not see his partner clearly. He is vulnerable and very easily seduced. Venus-Neptune aspects are one of the rare series where there is very little difference between the conjunction and the hard configurations. The main distinction is that squares and oppositions usually indicate greater certainty of pain and disappointment in love, and relationships which are more blatantly karmic, i.e. repayments of past-life debts. Also, the hard aspects are more consistent in producing spiritual disciples deeply committed to enlightenment and higher states of consciousness.

The person is restless and feels a void in the depths of his being. He craves perfection and longs for fulfillment. He is mystical and devotional by nature, and takes quickly to the spiritual path. Evolution comes most profoundly through bhakti yoga (the yoga of love and service) and the person is masterful at following his guru's guidance. There is strong creativity, imagination, and talent in all of the arts. The person is especially gifted in music, drama, film, and photography. He is kind, sympathetic, compassionate, and sensitive. He is refined and wants very much to do right by others. There is great loyalty and good character. The person forms powerful attachments to his loved ones.

As with most Neptune aspects the person is, in many respects, an escapist from the mundane world. He should avoid drugs and alcohol, and direct his otherworldly leanings towards meditation and other spiritual techniques. There is abundant intuition and psychic ability. The body is delicate, and the reproductive system may be at risk. The person should seek advice and counsel from friends and family regarding love relationships. He should beware of partners who are illusory, deceptive, and deceitful. Above all, he should not involve himself with alcoholic or drug-dependent partners. Women, particularly, should resist the temptation to martyr themselves by sacrificing their lives to emotionally deficient, parasitic-type lovers.

The person may need to work on self-confidence and self-love in order to attract an appropriate spouse who is worthy of his commitment. There is a need for detachment, discrimination, and practicality. The person has high ideals and is therefore susceptible to major disappointment. He may be seeking ecstatic, God-like experiences in love, and may consider sex too physical and gross an experience. There is great receptiveness and passivity. There is danger of laziness. Whenever Venus is significantly aspected by Uranus, Neptune, or Pluto, the person experiences less rules, regulations, and restrictions in his love life. Bisexuality is possible, as is confusion of sexual expression. John Belushi had an exact Venus square Neptune aspect. Mia Farrow has the opposition aspect within one and one half degrees.

"The purpose of life is not to be happy. The purpose of life is to matter, to be productive, to have it make some difference that you lived at all. Happiness, in the ancient, noble version means self-fulfillment and is given to those who use to the fullest whatever talents God or luck or fate bestowed upon them."

LEO ROSTEN

If Venus is trine or sextile Neptune, the person is the consummate love mate. He lives for romance, warmth, and human bonding. He understands, better than anyone, how to make relationships work. He spends much time and energy conceiving, visualizing, and finally manifesting idyllic love. He is generous, selfless, and giving. He wants to serve and please his partner. Venus trine Neptune, more than any other astrological aspect, indicates the likelihood of a predestined meeting of the person's soul mate on the earth plane. The person has been responsible and profoundly devoted in past-life love unions and is now receiving the good karma of his actions. He attracts a partner who is honest, loyal, pure, and benevolent. The spouse is also romantic, cultured, and spiritual. Money, comforts, and luxuries may intermittently appear throughout life as if by divine grace.

The person is refined, gentle, and soft. He is creative and expressive, and excels in all art forms. Music, poetry, drama, and painting or drawing are all favored. James Dean had the Venus-Neptune trine aspect within two and one half degrees. The person has a wonderful imagination and highly developed fantasy life. He is emotionally sensitive and among the most tender-hearted of the human race. He is kind, sympathetic, and compassionate. He does well in any healing or service-oriented profession. The person is extremely flexible, adaptable, and open-minded in his dealings with others. He compromises with his loved ones and seeks solutions which meet everyone's needs.

The person needs to be treated well and kindly. He should insulate himself from crude or offensive individuals, and create a protected environment. He is sensitive to negativity, opposition, and disapproval. The person is, by nature, the most innocent, open, and receptive being. Because of his vulnerable nature and sense of destiny in love matters, there is a strong craving for security and assurance from others. His greatest desire in life is to experience true love, which he will certainly do unless the rest of the birthchart is severely afflicted in such matters. Until the perfect spouse is found, life is like a subtle form of torture.

The person is dreamy and inspired. He is idealistic and wants to be surrounded by beauty, splendor, and grace. There is very great spiritual energy, which manifests most clearly and profoundly in the person's primary love relationship. The person is affectionate and sensuous. He is a luscious lover. There is a danger of laziness, passivity, and excessive submissiveness. The person has excellent taste. He is aesthetically-oriented and may occasionally be extravagant or wasteful. He never criticizes or condemns others.

According to Eastern gurus, marriage partners must be compatible on four levels; physical, mental, emotional, and spiritual. The person with the harmonious Venus-Neptune aspect never fails to succeed in spiritual harmony with his mate. The trine aspect is significantly more powerful than the sextile. The sextile indicates the opportunity to make the above characteristics a reality.

If Venus is conjunct Pluto, the person's greatest desire is to love intensely and completely, and to learn everything there is to know about human bonding. The person devotes tremendous energy to his love relationships, and is a master at passion and sexual technique. He is instinctive and extraordinarily gifted in flirting, courting, and mating. He enjoys the most wonderful merging with another soul that a person can experience in physical form. However, there may be a lifetime of deeply emotional, strenuous, or painful love affairs.

Because the qualities of Venus and Pluto are so incongruous, this conjunction presents one of the most challenging situations of all astrological aspects. Venus represents love — the natural, free-flowing energy of the universe and, in human life, the harmonious give-and-take of pleasure and affection. Pluto, on the other hand, is an influence of extreme sensitivity, depth, intensity, power, compulsion, control, etc. The two energies do not mix smoothly. Too much concentrated attention is, by nature, contrary to the gentle Venus experience. While the person will certainly possess great talent artistically, sexually, and in emotional depth, he will ultimately suffer on account of his consuming desires, cravings, and attachments. Also, although the Venus-Pluto conjunction is difficult for any individual, it is far more trying for women. This is because Venus, being one of the astrological indicators of females, represents some of the most intrinsic and essential features of feminine existence.

The person is too sensitive in love matters. He is naked and vulnerable in affections and passions. And he suffers the deepest hurt in moments when love does not go his way. Therefore, in attempts to avoid continual ego death-and-rebirth experiences, the person learns during childhood to manipulate his partner as well as his own feelings. Unfortunately, this is the worst possible response; it opens the way to relationships that are unbalanced, obsessive, or compulsive. The person would be wiser to embrace the challenge of emotional growth and soul transformation that he has so courageously chosen for himself. The person is sexy, sensual, and erotic. He knows how to please his mate and is extremely attentive in fulfilling his partner's most desired pleasures. His heart chakra (love center) is highly developed, and his best spiritual evolution comes through "bhakti yoga," the yoga of love, devotion, and service. He is interested in tantra (raising the kundalini energy by tapping the sexual forces). Or he may practice Taoist methods of sexual technique.

The person is insatiable in his desire for love and attention. There may be a profound insecurity; the person may be looking for a "soul mate" to fill the intense void he feels. The thought of rejection is his worst nightmare. The person is extraordinarily psychic, especially with his lover or spouse. He senses the other person's feelings and desires at the slightest change in their behavior. He is magnetic and very attractive to the opposite sex. He has the most earthy and natural quality about him. The person uses his physical beauty, sexual skills, and knowledge of how to please others to get his way. In being preoccupied with Venusian qualities the person may be highly vain. He is willing to do almost anything for his partner, and may expect the same in return.

Artistically, the person produces work which is deep, intense, moving, and even potentially disturbing. His purpose is to incite the passions and make a difference. Because Venus rules females, there is a strong chance that the person's mother is "Plutonian" — intense, controlling, psychic, manipulative, etc. The person has strong desires and must beware of the Scorpionic tendencies of possessiveness, jealousy, lust, and revenge. He should also relinquish the inclination to dominate or overpower others. Although the person is exceptional at lovemaking, there is the distinct possibility of sexual problems. This may be caused by a fear of genuine intimacy which would, of course, open the person up to the possibility of tremendous pain. Indeed, the person may feel so vulnerable in love matters that he chooses only partners whom he knows are at his mercy. The combination of his pure eroticism and cool, controlled manner helps him to attract infatuated lovers who are nearly possessed with desire.

The person is attracted to intense, powerful, famous, and spiritual partners. There is a desire to probe the mysteries of love, sex, and all of life's pleasures. The person especially enjoys breaking any sexual barriers society has erected. Bisexuality is possible. The person has complete sexual control, and extended periods of celibacy are likely. There may be love relationships where the mate dies or suddenly disappears. More than anything else, the person needs to learn surrender. He must let go of his attachments, learn to trust the universe, and relinquish the fierce control he exerts in life. William Jennings Bryan had the Venus-Pluto conjunction within two degrees.

If Venus is square or opposite Pluto, the person is at the mercy of uncontrollable passions. He has to endure a turbulent or volatile love life. In past lives he may have been insensitive, manipulative, or domineering with his spouse, and he now pays the price. There is a likelihood of one or more fated marriages where the person experiences enormous pain through his partner. The person is compulsive and insatiable in his need for emotional nourishment. He lacks balance and moderation. He may be obsessive about pleasure, and excessive in sexual behavior. He is erotic and libidinous, and his desires are extreme. There may be a jealous or possessive nature, and the person fears rejection in a major way. He may feel unworthy and unlovable, and therefore attract partners who are emotionally unavailable or incapable of tenderness and intimacy. The partner may be domineering, manipulative, intense, and just plain inappropriate. That person may also lack compassion and common decency.

The person is magnetic and charismatic. He is highly sensitive and psychic. He wants to examine all aspects of sexuality and learn everything he can about courting and mating. He enjoys breaking society's rules and is not bound by typical cultural standards. Bisexuality is possible. The person is an excellent lover and knows exactly how to please his mate in bed. Because of his inordinate vulnerability, he willfully tries to control his love partner as well as the relationship itself. Such attempts are futile, and there are likely to be incessant power struggles. The person may be used and exploited by his spouse, especially if Venus is opposite Pluto. The person is creative and talented, and may create powerful and profound works of art.

The person must resist the temptation to lie and engage in devious or ruthless behavior to get his way. He must cultivate strict honesty. Misuse of power will bring definite retribution and suffering. The person's bonds are intense. He loves as deeply as is humanly possible. There are instant erotic attractions throughout life, and the person emanates potent sexual vibrations at all times. His lovers may be famous or special. They may also die or disappear from the person's life without a note. The person may use sex as a manipulative device to get his way. In extreme cases, of course, prostitution is possible. Traditional astrological texts report that the person may be intense, imbalanced, and greedy about money. He may struggle with lust his entire life. Larry Flynt, publisher of a pornographic magazine, has the Venus-Pluto square aspect within two degrees. Renaissance artist Rafael had the opposition aspect within three degrees.

"It is not the critic who counts; not the man who points out how the strong man stumbled or where the doer of deeds could have done them better. The credit belongs to the man who is actually in the arena, whose face is marred with dust and sweat and blood; who strives valiantly; who errs and comes short again and again; who knows the great enthusiasms, the great devotion, who spends himself in a worthy cause; who, at the best, knows the triumph of high achievement, and at the worst, at least fails while daring greatly."

THEODORE ROOSEVELT

If Venus is trine or sextile Pluto, the person is the healthiest love partner. His past-life karma in heart matters is excellent, and he therefore attains the deepest, most rewarding love relationship with a mate who is compatible and sincere. The person is artistic, and has a great eye for beauty. He is loyal, devoted, and amongst the rare few who take complete responsibility for their love energy. He is resourceful, and maintains equanimity even during the most trying times of married life. His love is wise, profound, and highly spiritual. He is capable of immeasurable intimacy and does not fear his feelings. He is affectionate and tender, and understands the give and take of relationships.

The person may be a supremely gifted artist. He excels in music, drama, or any other art form. The great novelist Balzac had an exact Venus trine Pluto aspect. The Sculptor Rodin had the aspect within one degree. The person's work is deep and moving, never shallow or superficial. He is dedicated to his craft and his discipline in this realm knows no bounds. The person is appealing, magnetic, and charming. He has a strong sex drive and potent procreative powers. He is experimental about sex. He may find his true love at an early age and recognize that person in the blink of an eye. The sweetness of his marriage grows stronger by the day, and does not degenerate into boredom and monotony. The person gains great evolution and spiritual growth from married life. He gets a partner who is spiritual, powerful, and special. That person may also be charismatic and fascinating.

The person is happy and popular. He cares about the concerns of friends and family, and creates balance and harmony in his environment. He is flexible and adaptable, and creates relationships based upon mutual trust and respect. He is highly intuitive and knows exactly how to please each particular person. He may be good at earning and amassing wealth. The trine aspect is significantly more powerful than the sextile. The sextile indicates the opportunity to make the above characteristics a reality.

If Mars is conjunct Jupiter, the person is ambitious and motivated. He is the most energetic of individuals. His blood is strong and he is wonderfully confident. The person has a powerful presence and will be honored and respected in a big way. The person immerses himself fully in all endeavors and rarely gives up or quits. He is courageous, adventurous, and fun-loving. He is entirely action-oriented. The health is good and the person is productive. He is a natural leader.

The Mars-Jupiter aspect, indicating such positive and outgoing energy, is an extremely fortunate aspect in terms of success and accomplishment. However, there are a few drawbacks, due especially to the hot, malefic aspect that Mars bestows on Jupiter. The person will have little success or happiness in the areas of religion and spirituality. He may have arguments with gurus or spiritual teachers. He may also lack sensitivity, introspection, and self-reflection. There may be problems with allergies or the liver. The person may be arrogant and lacking humility. He may possess a hot temper. Also, because Jupiter is afflicted, there is a possibility that the person may be unlucky in a certain way. It is not that he encounters difficulties and struggles, or that he must endure failure; but the support of nature may simply be lacking. There will be isolated experiences or particular time periods when the person seems to be distinctly singled out as one with no "guardian angel."

The person makes an excellent showman or performer. He is good on stage and outshines all his peers. He is as dramatic and theatrical as an individual can be. He loves a good challenge and beats his competitors with ease. The person is honest, direct, and practical. He has nothing to hide. He sets tremendous goals and maintains unshakable faith in his abilities. He is loyal, and proud like a lion. The person is virile and sexually attractive. There is great masculine energy and a strong sex drive. The person excels in sports. He has a powerful and relentless ego. He is forceful and does well as a champion of causes. He is not shy in asserting himself or placing his personal desires above those around him. He is enthusiastic and enjoys playing the game of life on a grand scale. There may be abundant creativity and a powerful ability to inspire others. Pete Rose has the Mars conjunct Jupiter aspect within four degrees.

If Mars is square or opposite Jupiter, the person is an extremist. He lacks balance and moderation, does not know when to quit, and is often foolishly fearless. There may be poor judgement and an overly-confident nature. Many individuals with these aspects are impetuous, biased, and opinionated. The person may annoy others with conceit and exaggerated importance. He may give new meaning to the concept of arrogance. He excels in sports and loves to compete. He is a natural fighter and wins more often than not. There is a strong sex drive, and plenty of energy to get his desires fulfilled.

The person has a tendency to overextend himself. He may vacillate between extreme vitality and laziness. He may be overly indulgent in pleasures, and should be careful not too consume too many sweets or oils. As always with Jupiter afflictions, the liver is at risk. Though the person lacks common sense and temperance, success is favored. He takes risks easily and is impervious to the opinions of others. He is unyielding in his convictions. He is energetic and spirited. He is rarely, if ever, to be dissuaded from pursuing his goals.

The person may have a tendency to irritate or antagonize others. He enjoys winning, and bragging about his conquests. There may be difficulties with gurus or religious teachers. The person is intense in his beliefs, and may be known as a religious or philosophical fanatic. His energy is outward-directed, and there is a need for introspection and self-reflection. The person must take care not to produce sloppy or careless work. He may lack sensitivity, and lose friends on account of selfishness. The person is restless, and lives an active, physical life. He may be prejudiced and have troubles with authority. Traditional astrological texts declare that the person must avoid gambling and taking dangerous risks. He should work on modifying his excessiveness and extreme behavior, and consider the possibility of living a deeper, more rewarding existence based upon moderation, sensitivity, trust, and generosity. Martial arts master Bruce Lee had the Mars opposite Jupiter aspect within three degrees.

If Mars is trine or sextile Jupiter, the person is enthusiastic, spirited, and buoyant. He is dynamic, positive, and outgoing. Luck and success are favored, and the person is fortunate. He may be honored and respected during his lifetime. There is strong confidence, and the person is assertive in a non-threatening way. He is optimistic and straightforward. He hides nothing. He is cheerful and expressive. He enjoys life's adventures more than anyone.

The person is proud, loyal, and of good integrity. He is inspired and active. He excels in sports, and benefits through travel. He wants to learn and experience everything he can. Religion and philosophy are important areas of pleasure. The person may like to gamble or speculate. He has a powerful presence and may do well on stage. He is sexually healthy and has powerful procreative energy. The person is independent and enterprising. His spirit is irrepressible, his enthusiasm infectious. He is rarely, if ever, lazy. He fulfills his goals and ambitions. Tatum O'neil has the Mars trine Jupiter aspect within three and one half degrees.

In order for harmonious Mars-Jupiter aspects to be used to full advantage, the person needs to have strong discipline and depth of character indicated elsewhere in the birthchart. Otherwise, there is more vigor and excitement than tangible results. The trine aspect is significantly more powerful than the sextile. The sextile indicates the opportunity to make the above characteristics a reality.

If Mars is conjunct Saturn, the person lives a life of restrained impulses. His energy comes in spurts. Sometimes he is too controlled; at other times, he is too aggressive. The Mars-Saturn conjunction is a difficult one to endure as it is perfectly paradoxical. On one hand, restrictive-natured Saturn dampens every single impulse the person has the instant it occurs. However, Saturn also gives reality, form, and structure to the desire nature. Thus, the person vacillates between inhibiting his urges and fulfilling them with a vengeance. It is a frustrating way to live. It is decidedly painful during childhood, when restrictiveness from parents and authorities is already the order of the day.

The combination of the two traditional malefics may also give an overabundance of negative energy. The person is capable of extraordinary anger, coldness, malicious intent, and destructiveness. When his frustrations peak, he can experience fits of rage. He is capable of deviousness, and a profound or subtle meanness. He may experience a few colossal accidents in his time. As with all truly unwelcomed and difficult astrological aspects, the extremities of such behavior are likely to be experienced more readily during childhood and adolescence.

The person is an excellent problem-solver. He is adept in mechanics and any technical field. He is practical, down-to-earth, and good at advising others. The person is extremely courageous. He is tough and able to withstand adversity. Astrologer Robert De Luce had the Mars-Saturn conjunction within two degrees. There is a marked difficulty in decision-making. However, once the person chooses his path, he is wise and shrewd in his strategy. The person is highly libidinous and views sex as real, important, and significant. He will go to great lengths to satisfy his lust and increase his conquests. He is ambitious and craves power. The person may have difficulties with his father, resulting in lifelong scars of bitterness or resentment. He may have problems with personal discipline and authority figures. He may be intermittently plagued by petty fears, diffused energy, and restlessness. In his unrelenting inclination to restrain impulses the person makes an art form of procrastination and avoidance of minor commitments.

The person loses opportunities because of his inability to secure the moment. He does well in sports, the military, police work, or any Mars-oriented career. He is a dominant individual and may be a boss in his job. It is very important that the person eats well and gets plenty of rest in order to counteract the damaging effect of his energy-depleting psychology. He must also exercise. The person should learn to express his annoyances as they occur, rather than allowing them to accumulate and burst in a fury. The house placement of the Mars-Saturn conjunction may indicate an area of extreme difficulty. There is a distinct possibility that the person was reckless, rash, and irresponsibly aggressive in previous lives and is now paying the price. Above all else, regarding his dreams and visions, he must follow his heart. He should discipline himself to ignore the automatic, nearly-mechanical censoring voice in his head.

If Mars is square or opposite Saturn, the person's desires and impulses are subject to immediate restriction and censorship. The person suffers from a continual "push-pull" energy, and his life lacks ease, spontaneity, and grace. There may be a distinct lack of purpose and direction, causing frustration and a pervasive feeling of futility. The person gives up on his goals and ambitions because he is confused about how to properly assert himself and put his desires ahead of his peers and competitors. He is missing a sense of balance and appropriateness regarding aggressiveness, and fears that in order to genuinely pursue his aspirations he must be ruthless or merciless. Being uncomfortable with such options, he may simply choose to abandon his cravings and relinquish his passions. Or, even more commonly, he waits interminably for circumstances to conform to his desires, as if nature will magically fulfill his needs.

The person may start many projects which he never completes. He misses out on opportunities throughout life because of hesitation and failure to secure the moment. His judgement may be off and his timing poor. Some individuals with hard Mars-Saturn aspects are excessive about discipline. They are too austere, rigid, strict, and harsh. There may be difficulties with authority figures and the father, serving to create bitterness and pessimism. The person is well-advised to work on self-expression, self-love, and a sense of deserving. He must cultivate patience and determination, and remember that the journey of a thousand miles begins with a single step. When the person learns to perform consistent action towards his important goals, then he will leave his frustrated existence behind.

There may be a big temper. Because the person feels irrationally blocked, he may occasionally throw tantrums or experience fits of rage. He may be irritable or often negative. There may be deep selfishness due to feelings of scarcity and inadequacy. Traditional astrological texts report that the person vacillates too much. He may be very excited about an issue and later feel nothing at all. There may be difficulty in achieving a balanced sexual life. The person experiences extremes in this realm, i.e. periods of self-imposed abstinence and times of uncontrolled lust. Ted Turner has the Mars opposition Saturn aspect within four degrees.

If Mars is trine or sextile Saturn, the person feels a sense of purpose and direction, and actualizes his dreams consistently. He makes excellent use of his energy and actions. He is practical, down-to-earth, and has the greatest common sense. He understands form and structure as well as cause and effect. He is ambitious and industrious, and always succeeds in accomplishing his goals. The person is patient, disciplined, and hard-working. He pays attention to details and does not look for the easy way out. He is never lazy and he does not procrastinate. There is excellent mechanical ability. The person enjoys seeing a job through to its final, efficient completion. He is not interested in "get-rich-quick" schemes.

There is abundant leadership ability. The person handles responsibility well, as he is more concerned with results and productivity than ego and accolades. He is conservative, moderate, and controlled. He is serious and formal, and does not lose his temper. The person is very courageous and may be a pioneer in his field. He does not back down from a challenge. He is dependable, resilient, and determined. He is a survivor and always endures. He is an excellent fighter to have on one's side. The person is good in business, as he has powerful strength and fortitude to deal with competitors and adversaries. Michelangelo, Copernicus, and John Dillenger all had close Mars-Saturn trine aspects.

Instinct and willpower are pronounced. The person is calm, orderly, and uncluttered in his lifestyle. He is security-oriented and loves to build things. He may amass possessions as well as accomplishments over the years. He is good at overcoming obstacles. The trine aspect is significantly more powerful than the sextile. The sextile indicates the opportunity to make the above characteristics a reality.

If Mars is conjunct Uranus, the person lives a life of untamed energy and audacious activity. He is independent, impulsive, and highly stimulated. He is potentially rebellious. Above all, he craves excitement, spontaneity, and living life on his own terms. There is great courage and the person is never afraid to assert himself. He is original and intuitive. He reacts immediately and is impatient with slow, ordinary people. He enjoys being different. When he is focused and clear about his objectives he can realize his goals as quick as lightning.

There is a tendency towards hyperactivity. The person is high-strung and must guard against frenetic energy or rash behavior. He is head-strong and amongst the most obstinate of the species. Although there may be a distinct aversion toward routine, the person is extremely well-advised to adopt a regimen of martial arts, tai chi, hatha yoga, physical exercise, or any technique which helps him regulate and release his tensions. Since Mars-Uranus aspects are considered accident-prone, there is even more incentive to meditate or practice daily workouts.

The person hates pressure and restraint. He must therefore learn discipline, responsibility, and consistency as soon as possible. Otherwise, he will suffer the frustration of an erratic, inconsistent life. He lives instinctively and is rarely predictable. He may have an explosive temper. He is motivated and never lacking in enthusiasm. He is attracted to all endeavors that satisfy his need for a passionate, action-filled life. He loves racecars, flying, and the thrill of risk or danger. He is good in mechanics or any technical field such as architecture, engineering, drafting, etc. There may be leadership and inspirational ability, as well as a real talent for inventions.

The person is excited and experimental about sex. He wants a mystical, genius, or unconventional spouse. Because of his changeable and restless nature, he is wiser not to marry early. The person is strong-willed, direct, and blunt. He is determined and always on the move. If he discovers how to concentrate his efforts and master his volatility, he will live a rich and fascinating life of diversity.

If Mars is square or opposite Uranus, the person is overly independent, individualistic, and unconstrained. He is a non-conformist, and resents any kind of society-imposed morals or standards. He does not take to authority figures or the powers that be. There is an abundance of physical energy, and the person may be nervous, irritable, and high-strung. Many individuals with hard Mars-Uranus aspects are too easily excitable and, therefore, accident-prone. The person needs an outlet for his vivacious nature and frenetic energy, and should practice one of the martial arts. Or, he should engage in any active sport of his choice on a regular basis.

The person is unpredictable. He is impatient, too hurried, and often unreliable. He craves stimulation and excitement, and always wants to be busy. His life may be cluttered with many unfinished projects and incomplete affairs. There is a great need for patience, consistency, and composure. The person is extremely courageous. He fears nothing, except perhaps the loss of his independence. He is dynamic, pioneering, and decisive. He is a revolutionary who loves to challenge and change the order of things. Unfortunately, the person is also stubborn, unyielding, and as resistant as they come. He may be disagreeable for his own eccentric means of enjoyment. He wants what he wants, when he wants it. Therein may lie his greatest arrogance. He needs to learn how to object with dignity rather than rebelliousness.

The person is experience-oriented. He is original and intuitive. He is sexually exciting and follows his own impulses and desires. He is not bound by society's rules and mores. There may be emotional volatility, and the person may be direct, outspoken, and abrupt. He takes risks without a thought, and loves the thrill of danger. He is highly competitive. There may be a big temper. The person needs to develop perseverance, tolerance, and proper use of his indomitable will. He must tone down his extremist tendencies and learn to cooperate with others. Jacques Cousteau has the Mars opposition Uranus aspect within one degree, and Robert Redford has the square aspect within four degrees.

If Mars is trine or sextile Uranus, the person is inspired, ambitious, and successful. He exudes the most vital, spirited energy. He is original, creative, and extremely innovative. The person has his own ideas and never follows the crowd. He is a natural leader whose independence and powerful commitment are an example to others. There is a tremendous love, and need, for freedom. The person is determined and pursues his dreams and visions fearlessly. He is courageous, adventurous, and pioneering. He is not easily dissuaded or discouraged. He is persistent and unyielding.

The person is stubborn. He is opinionated, decisive, and of the strongest will. He does not look to avoid hard work or adversity. He is forceful and direct. There may be mechanical ability, and talent in any occult endeavor. The person is spontaneous and uninhibited. He is open-minded and never bound by rules, regulations, and tradition. He is intuitive, progressive, and different. He does not mind being considered eccentric or out-of-the-ordinary. There may be strong charisma and a most powerful sexuality. The person is excited about life and wants to experience everything the world has to offer.

As with nearly all Uranus aspects, the person needs discipline, depth of character, and staying power in order to make the best use of the above-mentioned abilities. There may be restlessness and a high-strung personality. The person is active, dynamic, and alert. He lives in the moment, and is incredibly resourceful. If the rest of the birthchart is strong, the person may achieve a great deal of accomplishment in his lifetime. The trine aspect is significantly more powerful than the sextile. The sextile indicates the opportunity to make the above characteristics a reality.

If Mars is conjunct Neptune, the person is psychically animated. He lives an ethereal, rather than physical, existence. He is blatantly clairvoyant and telepathic, though in many cases the person is unaware of any special talent since his abilities are so naturally ingrained. The person is idealistic, romantic, and undiscriminating. He is impractical, unrealistic, and has a difficult time in the world of humankind, due to his dreamy nature and altered perception of reality. The person is psychologically confused and restless in his soul. His longing for fulfillment is insatiable, and he is forever chasing happiness in the outer world (where, of course, it remains elusive). His imagination is too active and he is open to realms of existence closed to the average mortal.

The person is motivated by subconscious forces. He is powerfully affected by moods, feelings, and psychic impressions. He lives life by instinct and emotions. He is far too impulsive. The person needs to develop caution, discipline, and responsibility.

He is gullible, and easily deceived and exploited. Most importantly, he often feels like a helpless victim and lives his life as such. This is because Mars is badly dissipated by the dissolving influence of Neptune. The person has little will to confront others and take aggressive action. Because Neptune's weakening of Mars wreaks havoc with the ego, there is a profound fear of failure. However, the complex is quite subconscious and is revealed only in the person's inordinate inability to acknowledge any of his weaknesses or shortcomings.

The Mars-Neptune conjunction makes the person one of the best professional psychics, mediums, or channelers. He excels in art, music, photography, painting, magic, etc. He is tremendously magnetic and automatically enthralls and fascinates others. He is a vibrant mass of inspiration, seeking purpose and intention. Regarding sacred or mystical affairs he is the most responsive and "in tune" of all beings. Should he choose a life of mysticism or religious activity, he will find a most comfortable setting for his personality and temperament.

The person considers sex mysterious, magical, and spiritual. He feels a direct correlation between eroticism and the divine. However, he

208 may be disillusioned by the sex act itself, because he cannot relate to the physicality and earthiness of the experience. Some with the Mars-Neptune conjunction face bouts of impotence, while others occasionally attract partners who are impotent or become so during the relationship. The person is easily seduced and enjoys alluring others in the same enticing way. There may be serious sexual confusion and a world of sexual fantasies or role-playing.

There is likely to be an interminable confusion concerning desires and ambitions. Though it is not at all obvious, the person lacks faith in himself in a deep-seated way. He must cultivate a sense of confidence and self-worth, and realize that he deserves to accomplish his goals as much as anyone. Otherwise, he will experience major disappointment and frustration regarding his life purpose. On the positive side, because the person finds it so hard to place his desires above those of others and actively pursue his ambitions, he learns (in time) how to make things happen almost magically. He does this by telepathically communicating his needs and urges.

The person needs to get plenty of rest, eat well, and guard against poisons or other substances that could harm the bloodstream. He should avoid drugs and alcohol. Health may be delicate. The person must not overwork or enter stressful situations, since he is prone to diffuse energy even in the best of circumstances. Choice of friends and associates is of utmost importance since the person is, by nature, naive, idealistic, and vulnerable. Regarding love matters, advice from parents, friends, and other objective sources is definitely to be heeded. Excessive emotionalism is a problem.

The person should ponder whether his ideas are real or rosy, for he is prone to delusions of grandeur. The more powerful and positive the birthchart is, as a whole, the more serious the problem. This is because the person is very intuitive. Acutely sensing his potential destiny, the person feels a hair's breadth away from the goal. However, goals are rarely accomplished without action; for the Mars-Neptune person, the greater the potential, the greater the fear of failure and the less likelihood of action. The person may also have difficulty when expressing anger or dealing with enemies, competitors, and others who get in his way. Odd though it would seem, some people who have the Mars-Neptune conjunction do very well in sports. In such cases, their idealism is connected to Mars-type activities. More than anything, however, the person has trouble making his dreams and visions a reality (unless, of course, his desires are spiritually and mystically directed). Astrologer Dane Rudhyar had the Mars-Neptune conjunction within one and one half degrees. Former politician John Dean has the aspect within two degrees.

If Mars is square or opposite Neptune, the person has little ability to put his desires above those of others. The ego was not properly supported and nurtured during childhood by the parents or environmental factors. Therefore, the person lacks a solid basis for, or understanding of, personal success. He suffers from insecurity and low self-confidence, and needs to work diligently on his sense of deserving. The person is extraordinarily sensitive to criticism and disapproval. Underneath a calm exterior, he believes (consciously or not) that he is a failure. Facing his flaws and weaknesses may become particularly difficult. The person abhors competition, and his worst fear is to take a risk. He does not wish to open himself up to possible rejection.

Hard Mars-Neptune aspects are certainly amongst the most difficult astrological features, especially if close by degree. Aside from the problems caused by two particularly incompatible energies functioning in a discordant relationship, there is a serious feature of self-delusion present. Therefore, the person is rather incapable of recognizing the difficulties and complexities in his psyche. His desire nature and, more importantly, his ego are at the mercy of his well-developed imagination and animated fantasy life. Concerning his own nature, he sees and believes what pleases him. Though unaware of it, the persona he conveys to the world may be quite inconsistent with his true desires, needs, and wants. Regarding his purpose and life direction, he may delude or confuse even himself! There are simply too many unacknowledged fears in the subconscious mind. Above all, the issue of failure, which resides deeply in his heart, must be confronted and handled before the person can go on to lead the rich, rewarding, and successful life he may be capable of living.

The person is psychic and open to the astral realm. He is sensitive, receptive, and prone to be a medium. However, he is also gullible and vulnerable to suggestion. He is innocent and unsuspecting. He unwittingly invites deception or delusion from those around him. For these reasons, and because of a potentially obsessive personality, many traditional astrological texts warn that the person should avoid seances or major involvement in the occult. The person may be an ardent romantic. He is artistic, grandiose in schemes, and adores the hidden, mysterious side of life. There is a distinctly uncontrolled imagination which renders the person different and peculiar to the rest of the world.

210   He may, in certain ways, be considered odd or strange by others. There is a need for earthiness, discipline, and practicality, or the person will have little chance of functioning well in competitive society. He is absorbed in his imagination and fantasies. There may be a lack of consistency and follow-through.

The person lives for the gratification of sensual desires. He is an escapist from the mundane world and must diligently avoid drugs, alcohol, and any other path which takes him away from his responsibilities in the here and now. The person experiences no boundaries or check-points where his passions and cravings are concerned. A great deal of sexual experimentation is possible, as is bisexuality. The person may be preoccupied by, or obsessed with, lust and eroticism. He may become carried away by his senses. He is idealistic about sex and may consider love-making his path of merging with the Divine. In certain cases there is significant sexual confusion. The person may be unsure of his personal preference, and the issue is made more difficult since he immerses himself one-hundred percent in all sensual pursuits. Thus he may find himself enjoying both genders equally well.

Because the person has deep-down doubts about his worthiness, he is prone to attract critical or judgemental love partners. He may also possess an unconscious self-destructiveness, which eventually manifests as indulgence in some version of the sordid side of life. He may for a time associate with immoral, decadent, or profane individuals. Such alliances should obviously be guarded against, particularly since the person is so naive and easily thrown off-balance. In extreme cases, the person is affected by too many unconscious or repressed desires, and there is a possibility of severe sexual perversions or deviations. There may be times in life when the person genuinely contemplates suicide, but only because he has so little control over his imagination.

The person must be extra careful about his habits. He is easily led by his cravings, and may develop addictions or dependencies which interfere with his goals and ambitions. Most importantly, the person should surround himself with loving and supportive friends. He must try to set realistic goals by asking for advice from associates and loved ones. He should beware of pessimism, discouragement, and procrastination. The person is well-advised to read Sondra Ray's book "I DESERVE LOVE," and to participate in her "rebirthing" techniques. The person may also benefit from any form of psychotherapy which deals with reprogramming the unconscious mind. Females with hard Mars-Neptune aspects may have a particularly difficult time understanding men or masculine energy in general. Jimmy Hoffa had the Mars opposition Neptune aspect within three degrees.

If Mars is trine or sextile Neptune, the person wants to help. He is generous and his greatest pleasure is to serve and assist others. He is sensitive, perceptive, and has a wonderful heart. His motives are pure, and he is simple and selfless in wanting fulfillment for all. There is abundant talent in the arts. The person especially excels in music, drama, film, or photography. He is idealistic and inspired. When his imagination stirs him, he acts quickly and moves decisively towards the goal. Unlike most people, he is never afraid to pursue his most lofty dreams and visions. He is of excellent integrity and can certainly be trusted to keep his word. He is sympathetic, supportive, and always compassionate. John Denver has the Mars trine Neptune aspect within one degree.

The person is refined. He is honorable, humane, and pious in deed. He may be a very special healer. He is creative, and his greatest power comes from the spiritual world. He is good at planning schemes and organizing strategies. The person is sensuous. His emotions are strong and deep. He is flexible, adaptable, and rarely dominated by his ego. He succeeds in any service-oriented profession, and may enjoy occult or psychic work. The person is supremely blessed in being spared the need to prove himself through aggressiveness, competition, pride, and egotism. The trine aspect is significantly more powerful than the sextile. The sextile indicates the opportunity to make the above characteristics a reality.

If Mars is conjunct Pluto, the person is a reservoir of unlimited energy. He has more physical power than anyone. He is forceful and lives a life of desires and cravings. The person is action-oriented and does things in a big way. He is competitive, aggressive, and dominant. He is good in sports and always endures. There is a tremendous ego. Success is important, and the person may be relentless in pursuing his goals. When he is clear about what he wants, there is no doubt he will get his way. The person is, potentially, a human dynamo.

Although this aspect seems very fortunate, it is actually difficult to handle. There is a possibility that the person is deeply fearful of his mighty nature. During childhood he may have occasionally let loose his aggressions and forcefulness, and witnessed devastating effects. Or he may have received severe punishment for his actions. Furthermore, the person is very much aware of his intense strength. This potent conjunction of the two rulers of Scorpio produces massive potential; the person feels no build-in boundaries in a behavioral area, where rules are crucial. Violence is an all-too-apparent option. Therefore, the person may simply repress or deny his power nature altogether. Thus he may lose even the positive benefits that this aspect promises.

The person is sexually powerful. He is virile and sensuous, carnal and orgiastic. He may need lots of sex. His procreative and regenerative energies are strong. The person is healthy and muscular. He is proud, spirited, and confident. He is courageous and adventurous. He is persistent and enjoys a good challenge. Few planets function smoothly when conjunct Pluto (the indicator of vulnerability, compulsiveness, and control). Mars is not an exception. Since it represents masculinity, virility, and the macho, (or showy) aspect of ego, this aspect is especially hard for a man. He may feel unsure of his manhood and filled with a compulsive need to prove himself. Winning becomes of utmost importance. He may even question his sexuality. Worst of all, this the person is subject to an intense battle of competition with his father, and this can produce long-lived bitterness and resentment. The father may be competitive by nature, or he may feel threatened by an assertive and (consciously or unconsciously) challenging son.

The person must beware of the tendency to fulfill his desires by any means. There is a distinct tendency toward manipulation or using deceptive, devious tactics. In this way, the person is both shrewd and subtle. He is particularly uncaring about rules and regulations when they are in the way of his ambitions. There is potentially a fierce temper, and the person will experience the true meaning of rage in his lifetime. He is capable of realizing the greatest goals and accomplishments. But he must be diligent, rigorous, and responsible about the use of his power. If the Mars-Pluto conjunction is afflicted by aspects from other planets, the person may be cruel or ruthless in forcing his will on others. Paul McCartney has the Mars-Pluto conjunction within two degrees. Obviously, the fame he has achieved required profound drive and determination. Though the Mars-Pluto conjunction seems to contradict McCartney's gentle, easygoing personality, it is worth noting that toward the end of their relationship, all the other Beatles felt compelled to engage in a law suit against him that lasted nearly twenty years. Also, after convincing John Lennon not to quit the group, he secretly recorded a solo album in order to be the first Beatle with his own record!

If Mars is square or opposite Pluto, the person is driven by compulsive cravings to dominate and win. He is ambitious, competitive, and does not know the meaning of submission. He is willful, obstinate, and goal-oriented. There is phenomenal endurance, strength, and fortitude. The ego is intense, uncontrolled, and, in a word, inappropriate. The person wants to get his way. He is stubborn, resistant, and forceful. His desire nature is overdeveloped and he must beware of ruthless behavior and forcing his will on others. The person has enough energy to accomplish any purpose that comes to mind. In extreme cases there may be aggressive or violent behavior. The person would be cruel, relentless, and profoundly selfish.

There is an enormous sex drive and the person may use others purely for carnal pleasures. He is at the mercy of lustful desires, innate eroticism, and passions that do not abate. There may be a big temper or trouble with chronic anger. The person will certainly experience rage in his lifetime. He excels in sports and makes an excellent fighter. There is immense courage. Muhammad Ali, one of the most indefatigable fighters of all times, has the Mars square Pluto aspect within two and one-half degrees. The person has strong opinions of how things should be. He follows his own path and has trouble listening to others. He may often try to change or remold loved ones.

The greatest task in life is for the person to learn humility. He needs to explore the value of vulnerability and compromise. More importantly, he must confront his inordinate need for control, and realize the freedom to be gained from cooperation with nature and surrender to "the flow." He must eventually realize that if he continues to play life as a win-lose game then everyone suffers. Traditional astrological texts report that certain individuals with hard Mars-Pluto aspects are subject to violence, sexual abuse, rape, etc. This is especially true in cases where the person is unaware of (or has repressed) his massive desire nature, intense physical and sexual urges, and egocentric needs to dominate. In severe cases the person is reckless and has no regard for rules and regulations. He may be anti-social or engage in criminal activity.

Richard Pryor and General George Patton have (or had) the Mars square Pluto aspect within one and four degrees respectively. Machiavelli, the great master of "manipulative politics" had the opposition aspect within five degrees.

If Mars is trine or sextile Pluto, the person has great potential combined with the most potent energy. He can accomplish anything he desires, no matter how hard the work or difficult the struggle. His willpower is excellent and his actions are consistent and disciplined. He is successful. The person is resourceful, balanced, and healthy. He accepts responsibility for his desires and ego needs. There is strong confidence and leadership ability. No amount of work or struggle is too much if the person has a goal he wants to achieve. He is determined, and he immerses himself fully in his projects and endeavors. Albert Einstein and astrologer Robert Hand both have (or had) very close Mars trine Pluto aspects.

The person is virile and sexual. His procreative powers are strong. He is competitive in a good way. There is plenty of courage and the person enjoys a challenge. He is fearless, and does not allow problems to obstruct his success. The person is proud and noble. He excels in sports. He uses his instinct and intuition to gain the upper hand and win. There is strong blood and a powerful constitution. He is persistent and does not tire easily. He is creative in business, and is ambitious, dynamic, and decisive. There may be talent in metaphysics and the occult. The trine aspect is significantly more powerful than the sextile. The sextile indicates the opportunity to make the above characteristics a reality.

If Jupiter is conjunct Saturn, the person is of the strongest character and depth of soul. He lives with a great sense of responsibility and commitment. His goals are enormous and he attacks them with patience, discipline, and fortitude. The person knows how to bring form and structure to his most expansive dreams and visions. He understands tradition and convention, and works within societal confines to bring about the most radical changes possible. He is on the earth to break boundaries in whatever field he chooses. He knows instinctively what will work and what will not work. There is a remarkable singularity of purpose. The Jupiter-Saturn conjunction occurs approximately every twenty years. Typical examples of individuals who have used the energy to its greatest benefit are John Lennon, Timothy Leary, Christ, Mary Baker Eddy, Shakespeare, Nostradamus, Galileo, and John Glenn (the first astronaut to circle the globe).

Psychologically, the lifetime is by no means easy. The person feels entirely pulled apart by his paradoxical traits. He vacillates between optimism and pessimism, idealism and depression. Furthermore, Jupiter (the planet of luck and fortune) is quite harmed by the malefic energy of Saturn. The person has troubles with allergies and the liver. His sense of luck and joy are greatly toned down. Opportunities are limited, and the person learns early in life how to make the most of every possibility. He is good at succeeding in restricted situations. The person experiences more than his fair share of denial, austerity, and privation. He works hard, with no feeling of discontent or resentment. He expects to be given nothing, yet positively knows he will succeed in the end due to his persistence, diligence, and extreme practicality. He does not look for "get-rich-quick" schemes.

Ethics and morals are of supreme importance. The person lives a philosophically integrated life. He goes to great lengths to maintain his integrity and abide by his principles and convictions. He never yields to pressure. The person is greatly religious and spiritual by nature. However, because Jupiter is harmed by Saturn there will almost certainly be difficulties with gurus and religious teachers. There is a strong chance that the person will study and partake of numerous different religions in his life. In one way, the person is orthodox in his

218 approach. But he is also practical and exacting. Therefore, if and when problems arise he has no difficulty in moving on to a more significant and appropriate belief system.

Since all of Saturn's significations flourish by association with benefic Jupiter, the person is humble, responsible, and trustworthy. He is a natural leader and gains in wisdom with each passing year. He is respected and achieves a high status in his career. He may do well with real estate, carpentry, or construction. He drives a hard bargain and does not overpay.

The person lives with a sense of urgency and has high expectations for his life. He is therefore vulnerable to the possibility of disappointment which, in his case, leads to bitterness, discouragement, and pessimism. He feels burdened because he is only too aware of his inborn lack of luck. He may also be angry that the rest of humanity is constantly receiving opportunities while nothing ever comes his way. Also, much depends on the free will factor and the rest of the birthchart. If there is laziness, resignation, or inaction for any reason, the person will live a life of frustration and guilt for not realizing his innate sense of potential. It is reported that Jupiter-Saturn aspects (conjunctions, squares, and oppositions) are one of the most common features in the charts of suicides. The person must cultivate a sense of appreciation and avoid developing a chip on his shoulder. He must also follow his inclination towards unflinching honesty, since misdeeds bring almost instantaneous retribution.

The person is a perfectionest with a great need for order, authority, and control. He is a fascinating blend of restraint, discipline, and conservative method juxtaposed with radical, expansive, and progressive yearnings. He creates far-reaching structures which withstand the test of time.

If Jupiter is square or opposite Saturn, the person is overly concerned with the meaning of existence. He lives by a philosophy of duty, obligation, and responsibility. He may be so preoccupied with performing "right and significant action" that he forgets that personal enjoyment and happiness is one of the main purposes of creation. The person dreams of great achievements and grandiose accomplishments for the betterment of humankind. However, because he vacillates so dramatically between optimism and pessimism, he may lack the necessary consistency to fulfill his ambitions. There may be serious disappointment, disillusionment, and even bitterness on this account. The person wavers continually between expansion and contraction. Therefore, he is hard pressed to make wise and appropriate decisions. His life is a virtual struggle to learn balanced judgement. Not only does he neglect intuition, but his timing may be consistently, even humorously, off the mark.

The lifetime is not an easy one. The person must work extraordinarily hard to realize his goals. He is not favored by luck or opportunities. Furthermore, like the biblical character Job, the person is certain to be tested throughout his lifetime. He constantly meets with delays, and his patience is taxed to the limits. He continually finds himself in situations requiring long periods of waiting. In severe cases the person is depressed, gloomy, and frustrated. It is no coincidence that hard Jupiter-Saturn aspects are one of the most common features in the charts of suicide victims.

The person is an excellent worker for others. He is dutiful, disciplined, and efficient. He excels in any managerial or organizational capacity. He is conscientious and always aware of right and wrong. He has plenty of endurance, strength, and fortitude. He is good in the art of self-improvement. The person is sincere and genuine. However, he lacks spontaneity, imagination, and originality. He is overly solemn, and may not believe he deserves abundant pleasure, fun, and recreation. He is too philosophical for his own good. There may be allergies or other liver problems. The person is well-advised to avoid speculation and gambling. In the ancient system of Hindu astrology, Jupiter is known as the chief significator of children. Individuals with the Jupiter-Saturn opposition are likely to have difficulties with their offspring. There may be abortions, problems giving birth, or other such dilemmas.

220   The person is traditional, orthodox, and conservative. He thinks much about the past and the future. He is too sober and down-to-earth to deliberately pursue his dreams and visions. However, if the rest of the birthchart indicates a strong sense of idealism, then even the hard Jupiter-Saturn aspects will confer the ability to bring reality, form, and structure to the person's most fanciful aspirations. In such cases the person can make massive contributions to society, and even break the boundaries of his chosen field. The person is project-oriented. There are periods of intense expansion and growth, as well as profoundly boring, monotonous phases.

Religious difficulties are likely. The person may have the strongest faith in God during childhood, only to experience disillusionment as he matures. There may be problems with gurus or religious teachers. The person's devotional life, even more than the rest of his existence, is characterized by intervals of fervent idealism and hopeless discouragement. Because of his dual and fluctuating nature he does not know when to trust and when to be suspicious. He simply lacks the wherewithal to judge. He chases equanimity and reasoning power his entire life. The person is spiritually eclectic. He is discriminating, and therefore rather unlikely to stay with one particular guru or religious system.

For those with the Jupiter-Saturn opposition, the second half of life is more favorable than the first. The reason for this is clear if one is familiar with Hindu astrology. In the ancient predictive system, Saturn is known to "mature," or give its fullest effects, after the thirty-sixth year. Because it is aspected by benefic Jupiter (oppositions are considered neither good or bad, but depend on the benefic or malefic nature of the aspecting planet) the person will experience success in the Saturnian realms. Thus, he achieves honor, respect, wisdom, career promotions, success etc. during the second half of life.

In certain cases, there may be serious problems with college institutions or in obtaining higher knowledge. Also, some people with this aspect experience isolated instances of particularly bad luck. It is as if they are singled out by God or nature for some odd, perhaps karmic, reason. Sidney Poitier and Sigmund Freud have (or had) the Jupiter-Saturn square within one and two degrees respectively.

If Jupiter is trine or sextile Saturn, the person has the best judgement. He is responsible, broad-minded, and works for the good of the community. He is highly principled and stands up for his beliefs. The person works to correct any injustices he perceives around him. He is a natural leader, and may do well in politics. He is practical, earthy, and of great common sense. He is an excellent organizer and planner. Jeddu Krishnamurti and writer/researcher John Lilly both had the Jupiter-Saturn trine aspect.

The person is a hard worker and is always willing to pay his dues. He has the best ethics and morals. He has excellent timing and is likely to be extremely successful. Business and finance are favored. The person does well with investments and speculations. He is respected and has a very fine reputation. There is no difficulty in gaining higher knowledge or college degrees. The person is good at advising others. He is stable, modest, and wise. He is discriminating in his choice of spiritual teachers, and is rarely fooled by gurus or mentors.

There is plenty of optimism and a rather conservative nature. The person has respect for tradition and elders. He is extremely balanced in his analysis and conclusions. The trine aspect is significantly more powerful than the sextile. The sextile indicates the opportunity to make the above characteristics a reality.

If Jupiter is conjunct Uranus, the person thrives on knowledge, truth, and freedom. He is consumed with personal growth and spiritual evolution. He is excited, enthusiastic, and ever optimistic. He lives a fascinating life and experiences sudden luck at the last moment. Religion is a major concern and the person wants to do good and improve his chosen doctrine in any way he can. The person is a natural reformer and humanitarian. He is as progressive as they come.

The person is intuitive and metaphysically oriented. He loves the sciences and the occult. He is never bound by tradition, dogma, or rhetoric. He abhors routine and system. He loves new challenges and is the most adventurous of souls. He is restless, easily bored, and wants to make changes. Because the person is never swayed by rules and regulations, he is masterfully creative and inventive. The Jupiter-Uranus conjunction clearly suggests talent and potential genius. However, there must be significant discipline, responsibility, and organizational skills indicated in the birthchart (revealed through a well-aspected Saturn, an emphasis on earth signs, etc.) or the person's abilities will likely go unused, undeveloped, and unnoticed.

The person has strikingly quick and accurate intuition. His judgement is good, as is his common sense and objective intellect. The person is magnetic, appealing, and charismatic. He inspires others with ease due to his individuality, self-reliance, and self-integrity. He loves to travel and has many opportunities to do so. He is ever ready to pack his bags and secure the moment. He enjoys spiritual, eccentric, and out-of-the-ordinary type friends.

There is rebelliousness, egocentricity, and a most obstinate personality. The person should beware the tendency to argue and maintain fixed opinions. He must also consider who can, or cannot, tolerate his unpredictable actions and temperament. He may be willful, blunt, or tactless. There may be a kind of frenetic or "live wire" energy about the person. Sudden opportunities and good fortune may spontaneously occur — the person is always in a state of readiness, even expectation, for such occurrences. There is a tremendous love of new concepts, doctrines, and religions. The person is thrilled to share his knowledge and play his part in improving the world. Bob Dylan has the Jupiter-Uranus conjunction within three and one half degrees.

If Jupiter is square or opposite Uranus, the person is an extremist. He is eccentric by nature and is a rebellious, radical thinker. He is fanatical about truth, liberty, and freedom. He is independent, and may give new meaning to the concept of restlessness. He is perpetually critical, dissatisfied with the status quo, and feels it is his job to change things. The person is as adventurous as they come. He wants to try every stimulating endeavor known to humankind. He is overly idealistic and expects his greatest dreams and visions to be fulfilled in an instant. There may be serious disappointment on this account.

The person may excel in astrology or any occult field. He may break away from his given religion and engage in many different new age techniques and philosophies. His ideas are strange and his convictions intense. He may have ideological arguments on a regular basis. The person should choose a career which allows for a great deal of freedom, diversion, and personal creativity. He is stubborn and very strong-willed. He may be generally irritable and especially annoyed by slow, dull-witted individuals. He may be direct, brash, and tactless. He bluntly lets his feelings be known, and may easily offend others.

The person should not speculate or gamble. Though he believes that extraordinary luck is just around the corner, it is not. Many people with this aspect handle money poorly because of their misguided optimism. The person is fervent and spirited. He is a on a grand search for perfection and absolute truth. He has big ideas but may be quite undisciplined. He resents authority and restriction, and wants to do things his own way. The person takes lots of risks. He lives for the moment and does not bother about the future. He is original, creative, magnetic, and enthusiastic. However, he must resolutely guard against conceit. Because of his overconfidence he makes hasty, unwise judgements.

The person is extremely energetic and active. He is witty, clever, and of a keen mind. He may be amongst the most psychic of the human race. There is a strong need for patience, discipline, and responsibility. There may be a great deal of movement or travel in the person's life. He experiences more changes than the average individual. He must tone down his zealous attitude and try to see things more practically if he is to realize his goals and ambitions. James Dean and cultist Jim Jones both had the Jupiter-Uranus square aspect within one degree.

If Jupiter is trine or sextile Uranus, the person is an inspired lover of truth. He is intelligent, original, and occasionally brilliant. There is excellent judgement, a keen mind, and good philosophical depth. The person is open-minded and individualistic. He believes in fairness, and is always on the lookout for injustices within the system. There is excellent intuition, and the person is exceedingly lucky. He is well-liked, and others want to please him. Because of his infinite optimism, faith in himself, and belief in abundance, he is always taken care of. Great opportunities appear consistently throughout life. Large amounts of money come to him suddenly, as if by divine grace.

The person is active, energetic, and enthusiastic. He is original and inventive. He cares little for tradition and convention, yet is tolerant and respectful of the powers that be. He spends his life collecting and examining knowledge, and is thrilled to do so. He is responsible, wise, and makes profound use of what he learns. There may be talent or interest in astrology or the occult. The person may engage in progressive or new-age philosophies. He may demonstrate genius in his chosen field.

The person makes many long-distance journeys. He is fascinated by the culture and practices of foreign societies. The person is deeply absorbed in his experiences. He is interesting and lives a fascinating life. In some cases, the person is considered heroic for his commitment to improving conditions for his community or the masses. He has good principles and ethics. He is truthful and of fine integrity. He does not look to others to create his happiness. There is abundant creativity and inventiveness. The person hates restrictions, rules, and regulations. He champions the cause of freedom. He may have a religious or philosophical outlook on life. Astrologer/author Robert de Luce had the Jupiter trine Uranus aspect within two degrees. The trine aspect is more significant than the sextile. The sextile indicates the opportunity to make the above characteristics a reality.

If Jupiter is conjunct Neptune, the person is devotional, pious, and pure-hearted. He is religious and has unshakable faith in the divine. The person is compassionate, tender, and tolerant. He is generous and his love is unconditional. He is emotional by nature and irresistibly drawn to art, music, film, photography, and magic. He loves the sea and may choose a career on the water. Like Sir Lawrence Olivier, who had an exact Jupiter-Neptune conjunction, the person reaches for the most majestic, sublime, and spirited experience of life.

The person is psychic and regularly has prophetic dreams. He has powerful healing abilities and is significantly aided by his belief in a Higher Power. On the negative side, unfortunately, the person is too gullible. He has the most expansive imagination of anyone and, unless other birthchart factors balance this tendency, he may live a near-fantasy existence. He is unashamedly superstitious and often unfazed by logic. He may live in a dream world and flagrantly neglect to take important and necessary action. He may live with no sense of urgency at all. Since Jupiter rules judgement and is dissipated by the dissolving influence of Neptune, the person has little objectivity or perspective. He suffers indecision and confusion. Common sense is not his most abundant trait.

The person is optimistic and fun to be with. He has a good sense of humor, even under the worst of circumstances. However, this could be due, in part, to his different, impractical reality. The person looks for the good in others and is seriously offended by the harshness and insensitivity of humanity. There is a deep yearning for perfection and the person must beware his powerful escapist tendencies. Above all, he should avoid taking drugs, alcohol, and stimulants, as his liver would be almost immediately impaired. He is prone to allergies and strange, difficult-to-diagnose illnesses. He suffers more than his share of disappointment and disillusionment, especially due to his uneven judgement.

The person is patient, sympathetic, and hates injustice. He is capable of the most profound, subtle, and sublime love of God. Likely careers are those involving the monastic life, healing of the metaphysical sort, mediumship, gambling, investment enterprises, film, stage, photography, magic, ocean-oriented pursuits, or any Neptune-ruled activity. The person is self-indulgent and must learn to face reality. Otherwise, he has no chance of even coming close to fulfilling his desires and life purpose.

"I went to the woods because I wanted to live deliberately. To live deep and suck out all the marrow of life. To put to rout all that was not life, and not when I came to die, discover that I had not lived."

If Jupiter is square or opposite Neptune, the person is confused in his judgement. He is sentimental and affected by excessive emotions. He has difficulty distinguishing the real from the unreal. He has a great imagination but little common sense. He is idealistic and is easily fooled and exploited. He may see only the good in others. The person is extremely generous, sometimes to a fault. He always wants to help. He must develop a balanced sense of proportion and try not to waste or squander his energy. He is thrown off balance by wishful thinking, and his lifelong task is to learn discrimination and discernment.

The person may be an impassioned spiritualist. He loves the mystery, romance, and magic of life. However, he should be extremely careful in this realm because he is such an escapist. He is easily fooled by gurus and religious teachers. He is awed by their power and magnetism, and lacks the necessary prudence to protect himself. The person is prone to religious fervor. He is vulnerable, and always susceptible to disappointment and disillusionment.

The person has tremendous devotional urges. He is dedicated, faithful, and enthusiastic about spiritual growth. He is selfless, altruistic, and very empathetic. He is psychic and open to mystical realities that are closed to the average mortal. He excels in all kinds of social work. If the rest of the birthchart is strong, the person can make great use of his fanciful imagination. He may be a fine writer of fiction. Or he may do well on stage or in the film industry.

There is a need for discipline and responsibility. Many people with hard Jupiter-Neptune aspects neglect the requirements of daily life because of their infatuations and whimsical cravings. The person may be weak in character. He may be inconsistent, changeable, undisciplined, and incapable of ever realizing his goals. He must guard against strange, difficult-to-diagnose health problems which are caused by poisons and other substances specifically attacking the liver. Speculation and gambling are not favored. The person should beware of business dealings with associates who "promise the stars." There is simply too much naivete, and the person does not see straight.

Drugs and alcohol are particularly dangerous. The person has a sensitive liver and powerful escapist tendencies, which manifest as potential addictions. The person searches his whole life for perfection or nirvana. In some cases the person is too metaphysical for his own good. He may be superstitious and too psychically exposed. He has to be more precise in his work, and avoid making commitments he cannot fulfill. Marilyn Monroe, who experienced an inordinate amount of disappointment and disillusionment, had the Jupiter-opposition-Neptune aspect within four and one half degrees. Fidel Castro has the same aspect within two degrees.

> "Every person with an ideal faces the danger of being called a fool or a madman. Every great cause must be ushered into the world by a small majority of persons often denounced as cracked brains or ridiculous zealots. Someone said, "Nobody can be genuinely in earnest without appearing eccentric in a world where intensity is considered bad form."
>
> *REV. PAUL OSUMI*

If Jupiter is trine or sextile Neptune, the person is saintly. He does no harm to others and his greatest concern is to help. He is sympathetic and compassionate. He has the best heart. Because he finds his way to a service-oriented existence early on, he is assured a life of happiness and profundity for the rest of his days. He is sensitive, kind, sincere, and genuine. In short, he is a great human being.

There is a strong devotional nature. The person has unwavering faith in the divine. He is spiritual, reverent, and inclined towards religious enthusiasm and ecstasy. If other aspects of the birthchart confer, he may live a monastic life. He is mystical, intuitive, and good in the occult arts. He is inspired and always shares his religious and philosophical knowledge. He loves to pray and may occasionally rise to lofty heights of bliss.

The person is a visionary. He is a dreamer. There is a need for discipline, responsibility, and practicality if the person is to make the most of the harmonious Jupiter-Neptune aspect. He looks for the best in people and often misses the flaws and base motives of others. Because his intentions are so pure he has difficulty understanding corruption, greed, and selfishness. He is bewildered by politics and the "way of the world." The person is contemplative, receptive, and introspective. He is creative and has a wonderful imagination. He likes to consider the possibility of a utopian society where everybody wins.

The person is pleasant and easygoing. He is very artistic and may choose a career in music, drama, photography, or any endeavor where he capitalizes on his inspiration and aesthetic sensibilities. The person is romantic and spirited. He is highly intuitive and may have accurate insights and hunches. He loves magic and large bodies of water. The person is generous and willing to care for others. He will give up anything for his loved ones. There is an acute sense of right and wrong. In certain cases the person may be lazy or too passive. He may also be overly sentimental. He succeeds in hospital work or any other social service. Traditional astrological texts report that the person often receives conspicuously lucky benefits and that he is well-loved for his remarkable character. Marlon Brando has the Jupiter trine Neptune aspect within two and one half degrees. The trine aspect is significantly more powerful than the sextile. The sextile indicates the opportunity to make the above characteristics a reality.

If Jupiter is conjunct Pluto, the person is compelled to find the truth and have his life make a major impact. He is powerful, confident, and successful. He is a leader and desires to be the best in his field. There is outstanding enthusiasm and charisma, and the person does exceptionally well in selling his ideas to the masses. Mahatma Ghandi, Mick Jagger, and Lenin are typical examples. So are Willie Mays, Jackie Robinson, and dancer Martha Graham.

The Jupiter-Pluto aspect is a fascinating one. Planets conjunct Pluto become compulsive (even obsessive) forces, while planets conjunct Jupiter have their energies expanded and enlarged. Thus, the person does things in a very big way. He is definitely someone to be reckoned with. The magnification of Plutonian energy means the person has no trouble taking responsibility for everyone around him, even those outside his realm. He craves power and recognition. He has great healing ability. However, he is unlikely to become a healer unless other birthchart factors indicate the healing arts, since one-to-one activities will not be the most fulfilling.

Because the Jupitarian influence is intensified the person has the deepest need for a gratifying personal and universal philosophy. He simply must get to the truth. He will study or follow many different religions, even concurrently perhaps, and almost certainly make his way to some form of spiritual life. No matter what the level of consciousness or how earthly or mundane the person's direction, he will be open and receptive to metaphysics. He will have exciting spiritual experiences and will perceive no limitations or boundaries to the possibilities of existence. For this reason, he also believes in the fulfillment of his goals, however tremendous they may be. There is an acute sense of right and wrong. And yet, the person has great tolerance of differing philosophies and viewpoints.

Of all the planetary energies, Pluto (the planet of pure and unbounded potential) gives the most keen experience, or FEELING, of realness. Therefore, when combined with the planet of religion and philosophy, the influence is sure make the person a living embodiment of his beliefs and doctrine. He is willing to do anything for his principles

— nothing is more important. The person is royal, noble, and dignified. He is popular and will certainly receive recognition in his field. He has a wonderful sense of humor and almost never takes a depressive or negative outlook. He feels lucky and expects the best. The person is extremely ambitious and motivated. He is action-oriented. He is drawn to careers involving investments, banking, and anything connected with opulence. He may practice a metaphysical or healing-oriented profession if other birthchart factors concur. He must beware the tendency to dominate others or overindulge his desires.

"Forget about likes and dislikes. They are of no consequence. Just do what must be done. This may not be happiness. But it is greatness."

GEORGE BERNARD SHAW

If Jupiter is square or opposite Pluto, the person is extreme in judgement and compulsive about his religious and philosophical beliefs. He has no sense of mental proportion, and he lives with exaggerated attitudes. He may be intense and dogmatic in his ideas of right and wrong. He is arrogant about truth, and should beware of trying to force his convictions on others. His ego is big and he may be lacking in humility and self-reflection. He may be unaware of the price he pays for his know-it-all perspective and self-important demeanor. He is denied promotions, and misses out on significant opportunities, because of his unwilling-ness to compromise and consider differing viewpoints. Lenny Bruce had an exact Jupiter opposition Pluto aspect.

The person experiences tremendous ups and downs in his luck and money. He is on a lifelong quest to win the grandest financial prize society offers. He believes in himself wholeheartedly, and is likely to obtain extreme wealth at some point. However, he is just as apt to lose that wealth because of poor judgement and an intensely speculative nature. He takes too many unnecessary and unwise risks. The person loves power and wants to do everything on a massive scale. He is in need of limits and boundaries. There may be a serious tendency to misuse the knowledge he receives. He can easily be too fervent and fanatical.

The person may not be satisfied with traditional religious beliefs. He is interested in new-age philosophies and the occult. He is distinctly individualistic and independent where truth and knowledge are con-cerned. He is stubborn and fixed in his opinions and concepts. There may be problems with gurus, teachers, and college institutions. Because the person believes he is infallible, he may be wasteful and indulgent. He should be careful not to consume too many sweets and oils. He should also curb his self-righteous manner and try not to offend others with blasphemous talk.

If Jupiter is trine or sextile Pluto, the person is honorable and of the best morals. Because he learned fine values as a child he is blessed with a certain serenity and contentment for the rest of his life. His faith in God is unshakable and he is a positive influence wherever he goes. The person is enthusiastic, healthy, and enterprising. He understands human nature and is a fine organizer and coordinator. He makes a good leader and is never resented for his use of power. He enjoys managing large projects that make a big impact.

The person loves life and is extremely balanced in his optimism. He is patient, persevering, and purposeful. He has intense willpower and very good recuperative energy. He loves meditation, yoga, and the occult. His spiritual development occurs swiftly and with great ease. He is receptive to new ideas and gets more evolutionary growth than anyone. He craves new knowledge, and makes use of philosophical insights from myriad sources. He always seeks greater, more profound truth. He gets along well with gurus, religious teachers, and college professors.

The person uses his intuition wisely. He is mature, instinctive, and lucky. There is good vitality, and the person is strong and hearty. Luck is favored, as are legacies and inheritances. The person is focused, centered, and secure. He knows how to concentrate his energy in a way that is effective and successful. Because he bases his life on deep philosophical understandings, he is disciplined and of especially fine character. He knows the value and significance of human life better than anyone. There is a charm about the person, and certain individuals with this aspect may be quite pious and religious. Astrologer/author Grant Lewi had the Jupiter trine Pluto aspect within one degree. The trine aspect is significantly more powerful than the sextile. The sextile indicates the opportunity to make the above traits a reality.

If Saturn is conjunct Uranus, the person is an agent for change. He is rebellious, independent, and as strong-willed as they come. There will be numerous professions, and many ups and downs in that sphere. The person has powerful ideas of the way things should be and sees no practical reason to compromise. Unlike many ultra-independent types, however, the person definitely knows the meaning of discipline, responsibility, and hard work. Indeed, this aspect indicates a profound blending of conservative, traditional thinking along with radical and revolutionary desires. If the rest of the birthchart indicates strong direction and life purpose, the person will be extremely successful. He will break boundaries in his chosen field. Muhammad Ali and Barbara Streisand both have this aspect in their birthcharts.

The person may be spiritual, intuitive, and way ahead of the times. He will display genius in his early years. Science, metaphysics, and the occult are the most natural domains for the person's leadership, organizational, and progressive talents. There is great objectivity, and the person can analyze a situation quickly and accurately. He lives in the present and is ready to secure the moment.

Psychologically, the life is not an easy one. There is an innate struggle, from childhood, between security and freedom, stability and independence. Perhaps no other planetary conjunction can so generate tension and frustration. The person feels pulled apart in his soul and psyche by the merging of two such contradictory energies. He may be restless, irritable, volatile, or fitful. Leisure and recreation, or relaxing meditation techniques, should be regularly scheduled. The person is ambitious and determined. He is stubborn, obstinate, and does not give up. He abhors authority, though he is likely to become an authority figure himself. Free will is of chief importance to him.

There will be many major changes throughout life. The person is attracted to professions that are original, creative, and out-of-the-ordinary. He is open-minded, fair, and non-dogmatic. He is of a humanitarian nature and may be quite spiritual. Since Saturn has to do with authority, the father may have been strange, weird, occultish, or a genius. Or the father may have been an unstable, unpredictable force in the person's life. Traditional astrological texts warn that the person is prone to accidents because of his abruptness and abundance of nervous tension.

If Saturn is square or opposite Uranus, the person struggles to be both authoritarian and revolutionary. Thus, he is an eccentric type of rebel. He lives with a great deal of pressure, strain, and frustration, without understanding why. In one way, his thinking is detached, rational, and extremely progressive; however, he also is very attached to respect, obedience, and certain other cultural rules of order. He wants to be completely free to break traditions and customs when he feels the need. But at the same time, he wants to have everyone around him live entirely within the system. He hates to be restricted by rules and regulations, yet paradoxically imposes them on others! Thus, he may be disliked or considered hypocritical.

The person may be rigid or inflexible, and have precious little awareness of his shortcomings. He may seriously lack objectivity about his own character. Above all, the person does not appreciate others who disagree with his opinions. He has trouble with the powers that be, and his worst nightmare is to be at their mercy. The person may excel in occult studies. He needs a great deal of freedom and should try to choose a profession where he is his own boss. He may also be better suited to project-oriented work where his commitments are not terribly long-term. He lives by instinct and impulse. He may be highly creative and innovative. He may be an inventor. He may have many changes or ups and downs in the career. Because Saturn rules authority figures, the person's father may have been odd, changeable, or unreliable.

Traditional texts note the person's stubbornness, obstinacy, and egotism. Hard Saturn-Uranus aspects require a good deal of evolution, awareness, and an ability to laugh at one's quirky personality and personal needs. Otherwise, the person will have problems in all his relationships — personal, professional, romantic, etc. Newscaster Dan Rather has the Saturn square Uranus aspect within one and half degrees. Karl Marx had the same aspect within four degrees.

If Saturn is trine or sextile Uranus, the person is good at implementing progressive plans and actions. He knows how to combine traditional methods with innovative ideas. He is quite open to new ideas and concepts. He has a fine attitude about work, and he proceeds with caution and prudence. He is practical and has good common sense. He has organizational ability. The person loves knowledge and truth, and always wants to learn more. His most remarkable quality is his determination to expand and better himself. He is disciplined, patient, and persistent. He collects knowledge and puts it to excellent use.

The person may have talent in yoga, metaphysics, or the occult. He excels in the sciences and technical fields. He is good with details. Metaphysician Elbert Benjamin (pen named C.C. Zain) had the Saturn trine Uranus aspect within three degrees. There is strong willpower and endurance. The person does not give up easily. He is creative and has good concentration. He learns quickly from his experience and is not easily fooled. The person is simple and orderly. He likes to do things the right way. His thinking is original and ingenious. Traditional astrological texts report that the person is a great administrator. The trine aspect is significantly more powerful than the sextile. The sextile indicates the opportunity to make the above characteristics a reality.

If Saturn is conjunct Neptune, the person is a practical idealist. He is a romantic, visionary, and optimist by nature, but is much too pragmatic to spend his life chasing dreams which defy the odds. He must confront the dilemma of compromise on a daily basis. He has the most concrete sense of utopia, but is also more aware of the harsh realities of life than anyone. His lives a perpetual struggle between the perfect and the feasible. The person has a very real and eternal sense of God and the Divine. Therefore, he is unmoved by organized religion, convention, and tradition. He trusts his own spiritual experience implicitly and finds it superfluous to discuss or dissect such an intimate, organic process. Indeed, the person has developed his spirituality so thoroughly in previous lives that he feels no internal incompletion whatsoever. Thus, he has little inclination to practice evolutionary, self-improvement, or metaphysical techniques.

The person is drawn to the arts, especially music and drama. He sees in them a practical way to bring his sense of wonder, the miraculous, and the uplifting onto the physical plane. Also, because Saturn represents career and is conjunct Neptune, the person excels in any activity relating to the stage, the sea, magic, film and photography, oil, gas, etc. He values any endeavor that touches the soul and spirit. Because Saturn rules timing, the person is punctual and has excellent rhythm and tempo. Because Neptune dissolves the Saturnian energy, there may be an ascetic or non-attached quality to the life. The person does not concern himself with worldly possessions and needs, nor is he particularly fond of (or capable in) business, unless other aspects of the birthchart indicate.

Being spiritually whole, the person has no desire to escape from reality. He is never attracted by alcohol, drugs, and intense mystical movements. He relies thoroughly, and unconditionally, on his inner spiritual guide when he is confused or in need of support. This, however, is not at all obvious since the person is so extremely down-to-earth. Saturn rules authority, and thus represents the father to a certain extent. Therefore, the father will definitely exhibit some Neptunian characteristics. He may be spiritual, mystical, devotional, weird, or strange. Or the father may be ill with peculiar diseases, physically absent, or surrounded by odd conditions.

In many (if not all) cases, Saturn dramatically dampens the person's ability to pursue his dreams and visions. There may be seeming passivity which is, in fact, resignation. This causes moodiness and depression from not realizing one's talents and potentials. Ultimately, the person may be too narrow in his thinking. He should consider the imprudence of trading the ultimate joy of his existence for the attainment of daily practical amenities. He may also ponder whether his choosing practical realities is simply due to unconscious, irrational fears from childhood. He may feel a deep-seated insecurity about reality, thinking that nothing in his grasp is real or secure enough. This is because Saturn (which rules form, structure, and everything real and solid) is completely dissolved by Neptune.

There is likely to be a very strong sense of discipline, responsibility, and guilt. The person should beware of poisons or spoiled foods. He finds art a mystical experience. Abraham Lincoln had the Saturn-Neptune conjunction within three and one half degrees.

If Saturn is square or opposite Neptune, the person is dissatisfied and uncertain of himself. His security and sense of trust was undermined or violated during childhood, and the disintegration of his reality system was so great that he is suspicious and skeptical for the rest of his life. He feels victimized and does not want to open himself up to such disappointment again. The person may feel alone and isolated. He feels vulnerable and unprotected, and innately discontented. He needs to cultivate faith and hope, and guard against a defeatist attitude. Because Saturn and Neptune are both slow-moving planets (and therefore rather impersonal influences) this aspect should not be accorded too much significance unless it occurs in a tight orb (i.e., within three or four degrees).

The person may have problems with authority figures and his father. The father may have been strange, weird, alcoholic, or emotionally absent. Thus, the person did not receive a proper masculine base of confidence and assurance. He suffers from an unconscious, and perhaps unnoticeable, inferiority complex. He may need wealth, possessions, and all of society's status symbols in order to feel stable, safe, and secure. The person has a weak or impotent sense of idealism and devotion. He may trust scam artists and aggressive dealers, while doubting humble, sincere individuals. Mystical and occult endeavors are not favored. The person has trouble believing that which he cannot see, smell, touch, or taste. He is unlikely to pursue expansive dreams and visions. Indeed, he may feel frustrated, impatient, and lacking of a sense of purpose and direction.

The person may have trouble with guilt. Because Saturn is the natural ruler of the tenth house, there may be difficulties, deceptions, and strange occurrences in the career. The person may want to take calcium to protect his teeth and bones. Traditional astrological texts report that the person is beset by secret enemies, jealous individuals, and scandals. They also warn that in severe cases his general paranoia and negative attitude may fester into serious neurosis. Drugs, alcohol, and deep involvement in seances or the occult are also said to bring big problems.

If Saturn is trine or sextile Neptune, the person is an outstanding example of responsibility. He is hard-working and always willing to pay his dues, yet does not allow himself to be taken advantage of. He is spiritually integrated, idealistic, and of great common sense. He is as practical as they come, and uses his understanding of cause and effect to achieve his goals and ambitions. He is steady, dedicated, persistent, and exceedingly patient. His timing is excellent. He succeeds slowly but surely, one step at a time. Louis Pasteur had the Saturn trine Neptune aspect within two degrees.

Because all Saturnian qualities are so well-ingrained, the person is of very fine character. He is honest, loyal, fair, and pure-hearted. He is sincere, genuine, authentic, and trustworthy. He is devotional, and always does the right thing. There is good concentration, discipline, and self-restraint. The person is thoughtful and considers the feelings and opinions of others. He is loathe to hurt anyone. He is balanced and does not procrastinate.

The person has good business sense. He is perceptive and imaginative. He is realistic and down-to-earth. He may excel in any endeavor involving film, photography, or magic. Traditional astrological texts say that the person may be good in psychic, occult, or other secretive enterprises. The person may have fine organizational talent. He may understand religion and philosophy in the most profound and meaningful way. The trine aspect is significantly more powerful than the sextile. The sextile indicates the opportunity to make the above characteristics a reality.

If Saturn is conjunct Pluto, the person is compulsive about responsibility. He has an overdeveloped or distorted sense of duty and obligation. As a young child, the person may have been made to feel responsible for circumstances beyond his control. This conditioning may have occurred consciously or unconsciously, and may be related not only to personal events but also to those of society. Indeed, the child may have somehow felt he had something to do with destructive or negative worldly circumstances. As a result, he has no accurate perspective concerning the effects and consequences that are genuinely his responsibility. He lives with feelings of guilt that are far more deeply ingrained and difficult to correct than those generated by other Saturn aspects. When personal planets, such as the Sun, Moon, Venus, etc., are aspected by Saturn, the person FEARS he is guilty, responsible, inadequate, and to blame. When Pluto is involved with Saturn the person positively knows it! The experience, in most cases, is quite unconscious and suppressed. But the person is still motivated by such feelings.

The person enters situations which ensure struggle, hardship, privation, and no possibility of fulfillment. And yet he resists change with a resoluteness that defies logic. His stubbornness is severe, yet the person is not a typical "bull-headed" type. It is simply that there are irrational fears in the psyche which the person refuses to deal with because each and every impulse the person has is felt to be real, lasting, permanent, and cast in stone. Considering such psychological workings, where would be the impetus to attempt change or transformation?

On the positive side, the person is self-disciplined and self-motivated. He can endure anything and will never give up. He is excellent with form and structure and can build creations which will last eons. He appreciates tradition and convention for what they are worth. The person is proud, self-denying, and always willing to sacrifice. There may be great spiritual power if other aspects of the birthchart reveal a religious, occult, or metaphysical nature. However, in most cases the person is exceptionally earthbound. The person is a very strong soul, never lacking in character. He is deep, honorable, and does not look for the easy way out. No one grasps the meaning of commitment better than he. Alan Watts, Walt Whitman, Orson Welles, and Prince Albert all had Saturn-Pluto conjunctions.

The person has a troubled relationship with authority. Although he is a conservative type who is predisposed towards tradition and orthodox methods, he may have an extreme distaste for law and the powers that be. He simply does not trust individuals above his position. Indeed, he lives as a law unto himself. He tends to boss or dominate others when he can. Also, he may use manipulative or devious means to get his way. He is overly serious and lives with a constant sense of pressure and frustration. A sense of humor should be cultivated.

The person feels like a misfit or outcast, and identifies with the suffering and downcast members of society. He is always aware of his limitations and feels them acutely. He is quite secretive. The person may be too severe or of an austere disposition. He is capable of cruelty, resentment, and hard-heartedness. He may be depressive or defensive. He should be sure to take plenty of calcium as the teeth and bones could be much afflicted. The house position of the Saturn-Pluto conjunction will reveal an area of great restriction, discipline, and attention. The person may have been missing a conscience during previous lives and is now paying the price.

If Saturn is square or opposite Pluto, the theme of the person's life is karmic repayment of past-life debts. There is an inordinate amount of difficulty, hardship, and suffering. Success is delayed, and the person is at the mercy of circumstances beyond his control. His life is plagued with long-term obstacles. The person is intensely ambitious and persistent. He has a big ego and is of very strong character. He is quite likely to achieve his goals and aspirations. However, he must guard against a workaholic nature. He is rigid and inflexible in his understanding of responsibility and discipline. He goes overboard in duties and obligations, and must remember to structure fun and recreation into his life. Some individuals with hard Saturn-Pluto aspects sacrifice important aspects of their character, and/or entire periods of their lives, to care for loved ones or to take care of complex predicaments.

The person has a tendency to get stuck in tedious situations. He resists change with a vengeance, even when change is in his own best interest. He is stubborn, and does not listen to others. He lives with psychological issues revolving around power and control. He does not like authority figures and would like to dominate others. There may be a distorted, or perverted, sense of responsibility. The person may be motivated by unconscious guilt feelings carried over from early childhood. He should be careful not to suppress or inhibit his creativity and self-expression. Some hard Saturn-Pluto individuals are selfish, self-destructive, and hedonistic (a rebellious reaction to their frustrating and arduous life).

The person is extremely serious. He may be a leader and accomplish a great deal. His greatest task in life is to learn flexibility, humility, and openness to the advice and support of friends and loved ones. He must at some point consider that his perceptions and convictions are unduly colored by the extraordinary and peculiar demands he has had to endure. Traditional astrological texts report that the person may be cruel, harsh, narrow, and even mean-hearted. Given the potential adversity the person has to bear, such behavior is not hard to imagine. However, much depends upon the birthchart as a whole. Certain individuals with these aspects are profoundly sacrificial and self-negating, while others respond with crude, more defiant conduct. James Dean had the Saturn-Pluto opposition within one degree.

If Saturn is trine or sextile Pluto, the person is a mature human being. He sees himself as the cause of his experiences, never the victim. He is responsible, serious-minded, and as resourceful as they come. The person has strong ambitions and is likely to be successful. He has a sense of destiny and purpose. Once aware of his goal, he climbs steadily towards the top. He is determined, hard-working, and consistent. He is reliable, and very conscious about keeping his word. The person has intense willpower and discipline. He is enormously practical and of good common sense. His vision and perspective are profound, and he makes an excellent leader, organizer, or administrator.

The person is real. He does not lie, play games, or beat around the bush. He learns quickly from experience, and is concerned with practice, not theory. He understands cause and effect, and form and structure. His designs and constructions are long-lasting. The person works hard to improve himself in areas where he feels weak. He is conservative and moderate in behavior. He is rarely out of control or at the mercy of obsessions or infatuations. He compromises without difficulty and his greatest concern is making life work properly. He does not give in to petty or vengeful conduct.

Concentration is good and the person is thorough. He embraces Maharishi Mahesh Yogi's spiritual teaching; "see the job, do the job, stay out of the misery." He excels in research endeavors, and may enjoy astrology, metaphysics, and the occult. He does not tire easily and he is not a quitter. The person may be quite spiritually evolved. The trine aspect is significantly more powerful than the sextile. The sextile indicates the opportunity to make the above characteristics a reality.

The Uranus-Neptune conjunction occurs approximately every 170 years. The next one happens in 1993. It is to be deduced that the aspect will not be an easy one personality-wise. Furthermore, the house position of the conjunction is likely to be an area of great difficulty, tension, and lack of control. The person will experience intense confusion regarding his independence, self-reliance, and individuality. He may feel no inner confidence regarding his own creativity, originality, and inventiveness. At the same time, however, there may be the greatest idealism, romanticism, and visionary nature about the possibilities of human existence.

The person may have extraordinarily unique and special talent in the realms of religion, philosophy, devotion, and metaphysics. He may have the most natural understanding of the true nature of reality. He will grasp, from birth, the concept of maya (illusion) and the futility of materialism. He will perceive the potential for utopian life and help make it a reality. There are likely to be extreme escapist tendencies and therefore the person should avoid drugs and alcohol altogether. Extrasensory perception will be acute and abundant.

Some individuals born during the last Uranus-Neptune conjunction (around 1820 or so): Karl Marx, Walt Whitman, Clara Barton (originator of the Red Cross), and Mary Baker Eddy (the founder of Christian Science).

If Uranus is conjunct Pluto, the person feels compulsive independence in the depths of his soul. He is on the earth to break down existing conditions and bring about a new social order. The person feels free, uninhibited, and self-reliant. He has no admiration for tradition, convention, and the order of the day. Indeed, he may fail to understand the purpose of rules, regulations, and cultural practices until late in life. The person is extremely enlightened in the sense of non-attachment and the ability to live absolutely in the moment. Unfortunately, however, there is no breadth of perspective. The person lives entirely from experience and must learn each and every lesson on his own, often the hard way. There is an egocentricity about such behavior, and the person should be made aware that, in the end, there will be serious consequences to pay for ignoring the wisdom of society and its elders. The person takes many actions which feel logical and appropriate at the time but which are errors in the long run. Discipline, restraint, moderation, and responsibility are an absolute must if the person is to realize his potential and fulfillment.

More than anyone, the person is tolerant of differing viewpoints and philosophies. He is highly intelligent in his comprehension of religion and is unlikely to be fooled in this realm. He knows all paths lead to the same universal source and he is aware of his role in helping to create a new world of unity, compassion, and acceptance. Being unimpressed by formality and the superficial, the person quickly makes his way to the reality of things. His intuition is accurate and deeply ingrained, and he trusts himself unquestionably. There is not the slightest hint of prejudice or bigotry and the person never passes judgement on others. He is exciting, talented, and thrilled with life. He does well in science, astrology, computers, aviation, or any endeavor which is ahead of the times. However, there may be profound impatience, impulsiveness, or anti-social leanings. Discretion, prudence, and respect for wisdom is needed.

The person may be a supreme revolutionary. He breaks tradition without concern and knows full well that anything is possible. There may be deep religious or metaphysical experiences. The person is a humanitarian in his soul but he may be too egocentric or selfish to devote his life to helping others. He must beware abruptness and the temptation to live as if he is the center of the universe. If Saturn is powerful and well disposed in the chart and the person achieves significant maturity and depth, then he may be a great pioneer and innovator.

Psychologically, the Uranus-Pluto conjunction is extremely difficult. A great deal of self-compassion and understanding is necessary if the person is ever to come to a sense of peace and contentment, and realize his potential. The biggest problem: while Uranus is the planet of independence and individuality, it also rules Aquarius, the sign of society and public concern. Therefore, since the person's Uranian energy is nearly obsessive, he is extremely independent and individualistic. But at the same time, his basic values and way of perceiving life are (paradoxically) more social than personal. Very early in life, he sees the evils and injustices perpetrated on the masses. He is keenly aware of the need for societal change and transformation. And he is by nature original, innovative, and extraordinarily inspired and spirited.

Unfortunately however, he is so detached and separate from the world that he feels alien, alone, and unable to influence the situation. The existing order is so radically different from what he believes it should be that he cannot even decide where to begin his work. Furthermore, his independence is so extreme that he does not feel connected or bonded to others of his era. All individuals experience a generation gap at some point in their lives, but the Uranus-Pluto person ALWAYS lives with one. On yet another level, the person may find himself entirely unmotivated to engage successfully in life; he finds himself stuck in a system which he disagrees with, and that he had no part in creating. Thus, he may antagonize everyone around him with complaints and criticisms, while remaining conspicuous for lack of action. In short, the person is unwilling to pay his dues. And while he suffers massively because of it on an intimate level, he refuses to admit any concern or apprehension because his most important values are societal. Indeed, the person is largely unaware of personal pain. He may often "bite his nose to spite his face." It is a difficult situation, and in some sense a tragic waste of enormous potential. No one is more animated, enthusiastic, proud, creative, visionary, and ingenious than the Uranus-Pluto person.

More than anything, the person must come to realize that he is one of God's children. He therefore deserves to have his intimate needs fulfilled as much as society needs his attention. Indeed, it is only when he is personally fulfilled to a meaningful degree that he can be of real benefit to others and community. He must also meditate on the taoist mantra, "the journey of a thousand miles begins with a single step." The last Uranus-Pluto conjunction occurred during the early nineteen-sixties, when enormous societal change and transformation took place.

The last Neptune-Pluto conjunction occurred around 1891 and brought about an abundance of spiritual proponents and great Neptunian individuals. The next time of the aspect will be in the 2300s. It is to be deduced that the future generation born with Neptune conjunct Pluto will be highly clairvoyant, metaphysically-oriented, extremely devotional, and highly evolved. One can only speculate about the intense advances scientists and metaphysicians will make regarding new forms of energy, alchemy, religion, philosophy, astral travel, and space exploration. Great strides will also be made in the area of film, photography, magic, and theatre.

Some of the individuals born during the last Neptune-Pluto conjunction, which was in effect at least between 1887 and 1895, are as follows: Rose Kennedy, Mae West, Charlie Chaplin, Dame Edith Evans, Eugene O'Neill, the philosopher Heidegger, Dane Rudhyar, Wilhelm Reich, Krishnamurti, Kirpal Sing, Meher Baba, Buckminster Fuller, and Paramahansa Yogananda. An impressive list, to say the least.

The following aspects between outer planets occur for such long periods of time they are considered generational. They are more useful in analyzing social trends than individual behavior.

URANUS SQUARE OR OPPOSITE NEPTUNE

URANUS TRINE OR SEXTILE NEPTUNE

URANUS SQUARE OR OPPOSITE PLUTO

URANUS TRINE OR SEXTILE PLUTO

NEPTUNE SQUARE OR OPPOSITE PLUTO

NEPTUNE TRINE OR SEXTILE PLUTO

SERVICES OF JAMES BRAHA AND HERMETICIAN PRESS

James Braha
Hermetician Press
P.O. Box 195
Longboat Key, Fla. 34228

Website   www.jamesbraha.com
E-mail   brahas@earthlink.net

All orders can be made through e-mail (using credit cards MC/VISA/DISCOVER) or postal mail using James Braha/Hermetician Press address above.

Books by James Braha

*Ancient Hindu Astrology for the Modern **Western Astrolger**, $21.95*
*How To Be a Great Astrologer; the Planetary Aspects **Explained**, $19.95*
How to Predict Your Future; Secrets of Eastern and Western Astrology, $22
Astro-Logos; Revelations of a Hindu Astrologer, $9.95
The Art and Practice of Ancient Hindu Astrology, $29.95
                              Add $1.50 per book for shipping and handling.

James Braha Eastern & Western Astrology Computerized Birthchart Report
Beautifully bound, 60+pages, full text by James Braha includes full interpretations of Hindu planets in houses, Hindu *dasa* and *bhukti* periods for 15 years, transits of Western "outer planets" for 3 years, Western natal astrolgical aspects, South Indian Hindu horoscope with *dasa - bhukti* periods, Western horoscope. $50.

Hindu Full - Life Birthchart Interpretation by James Braha
In-depth analysis of natal Hindu horoscope and future ***dasa*** and ***bhukti*** ***periods*** (with full astrological explanations). 60 to 90 minutes long, given by phone and recorded on cassette tape. Includes gemstone recommendations, mantra and *yagya* prescriptions, as well as transits, progressions, and *dasa-bhukti* periods and subperiods. More in-depth for next 3-4 years. For details, call James Braha at (941) 387-9101, or call directory assistance for James

Braha in Longboat Key, Florida.

Hindu Astrolgy Software - Haydn's Jyotish

Calculates all 16 *varga* charts, *nakshatras*, *dasas*, *bhuktis*, and sub-bhuktis. Includes options for English or Sanskrit, North or South Indian chart formats, and explanatory comments on planets and houses (Note:This is not an interpretive program).Extremely user friendly. DOS PC or MAC. $110.

American Council of Vedic Astrology (ACVA)

One of the purposes of ACVA is to promote Vedic astrology in the West through their yearly conferences and certification programs. For more information, contact Dennis Harness at (928) 282-6595.

Excellent Horary Astrologer

Lee Lehman - (321) 728-2277 (answers questions based on William Lilly's 16th century techniques).

To Have Large Yagyas Performed in India

For 3-day or 7-day *Yagyas* performed in India, contact Yves DeCarie - (450) 463-3636, or visit his website www.yajna.com

Temples Where One-hour Yagyas Can be Obtained

Sri Shirdi Sai Baba Temple	Hindu Temple of Greater Chicago
3744 Old William Tell Highway	12 South 701 Lemont Road
Pittsburgh, Pa. 15235	Lemont, Illinois 60439
Ph. # (412) 374-9244, (412) 823-1296	Ph. # (630) 972-0300

Gemstone Information

Jay Boyle 1-800-559-5090   See www.astrologicalgem.com

Catalogue of Hindu Astrology Texts, Chanting Beads, and Deity Pictures

21st Century Books
401 N. 4th St.
Fairfield, Iowa 52556
Phone 1-800-593-2665

Computer Calculated Hindu Charts With Dasa-Bhuktis

ACS Astro Communications Service
PO 34487, San Diego, Calif. 92163-4487   Phone 1-800-888-9983

READING LIST

The following is a list of suggested reading on Hindu and western astrology. Out of the hundreds of popular books that exist, these are my clear favorites.

WESTERN ASTROLOGY TEXTS

Arroyo, Stephen. *Astrology, Karma and Transformation.* Sebastopol, CA: CRCS Publications, 1978.

Carter, C.E.O. *Astrological Aspects.* Wheaton, IL: Quest Books, The Theosophical Society.

—— *The Principles of Astrology.* Wheaton, IL: Quest Books, The Theosophical Society.

Hand, Robert. *Horoscope Symbols.* West Chester, PA: Whitford Press, 1981.

—— *Essays in Astrology.* West Chester, PA: Whitford Press, 1982

—— *Planets in Composite.* West Chester, PA: Whitford Press, 1975

—— *Planets in Transit.* West Chester, PA: Whitford Press, 1976.

—— *Planets in Youth.* West Chester, PA: Whitford Press, 1977.

Hickey, Isabel. *Astrology: A Cosmic Science.* Sebastopol, CA: CRCS 1992.

Houck, Richard. *The Astrology of Death.* 1994. P.O.Box 8925, Gaithersburg, MD 20898: Groundswell Press.

Lewi, Grant. *Astrology for the Millions.* St Paul, MN: Llewellen Publications, 1990.

Sasportas, Howard. *The Twelve Houses.* Great Britain: The Aquarian Press, 1985.

Tompkins, Sue. *Aspects in Astrology.* Dorset, England: Element Books, 1989.

Zain, C.C. (a.k.a. Elbert Benjamin) - *Delineating the Horoscope.* Los Angeles, CA: Church of Light, 1950.

HINDU ASTROLOGY TEXTS BY WESTERNERS

Braha, James. *Ancient Hindu Astrology for the Modern Western Astrologer.* Hollwood, FL: Hermetician Press 1986.

Dreyer, Ronnie Gale. *Indian Astrology.* Wellingborough, Northamptonshire, England: The Aquarian Press, 1990

Frawley, David. *The Astrology of Seers.* Salt Lake City, UT: Passage Press, 1990.

Hopke, Tom. *How to Read Your Horoscope.* Honolulu, HI: Vedic Cultural Association, 1987.

Defouw, Hart and Svoboda, Robert. *Light on Life.* New York, NY: Penguin Books (Arkana). 1996.